THE SOUL OF JUDAISM

RELIGION, RACE, AND ETHNICITY

General Editor: Peter J. Paris

For a complete list of titles in the series, please visit the New York University Press website at www.nyupress.org.

The Soul of Judaism

Jews of African Descent in America

Bruce D. Haynes

NEW YORK UNIVERSITY PRESS

New York

NEW YORK UNIVERSITY PRESS
New York
www.nyupress.org

Library of Congress Cataloging-in-Publication Data
Names: Haynes, Bruce D., 1960– author.
Title: The soul of Judaism : Jews of African descent in America / Bruce D. Haynes.
Description: New York : New York University Press, [2018] | Series: Religion, race, and ethnicity | Includes bibliographical references and index.
Identifiers: LCCN 2017044867 | ISBN 978-1-4798-1123-6 (cl : alk. paper)
Subjects: LCSH: African American Jews—History. | United States—Ethnic relations. | Jews—Identity.
Classification: LCC BM205 .H376 2018 | DDC 305.6/9608996073—dc23
LC record available at https://lccn.loc.gov/2017044867

New York University Press books are printed on acid-free paper, and their binding materials are chosen for strength and durability. We strive to use environmentally responsible suppliers and materials to the greatest extent possible in publishing our books.

Manufactured in the United States of America

10 9 8 7 6 5 4 3 2 1

Also available as an ebook

CONTENTS

Introduction

Opening the Gates

I don't know about no heaven. I don't know about no hell. . . .
All I want to do is qualify.
—Rabbi Bill Tate, Beth Shalom Synagogue, Brooklyn, 1999

Relations between blacks and Jews have been both romanticized and vilified. Some point to the fellowship between Rabbi Abraham Joshua Heschel and Reverend Martin Luther King Jr. as evidence of a natural alliance, while others cite the riots in Crown Heights, Brooklyn, as confirmation of a more insidious relationship. Jews have been accused of abandoning their commitment to racial equality and affirmative action policies, while blacks have been charged with embracing anti-Semitism and racial nationalism. The relationship between blacks and Jews has seesawed between a "Grand Alliance" and a "peculiar entanglement" (Salzman and West 1997).

The modern seeds of disaffection can be traced to the restructuring of race categories in the late nineteenth century, a time when blacks and Jews encountered one another in urban metropolises like Philadelphia and New York. Of special importance was the period between 1870 and 1920, when some two million eastern European Jews immigrated to the United States and when modern racial classifications were solidifying (Hattam 2007; Lederhendler 2009; Treitler 2013). Jews had fled the *pogroms* and persecution of eastern Europe and hoped to remake themselves in America. At the same time, over one million blacks were fleeing the inequities and mob violence of the rural Jim Crow South to remake themselves in the industrial North and Midwest. Yet Jews—who had been viewed as racially distinct in Europe—were able to reframe themselves as ethnics, and therefore whites, within an emerging black-white binary that determined all civic, social, political, educational, residential, labor, and cultural boundaries and opportunities.

This ability of Jews to cross the "color line" and wield economic and political power like other whites has long stoked resentment from blacks. James Baldwin articulated the offense in his 1967 essay "Negroes Are Anti-Semitic Because They're Anti-White":

> In the American context, the most ironical thing about Negro anti-Semitism is that the Negro is really condemning the Jew for having become an American white man—for having become, in effect, a Christian. The Jew profits from his status in America, and he must expect Negroes to distrust him for it. The Jew does not realize that the credential he offers, the fact that he has been despised and slaughtered, does not increase the Negro's understanding. It increases the Negro's rage. (Baldwin 1985)

During the 1990s, black and Jewish intellectuals across the nation were engaged in a public exchange over the character of Jewish-black relations. A cacophony of voices from the Left and the Right entered the fray, debating the nature and character of Jewish involvement in transatlantic slavery and the civil rights movement, the role of black separatism, and the perception of growing black anti-Semitism and Jewish racism (Sleeper 1990; Martin 1993; Berman 1994; Crouch 1995; Diner 1995; Friedman 1995; Lerner and West 1995; Salzman and West 1997). While a clear tendency could be observed among ghetto-bound black Americans to reject the idea that any authentic relationship had ever existed, liberal Jews like Lerner romanticized a common history of persecution and commitment to civil rights, just at a time when many Jews were in fact abandoning that commitment (Steinberg 2001b). Meanwhile, a new narrative was quietly unfolding off center stage: individuals who self-identified as both black and Jewish began gaining national attention and even legitimacy. Their presence challenged traditional narratives that relegate blacks and Jews to two mutually exclusive social categories.

This book traces the history of Jews of African descent in America and the counternarratives they have put forward as they stake their claims to Jewishness. It examines their struggles as blacks to be recognized as Jews in an era in which Jews have "become" white (Brodkin 1998). In claiming whiteness, Jews have had the freedom to express their identity in fluid ethnic terms, while African Americans have continued to be seen as a fixed racial grouping despite obvious cultural and phenotypical variations. Yet, this book argues, such divisions have always been in flux, and an examination of the relations between black and Jewish identity pushes us to reconsider the relationship between race and ethnicity.

The National Jewish Population Survey (NJPS) conducted in 1990 was, at the time, the most comprehensive study of the American Jewish population to date.[1] It sampled 2,441 households[2] in which at least one member self-identified (or had once self-identified) as Jewish and found that 2.4 percent of the sample, or an estimated 125,000 individuals,[3] also identified themselves as black.[4] The enormous size of this population caught researchers by surprise but came as no shock to black Jews themselves, who have estimated their numbers to be as high as 1.2 million (Holmes 2006). In the late 1990s, news reports placed the numbers of black Jews closer to about 200,000.[5] More recently, researchers at the Institute for Jewish and Community Research suggested in their 2005 book, *In Every Tongue: The Racial and Ethnic Diversity of the Jewish People*, that 7 percent of all American Jews, or some 435,000 people, were either black, Hispanic, Asian, or Native American (Tobin, Tobin, et al. 2005). But the true number of black Jews largely depends on how we define a Jew. Conservative estimates use a more rigid *halakhic* definition— that is, a definition in accordance with traditional Jewish law—which recognizes only those who have undergone formal conversion or were born to a Jewish mother. In 2013, the Pew Research Center surveyed over 3,400 American Jews, reporting its findings in *A Portrait of Jewish Americans: Findings from a Pew Research Center Survey of US Jews*. In a conservative analysis of the data, sociologist and demographer Bruce A. Phillips estimated that some 7 percent of the roughly 5.3 million Jewish adults in the US identified as nonwhite, and at least 1.7 percent, or about 90,100 persons, identified as non-Hispanic black (Alexander and Haynes 2016).[6] Meanwhile, Brandeis University conducted its own study in 2013 and found that 12 percent of American Jewish adults were nonwhite and 1.9 percent were black.[7]

If the actual number of black Jews seems elusive, so too is any single Afro-Jewish identity or community. Black Jews are found within the Orthodox, Conservative, Reconstructionist, and Reform movements, as well as in denominations and approaches that push the boundaries of normative Judaism. For the sake of clarity, I distinguish between *black*

Jews (those who are born to or adopted by a Jewish parent or who have *halakhically* converted to Judaism) and *B*lack Jews (members of indigenous black American groups, some of whom trace their Jewish roots to Africa and the Caribbean, and who favor the descriptor "Hebrew" or "Israelite"), with the caveat that individuals often cross boundaries and move between communities (Chireau 2000; Landing 2002).[8] For example, Rabbi Capers Funnye has his roots in the Hebrew Israelite movement but later converted to Conservative Judaism. Today he maintains ties to both communities. He is the spiritual adviser of the Beth Shalom B'nai Zaken Ethiopian Hebrew Congregation in Chicago; he also serves on the Chicago Board of Rabbis and on the boards of the American Jewish Congress and the Jewish Council on Urban Affairs. In June 2015, he was elected as chief rabbi of the International Israelite Board of Rabbis of the Ethiopian Hebrews.

I have encountered many such examples of boundary crossing throughout my research. One participant, an Ethiopian-born Jew who had settled in the Hasidic community of Crown Heights, Brooklyn, expressed a deep religious connection with his Hasidic community but also yearned for the comfort of other blacks and occasionally attended services at an Ethiopian Hebrew congregation in Crown Heights. I met one black convert who felt more alienated among American Ashkenazi Jews and more at home among the Karaites,[9] a Jewish sect that originated in Baghdad, relies solely on the Tanakh (Hebrew Bible), and rejects the oral tradition (including the Talmud and Mishnah) of rabbinic Judaism (Zenner 1989; Hirshberg 1990).[10] Are these individuals "black" or "Black" Jews? Ultimately, the terms are merely analytical abstractions, conveying at best "ideal types"—a concept introduced by the German sociologist Max Weber to provide a common basis for analyzing structural forms and meanings (Hekman 1983).

Black Jewish groups first emerged during the late nineteenth century, just as eastern European Jews were arriving en masse in American cities. Since that time there have been distinct manifestations of Judaism in the religious practices and identities of various African American religious movements, including the loosely defined Hebrew Israelite movement. These groups vary from religiously observant congregations, such as Congregation Temple Beth'El in Philadelphia and the Commandment Keepers in Harlem, to Christian Israelite congregations, such as the

Church of God and Saints of Christ. They encompass black nationalist groups, such as the Black Hebrew Israelites of Worldwide Truthful Understanding, whose "public performances of Black Jewishness" represent, as urban anthropologist John L. Jackson Jr. puts it, "displays of black masculinist spirituality" (Jackson 2005). And they extend to self-identified Israelites who have traveled to Israel or attended *yeshiva.*[11]

The last fifty years have brought unprecedented diversity to American Jewish communities. In 1965, a shift in immigration policy brought Jews from Yemen, Syria, Ethiopia, Morocco, and Mexico to the US. In addition, a small but growing number of nonwhite Americans have converted to Judaism over the last five decades (Tobin, Tobin, et al. 2005; Kaye/Kantrowitz 2007). Perhaps the most significant development is the rise in interracial marriages—particularly between black men and Jewish women—since the civil rights era. In many cases their children have been raised with both black and Jewish identities. Until the historic *Loving v. Virginia* Supreme Court decision of 1967, antimiscegenation laws throughout much of the nation criminalized intermarriages and delegitimated their children (Zack 1993). The court's ruling challenged the hegemony of the "one-drop rule" and opened new possibilities for the offspring of black-white marriages to claim a biracial or multiracial identity.[12] Parents of multiracial children mobilized to petition the Office of Budget Management to include a multiracial category on the 2000 census (Daniel 2001). Today, with one in forty Americans self-identifying as "multiracial," many scholars maintain that the one-drop rule has become obsolete (Hollinger 2005; Roth 2005). Some have called for a new language of identity (Somers 1994; Brubaker and Cooper 2000). The categories become multilayered when dimensions of ethnicity and religion are added to the mix.

Judaism embodies both of these dimensions, and its intersection with race yields new and often-shifting identity constructions. In their 2016 book, *JewAsian: Race, Religion, and Identity for America's Newest Jews,* the sociologist Helen Kiyong Kim and her partner Noah Samuel Leavitt, associate dean of students at Whitman College and former advocacy director for the Jewish Council on Urban Affairs, explore the racial, ethnic, and religious dimensions of identity among Jewish Asian American children and find that "how one identifies racially cannot be isolated from one's social interactions and larger context." Indeed, the highlighting of one dimension complicates assumptions about the other (Kim and Leavitt 2016). Like the American multiracial population in general, the staking of new identity claims has been articulated by monoracial and biracial black Jews alike.

Early attempts at dialogue between the Jewish mainstream and Black Hebrew and Israelite groups in the United States went largely unnoticed by most American Jews. One of the more significant encounters occurred in 1964, when Irving J. Block, an ecumenically minded Conservative rabbi and founder of the Brotherhood Synagogue (Beit Achim) in Greenwich Village, teamed up with Yaakov Gladstone, a Canadian Jew (who at the time was teaching Hebrew songs to members of the Hebrew Israelite Congregation of Mount Horeb in the Bronx), to found Hatzaad Harishon (The First Step). The vision of Hatzaad Harishon was to bring Jewish community assistance to black Jews, while also bringing "black and white" Jews together (Berger 1987). The group's board was what Jewish educator and activist Graenum Berger called "a mixed group of black and white Jews, including some 'black' rabbis and white rabbis." Initially, Hatzaad Harishon had many successes: Some black Jewish children received scholarships to Jewish schools, and several Hebrew Israelites enrolled in seminaries to study Jewish education. Some joined Ashkenazi congregations, some formally converted, and some spent summers in Israel. Between 1966 and 1972, members even produced a mimeographed newspaper that had national circulation (Berger 1987). Rabbi Block, who had "trained" young black Jews for their bar mitzvahs, believed that it was "time—and long overdue—to integrate Black Jews into activities of the mainstream American Jewish Community" (Berger 1987; Block 1999). Yet while Hatzaad Harishon disrupted the dominant narrative of Jews as white people, the group was consistently plagued by internal disagreement over the definitions of Jewishness (Fernheimer 2014). It disbanded in 1972.

Still, the first Black Jews to draw significant public attention were not American-born but Jews from Africa. Although some eight thousand Ethiopian Jews had already been secretly moved to Israel via Sudan by the 1980s, the 1984 Israeli airlift, code-named Operation Moses, brought international attention to their plight.[13] The Ethiopian Jews, also known as the Beta Israel (House of Israel), had been persecuted by Christian Ethiopians and were under threat of starvation in the Gondar Province and surrounding areas. Word of their rescue was widely publicized on January 4, 1985, when the *New York Times* reported that Israel had air-lifted ten thousand Ethiopians. Over the next several years, under the widely publicized Operation Queen of Sheba (1985) and Operation Solomon (1990), close to another sixteen thousand Ethiopian Jews were flown into Israel. By 1996, there were fifty-six thousand, and by 2002, some eighty-five thousand Ethiopian Jews were living in Israel, including twenty-three thousand who had been born there. The vast majority were employed in agriculture and manufacturing and were concentrated in the cities of Netanya, Rehovot, Haifa, Hadera, and Ashdod (Weil 1997; BenEzer 2002; Parfitt and Semi 2005; Spector 2005). In the wake of this new attention, other self-identified African Jews, such as the Lemba of southern Africa, the Abayudaya of Uganda, the Igbo of Nigeria, and even the Tutsi of Rwanda, began seeking recognition as Jews, although with varying success. Some have described this identity quest in West and sub-Saharan Africa as a "Jewishly related phenomenon" (Lis 2014; Brettschneider 2015).

Here in the United States, black Jews grew more vocal as well. In 1988, the civil rights activist Julius Lester chronicled his Orthodox conversion to Judaism in *Lovesong: Becoming a Jew*. In 1996, James McBride told the story of his Orthodox Jewish mother and black father in pre-civil rights America in *The Color of Water: A Black Man's Tribute to His White Mother*. In 2001, Rebecca Walker, the daughter of acclaimed civil rights lawyer Mel Leventhal and renowned author Alice Walker, wrote the *New York Times* best seller *Black, White, Jewish: Autobiography of a Shifting Self*.[14] Other black Jews who have risen to prominence include author Walter Mosley, civil rights lawyer Lani Guinier, actors Yaphet Kotto and Lisa Bonet, former Charleston police chief Reuben Greenberg, musicians Lenny Kravitz and Joshua Redman, gospel singer Joshua Nelson, and New York publisher Elinor Tatum, as well as, of course, the entertainer Sammy Davis Jr. They also include in-vogue performers like Yitz Jordan (a.k.a. Y-Love), an Orthodox hip-hop artist, and the Canadian-born black Jewish rapper Aubrey Graham (a.k.a. Drake).

Professor Lewis Ricardo Gordon, a secular Jew and founding member of the Caribbean Philosophical Association and Temple University's Center for Afro-Jewish Studies (founded in 2004), traces his Judaism through his Jamaican mother and calls his "New World" Judaism a "creolized world" that enabled "the possibility of black normativity" (Tobin, Tobin, et al. 2005). His embrace of secular Jewishness stands in stark contrast to the religiosity of groups like Beth Elohim Hebrew Congregation in St. Albans, Queens, which describes its customs as being more closely aligned with those of the contemporary Conservative movement, "with clear Conservative and African American influences," as its web page explains. "For example, a layperson would notice that we maintain separate seating for men and women in our sanctuary, but we believe in the complete equality of women. We allow travel on Shabbat, follow a biblical definition of kosher foods that prohibits the eating of pork and certain kinds of sea food but does not require the separation of milk and meat products." The congregation also observes the Jewish holy days of Passover, Rosh Hashanah, Yom Kippur, Chanukah, Tu Bishvat, and Purim.[15] Yet despite these many commonalities with observant Ashkenazi[16] and Sephardi[17] Jews, members distinguish themselves as Hebrew Israelites or simply Hebrews—terms they feel resonate with their African roots.

This viewpoint, that the Israelite is part of a particular Jewish tradition that evolved through the African diaspora, has been echoed by the Hebrews and Israelites whom I interviewed for this book. One participant in the study, a member of the Church of God and Saints of Christ—which, according to its website, is "the oldest African-American congregation in the United States that adheres to the tenets of Judaism"—explained, "The distinction between having a Jewish identity per se for yourself versus having an Israelite identity is that the notion of an Israelite allows you to not have to dispense with your African American cultural heritage and identity."

In *Stepping into Zion: Hatzaad Harishon, Black Jews, and the Remaking of Jewish Identity*, the Jewish studies and rhetoric scholar Janice Fernheimer argues that Black Hebrews and Israelites have employed a rhetorical strategy of "interruptive invention" to challenge a dominant narrative or paradigm and that the simple articulation of "a new or revised concept, term, identity, definition, or idea" can tear at and, in time, rupture that paradigm, making "rhetorical space for further discursive invention to occur" (Fernheimer 2014). In fact, many Black Hebrews and Israelites have drawn upon the same rhetorical strategies that whites have long employed. Through biblical exegesis, they have placed themselves at the center of the Hebrew Bible—the quintessential story of exile and return, of bondage, deliverance, and redemption—and rewritten themselves back into history. Just as religious studies scholar Edward E. Curtis IV observes in his work on Black Muslims, these new narratives link religion to the historical destiny of black people as a whole (Curtis 2005).

Cohane Michael Ben Levi, an Israelite who recognizes the charismatic self-proclaimed messiah Ben Ammi Ben-Israel as the "Anointed Messianic Leader of the Kingdom of God," invokes "Jew" and "Israelite" as related but contrasting terms, the former meaning "white Jew" and the latter signifying those legitimately descended from the ancient Hebrews. He spends much of his book, *Israelites and Jews: The Significant Difference*, reiterating that "so called Negroes" are in fact "Israelites" and argues that "the Israelites like the Egyptians were Black People" (Levi 1997).

Racial Projects

The counternarratives of Israelites like Ben Levi, which challenge the prevailing account of biblical history, might be seen as "racial projects." A racial project is a concept put forth by sociologists Michael Omi and Howard Winant to explain the dynamic between the meanings one attaches to race and the distribution of social resources in accordance with these meanings. The concept, integral to Omi and Winant's theory of racial formation, links the abstraction and symbolism of race—how race is articulated, interpreted, and represented through language, imagery, and media—to concrete structural outcomes, such as access to tangible goods and resources. It links structure with representation (Omi and Winant 2014). "Racial projects do the ideological 'work' of making these links," they write in the second edition of their seminal work, *Racial Formation in the United States: From the 1960s to the 1990s*, connecting "what race *means* in a particular discursive practice and the ways in which both social structures and everyday experiences are racially *organized*, based upon that meaning" (Omi and Winant 1994). Thus, the challenges of Black Jews to rabbinic hegemony—through biblical exegesis and the reinterpretation of key terms, verses, and passages—can be seen as a competing racial project to redefine the role of blacks in world history and to claim the favored status of the chosen people.

One could argue that Jews have also engaged in racial projects since arriving in the United States. At the turn of the twentieth century, eastern European Jewish immigrants were eager to shake off the yoke of Orientalism and to recast themselves, first as Westerners and later as white ethnics, in order to gain both social acceptance and access to valued social resources. What was once stigmatizing to European Jews, however, presented a new racial paradigm for American blacks. Indeed, early Black Jewish groups emerged during this same period. Embracing an Orientalist framework and situating themselves within an East/West binary by claiming descent from the ancient Israelites, they introduced new narratives that elevated their place in history. Religion scholar Judith Weisenfeld's historical investigation of the Commandment Keepers Ethiopian Hebrew Congregation argues persuasively that the cosmopolitan environments of northern cities like New York, Chicago, and Philadelphia between the 1920s and 1940s encouraged new religious movements in which people of African descent actively reshaped racial meanings through their engagement with religion, identifying themselves as Moorish, Asiatic, Ethiopian Hebrew, and even raceless (Weisenfeld 2016).

This book uses the case of black Americans who embrace Jewish identity to argue for a more fluid relationship between race and ethnicity than has generally been appreciated and to demonstrate how racial projects emerged within the context of religion. The counternarratives employed by Jews of African descent call attention to their agency and their ability to reassert their humanity and worth as people of the book.

The claim of Black Hebrews that Judaism is a black religion seems no more groundless than those articulated by Jewish pundits like Rabbi Harold Goldfarb, who insisted in 1977 that blacks can't be Jews because Jews are Europeans and therefore white. Goldfarb, then executive director of the Board of Rabbis of Greater Philadelphia, asserted that "a white man who claims to be Jewish is in fact a Jew, unless there is reason" to doubt his claim (Goldfarb 1977). Based on such reasoning, no person of African descent would have a foundation for making a claim as a Jew, short of proof of formal conversion.

A Jew is someone who both considers himself or herself to be Jewish and is considered to be Jewish by relevant others (Dashefsky, Lazerwitz, et al. 2003). Yet determining who the "relevant others" are can be a thorny question. For Orthodox Jews, the answers to the most important questions in Jewish law lie not in the Torah itself—the most sacred text of the Jewish religion—but in a trove of teachings, opinions, interpretations, and commentaries transmitted by rabbis in the centuries following the destruction of the Second Temple in 70 CE. While these writings form the core of rabbinic Judaism, multiple opinions on any given topic are presented and weighed against one another without any definitive conclusion provided.

Early Judaism evolved from a temple-based to a book-based religion marked by exegesis (Neusner 1995). After the destruction of the Second Temple, the Hebrew Pentateuch—that is, the Five Books of Moses—became the center of Judaism. The handwritten scroll of the Pentateuch, the Torah, became a ubiquitous foundational reference point of rabbinic religion (Neusner 1995). As a document written without vowels, many words of the *Sefer Torah* required contextual interpretation, which was provided by an oral tradition that became the domain of trained rabbis. Thus, the reciting of the Torah on the Sabbath was more an act of recitation of a known discourse, based upon the possession of specialized knowledge, than a deciphering of text (Neusner 1995). Specialized knowledge remained located within the rabbinate, which solidified their power as gatekeepers in determining who is a Jew.

Around 200 CE, Rabbi Yehudah HaNasi (Rabbi Judah the Prince) recorded and systematized the Oral Law—the legal commentary on the Torah—into sixty-three tractates, known as the Mishnah. Succeeding generations of rabbis wrote their own commentaries in a series of books called the *Talmud Yerushalmi* (Jerusalem Talmud), widely known as the Palestinian Talmud, around 400 CE (Steinsaltz 1976; Telushkin 1991). A century later, Babylonian Jewish scholars recorded a more extensive set of discussions and commentary, known as the *Talmud Bavli* (Babylonian Talmud). The Mishnah and later rabbinic commentaries, known as the Gemara, together comprise the Talmud (Telushkin 1991; Neusner 1995).

Talmudic scholars, the laureates of rabbinic Judaism, note special status for the *ba'al teshuva*, which translates as "master of return" and refers to one who returns after a lapse to a fully observant Jewish life. In fact, the Talmud notes, "In the place where a *ba'al teshuva* stands, a perfectly righteous person cannot stand" (Berachot 34b; Sanhedrin 99a). Many of those who identify as Israelites or Hebrews fall outside the bounds of rabbinic Judaism yet refer to themselves not as converts but "reverts," souls who were lost, ignorant, or had been disconnected from their true Jewish selves.

At the turn of the nineteenth century, just as Jewish claims to whiteness and Western roots were winning adherents, some blacks found religious expression in Judaism and took on Hebrew identities. An early precedent for nonrabbinic Judaism occurred within the context of eighth-century Islam, when a sect of Jews rejected mainstream rabbinic practice in favor of a more Bible-based religion that developed its own set of legal exegeses from Torah (Astren 2004). Known as Karaites, they carried the status of *safek akum*—that is, their legal status as Jews was questioned within the rabbinic world, and their identities as Jews were placed in doubt (Bleich 1975). While Karaite practice remains active in America today, it is not recognized as part of modern-day Judaism.

Another challenge to rabbinic hegemony came later during the nineteenth century from Kansas, Philadelphia, Chicago, and New York, where organized groups of Negro Americans who self-identified as Jews, Israelites, or Hebrews claimed their own right to interpret scripture (Landing 2002). Tudor Parfitt, a distinguished scholar and expert on Judaizing movements, argues that the conversion of black slaves to Judaism in both Amsterdam and the Caribbean during the colonial period, along with persistent rumors of lost black Jews in Africa, contributed to the belief among millions of people of African descent that they descended from the ancient Hebrews (Parfitt 2013). Religious scholar Allen Dwight Callahan, former professor of New Testament at Seminário Theológico Batista do Nordeste (Brazil), shows that, among African Americans, the most widely cited verse in the Bible is Psalms 68:31 (Callahan 2006):

> Princes shall come out of Egypt;
> Ethiopia shall soon stretch out her hands unto God.[18]

While the psalm is actually a celebration of the centrality of the Temple in Jerusalem, the verse has often been taken as a prophecy of the exaltation of African peoples. It held special importance for early African American Hebrews (Landing 2002). The early groups relied on translations of Greek and Latin texts that themselves were translations of the Hebrew Bible. As a result, some terms lost their original intent. For example, the Hebrew term *kush*, which refers to a vast region encompassing "the area south of Egypt descending into Central Africa and extending east to the Red Sea," was translated as "Ethiopia," thus perpetuating the link between color and geography that had existed in early biblical discourse (Goldenberg 2003).

Scholars situate the roots of organized Black Judaism in the Protestant Pentecostal movement of the nineteenth century (Baer and Singer 1992; Fauset 2002; Landing 2002). Two distinct black Protestant groups emerged, both founded by Masons. The first was the Church of the Living God, founded in Arkansas in 1888 by former slave William Christian (Landing 2002). Christian's teachings were a form of Judaic Christianity that was rooted in his claim to genealogical descent from the ancient Israelites, a strict adherence to the Ten Commandments, and an embrace of Jesus as an Israelite (Landing 2002). Without a Torah scroll or knowledge of Hebrew, members interpreted their Judaism and constructed their liturgy using Christian elements (Landing 2002). The second group was the Church of God and Saints of Christ, founded in Kansas at the turn of the century by William Saunders Crowdy, a former Baptist deacon and Union Army cook (Landing 2002). Crowdy set up tabernacles in Lawrence, Emporia, and Topeka, Kansas; and later in Sedalia, Missouri; Chicago; Philadelphia; New York City; and eventually South Africa, ordaining men as needed. Like William Christian, Crowdy believed in direct genealogical descent from the ancient Israelites. His group also engaged in such biblical practices as eating unleavened bread and foot washing, which were likely holdovers from their Pentecostal roots (Landing 2002).

Historian James Landing speculates that the Crowdys, as the community is often called, provided the ideological seedlings for Black Judaism to mushroom in Chicago and New York. Although groups with varying identifications as Jews mingled in these cosmopolitan settings, any connection between the Crowdys and Black Hebrew groups like the Commandment Keepers is purely speculative. The latter, which had a strong Caribbean membership in New York, appears to be the first group to link traditional Judaism with an idea of nationalism and race that explicitly substituted blackness for whiteness. They were also among the first to argue that all blacks were Jews. Today, the group situates itself within a normative rabbinic style of Judaism mixed with its own Afro-American traditions.

Re-staking Identity

During the 1990s, many biracial Jews, black converts to Judaism, and Black Hebrews took to organizing. In December 1993, the California African American Museum in Los Angeles sponsored the symposium "Where Worlds Collide: The Souls of African-American Jews." Two years later, the Alliance of Black Jews was formed (Wolfson 2000). One of its founding members, a biracial woman born to a Jewish mother of German descent and an Ethiopian Jewish father, described to me its first meeting, which was held at Rabbi Funnye's Beth Shalom B'nai Zaken Ethiopian Hebrew Congregation in Chicago:

> We had to have a kosher lunch because we were in his [Funnye's] building. But then we went to Leon's Barbeque, like a whole group of us. And we got a picture of us in front of Leon's saying *treif* [not kosher]. We didn't get ribs obviously.

The group soon disbanded, but other organizations quickly stepped in to fill the void. The Ayecha Resource Organization was founded in the early 2000s by Yavilah McCoy, a black Orthodox diversity consultant and recipient of a Joshua Venture Fellowship, to provide support, information, and resources for "Jews of Color" and "Jewish diversity."[19] MORESHET: Network of African Heritage Jews, founded in 2000, is an Internet-based outreach program run by a group of international volunteers under the auspices of America's Black Holocaust Museum in Milwaukee, Wisconsin, and in partnership with the American Jewish Committee.[20] In 1997, the Institute for Jewish and Community Research in San Francisco, under the directorship of the late Dr. Gary Tobin and his wife Diane, began a research initiative and community-building project called Be'chol Lashon, meaning "In Every Tongue." It advocates a more open attitude towards those who would like to convert or return to Judaism and argues that, given the increasing rates of out-marriage to non-Jews, the shift is critical to the Jewish people's survival. Its website invites viewers to "imagine a new global Judaism that transcends differences in geography, ethnicity, class, race, ritual practice, and beliefs. Discussions about 'who-is-a-real-Jew' will be replaced with celebration of the rich, multi-dimensional character of the Jewish people." The group has created a national network of multiethnic-multiracial Jews, supports multicultural Chanukah and Shavuot celebrations in the Bay Area, and holds an annual "think tank" that brings together Jews from Uganda, Ethiopia, and southern Africa, as well as representatives from the United States and Australia. By 2005, a conference entitled Jewish Leaders of Color was held at New York University's Bronfman Center for Jewish Student Life. Combined with a strong Internet-based support system, these events have greatly enhanced communication between black Jews and other Jews of color and have created a forum for addressing issues of cultural and color diversity within the Jewish American community.

With the proliferation of the Internet in the late 1990s and user-friendly search engines like Google (founded in September 1998), many self-identifying black Jews from different backgrounds and sometimes isolated circumstances began to communicate and refine collective identities as black Jews, Hebrews, and Israelites. Computer-supported social networks have become a prime location for sustaining alternative social identities, where boundaries are more permeable, interactions more diverse, and hierarchies more recursive. The black Orthodox Jewish blogger, MaNishtana, maintains a website (https://manishtana.net/) and Twitter account (@MaNishtana) in which he documents his experiences as a Jew of color. A Facebook group, Black and Jewish, provides a forum for exchanging information and resources, such as family histories, personal biographies, books, theological orientations, and ritual practices.[21] In 1998, the Yahoo! Group Aframjews—the self-proclaimed "premier online community for Jews of African Heritage"—was launched. Ayecha, which ceased operating in 2008, began operating a Yahoo! Groups Listserv for "born and converted Jews of Color" in January 2001. Other groups, such as the New York-based Kulanu (All of Us), founded in the early 1990s by Jack Zeller, have supported "lost" Jews and "emerging Jewish communities," mostly on the African continent, bringing them into contact with Western rabbis and often helping them with conversion. As a result of these initiatives, many Jews of African descent have been encouraged to come together, talk, reflect, and debate what it means to be black and Jewish, both within and outside the global black and Jewish communities.

A parallel re-staking of identity claims has occurred within Judaism itself. In 1983, the Reform Jewish movement broke with eighteen hundred years of rabbinic tradition and began recognizing Jews of both patrilineal and matrilineal descent.[22] The shift had huge repercussions for biracial Jews who traced their Jewish ancestry through their fathers. As American Jews began to experience less anti-Semitism and to marry non-Jews, the Jewish community became fearful of losing community altogether. Debate over the "loss of community" was reinvigorated with the publication of the 1990 National Jewish Population Survey, which reported a shrinking commitment by American Jews to Judaism and to the Jewish community. As social scientists described "a crisis of community," one major institutional response by Reform and Conservative institutions has been to promote Jewish ritual practice, outreach to the non-Jewish partners of members, and interethnic marriage. A few have even advocated for actively seeking converts (Tobin 1999). A second, less visible response has been to reach out to disenfranchised Jewish populations and connect them to the global Jewish community. Organizations like Kulanu have focused on embracing "Lost Jews" in foreign lands, and some activists have turned the cause into a thriving business. For example, the musician, educator, and activist Jay Sand writes and sings about isolated Jewish communities and has founded a world music and culture program for children, called All Around This World (www.allaroundthisworld.com). Other organizations, like Be'chol Lashon, are structured to help black Jews help themselves.

Meanwhile, an increasing number of American Jews are nonobservant. The scholar of American religion Barry Kosmin sees this lack of ritual observance as part of a larger trend towards the Protestantization of American religion (Kosmin and Lachman 1993). Although 47 percent of affiliated Jews were members of the Conservative movement, many of them did not define themselves as observant. In addition, most American Jews (38 percent) considered themselves Reform, although far fewer were affiliated with any particular congregation (Kosmin and Lachman 1993). According to the 2013 Pew Research Center survey of US Jews, one in five American Jews identify as having no religion (Pew Research Center 2013). Unlike Jews in other countries, non-Orthodox Jews in the United States account for the majority of both self-identified and practicing Jews (Aviv and Shneer 2005). Thus, the continued reliance on traditional Orthodox rules of membership to judge the legitimacy of blacks who make claims to Judaism not only presumes neat and clean group boundaries but also defies the post-World War II trend towards individualization, secularization, and recognition of patrilineal descent among American Jewry.

In February 2002, the Israeli Supreme Court entered a significant ruling that will influence future debates regarding who is a Jew. It held that individuals converted by the Conservative and Reform movements should be listed as Jews on the official population registry. Still, many Orthodox, Conservative, and even secular Jews continue to cling to biological notions of group membership and consider even unaffiliated and nonreligious matrilineal Jews more "Jewish" than converts (Tenenbaum and Davidman 2007). Given this entrenched bias among American Jews, the barrier facing ritually observant African American Jews with no matrilineal ties seems almost insurmountable.

Past scholars have largely treated Black Hebrews and Israelites as exotic, militant, and nationalistic sects outside the boundaries of mainstream Jewish thought and community life. Anthropologists and sociologists have tended to lump all Black Jewish groups—along with Black Muslims—into a single category, labeling them as messianic nationalist sects (Baer and Singer 1992; Kosmin and Lachman 1993). Yet black separatist groups like the Nation of Yahweh, which have been likened to cults and condemned as hate groups, have been widely dismissed by Hebrew Israelites and black Jews alike.[23] In short, because some forms of Black Judaism and, more generally, African American religious practice evolved a cosmology of the "chosen people," scholars highlight the politically racial component of their theologies and conflate vastly different groups as belonging to the same general belief systems (Dorman 2013).

Three works have shaped contemporary understandings of Black Jews: *The Black Jews of Harlem: Negro Nationalism and the Dilemmas of Negro Leadership* (1947) by Howard Brotz; *Black Jews in America: A Documentary with Commentary* (1978) by Graenum Berger; and *Black Judaism: Story of an American Movement* (2002) by James Landing. All, unfortunately, conflate self-identified nationalists, assorted Garveyites, and messianic nationalist sects. Berger's book, considered the most comprehensive study of African American Jews to date and authorized by the Commission on Synagogue Relations of the Federation of Jewish Philanthropies of New York, ignores the rise in black converts to Judaism, children of Jewish and African American parents, and adoptions of African American and Ethiopian children by Jews of European descent. It concludes that few bona fide black Jews exist in the United States and that "most have invented and accepted a mythology about their origins, which makes it difficult for them to achieve acceptance and integration within the Jewish community, whether in America, Ethiopia, or Israel" (Berger 1978). While much scholarship has characterized new Afro-American religious moverments as "messianic nationalist" (Baer and Singer 1992), many black Americans who self-identify as Jews, Hebrews, or Israelites are not nationalist, nor do they believe that their spiritual leaders are messiahs. Even Christian Israelite groups, such as the Church of God and Saints of Christ, view Jesus as only a prophet.

Rather than explore centuries of African-Jewish contact in the New World and the influence of Judaism and Jewish culture on transatlantic black populations, Berger and others situate African American collective identity within the confines of the Protestant revival of the eighteenth and nineteenth centuries. They claim that through a syncretic reinterpretation and allegorical identification with the ancient Israelites of the Christian Bible, blacks constructed new identities as Israelites and "literally *became* Jews" (Chireau 2000).

According to the sociologist Eviatar Zerubavel, the multiple ancestries of African Americans are hidden behind varied attempts of people in the Americas to "cut off entire branches of their essentially multiracial family trees in an effort to fabricate 'pure' genealogies that are virtually devoid of any 'embarrassing African ancestors'" (Zerubavel 2004). Pedigrees provide both status and identity, and consanguinity (blood) is the most prevalent claim to having Jewish roots, especially when it is carried through the maternal line.

Many groups today have taken on the term "diaspora" to characterize their exile or simply their immigration to a new home country and have become preoccupied with obtaining proof of their ancient origins. The story of the biblical exodus of the Jews from Egypt (Exodus 12:38) serves as an archetype of nationhood in the Western imagination. Over the centuries, such varied groups as the Celts, Sami, Finns, Inuit, Maya, Berbers, Igbo, Zulu, and Native Americans have traced their origins to one of the lost tribes (Benite 2009; Parfitt 2013; Lis 2014). Sociologist Stanford Lyman has conducted a sociological interpretation of what he calls the "mytho-historical legend" of the Lost Tribes and concludes that since 721 BCE, when Assyria overtook the Northern Kingdom of Israel, "every aspect of the history—and the very existence—of the ten tribes of Israel is fraught with existential controversy and epistemological conundrums" (Lyman 2001). While much attention has been given to the Beta Israel of Ethiopia, who have been officially recognized as the lost tribe of Dan, there is greater biological merit to the claim of the Lemba, a southern African group that has been found to carry—with the same frequency as European Jews—the signature haplotype, or combination of genetic markers, identified with the ancient Hebrew population. Beginning in the late 1990s, some Lemba formally converted to Conservative rabbinic Judaism as a way to establish legitimacy within the global Jewish community (Thomas, Parfitt, et al. 2000). Other groups, such as the Abayudaya of Uganda, who do not claim to be descended from the ancient Israelites, have undergone formal conversion (Twaddle 1993).[24] The precedent of the Beta Israel emboldened some sub-Saharan African groups who self-identify as Jewish to seek official recognition. An estimated thirty thousand Igbo in southern Nigeria now trace their lineage to ancient Israel, citing such practices as male circumcision on the eighth day, separation of women during their menstrual cycles, the blowing of a ram's horn, and a mourning period that bears some resemblance to the Jewish *shiva*. Some have formally converted, while others resist, believing that to do so would undermine their claim that they are already Jewish (Bruder 2008; Bruder 2012; Lis 2014; Parfitt and Fisher 2016).

Claims to an unbroken ancestral history bolster the notion that the Jewish people constitute a biological group. The search for the genetic history of the Jewish people or an identifiable set of Jewish genetic markers is testament to how we continue to reproduce these notions (D. B. Goldstein 2008; Osterer 2012). Scholars are only now beginning to reevaluate common understandings of Jewish identity and to recognize that, like the ancient Israelites, modern-day Jews are a "mixed multitude"—that is, descended from multiple tribal and ethnic origins rather than a common ethnic or racial stock (Biale 2006).

The Author's Quest

My own interest in the world of black Jews was sparked in 1995, when I joined the faculty of Yale University as an assistant professor in the Sociology and African American Studies Departments. My Jewish wife and I had moved from Manhattan to the Connecticut suburbs, where she began searching out Jewish communities, or "*shul* shopping," as the expression goes. We joined an egalitarian Conservative synagogue in New Haven, where a number of interfaith couples were also members.[25] There I noticed a scattering of people who looked black and who regularly attended Shabbat services. At Yale as well, I came across blacks who identified themselves as Jewish or Hebrew. I became fascinated by, what seemed to me, a new phenomenon and wondered how these Jews fit in with the popular narrative of a broken alliance between blacks and Jews. This was also a period of heightened Jewish angst over scapegoating by black provocateurs, such as Minister Louis Farrakhan and Khalid Abdul Muhammad of the Nation of Islam and Professor Leonard Jeffries of the City University of New York.

I began to tap into my own personal network of mostly European-descent (Ashkenazi) Jews from the New York metropolitan area in order to locate people of African descent within mainstream Jewish communities and to learn more about rabbinic Judaism and Jewish life. I used the Internet to contact people who had organized websites for or about black Jews. Some of these individuals proved critical in helping me to develop a seminational snowball sample. I took a few missteps in my early forays in the field and was upbraided by potential participants for presuming that they had not always been Jewish. I quickly learned to strip my questions of presumptive language.

By December 1998, I was well entrenched in a number of semiautonomous but overlapping networks of people who self-identified as black and Jewish (or Hebrew/Israelite), and I was a member of two web-based Listservs. Some individuals were connected to loose networks of black Jews in cities like Chicago or San Francisco, while others were isolated in cities like Allentown, Pennsylvania. I came into contact with individuals who had monoracial and biracial ancestries, with converts to Judaism, and with normative Jews by birth. They represented the full spectrum of mainstream Judaism—Orthodox, Conservative, and

Reform movements—but some traversed the boundaries, engaging in nonrabbinic forms of Judaic religious practice.

My networks of self-identified black Jews, Hebrews, and Israelites spanned across the nation to include people from New York, Connecticut, California, South Carolina, Illinois, Massachusetts, and Wisconsin, and even beyond the United States to Australia (where one participant had recently moved). The core of the data that undergirds this book is drawn from in-depth interviews, conducted between 1998 and 2003, with twenty-five participants—thirteen men and twelve women. Interviews were structured chronologically around participants' life histories. Most were conducted in participants' homes and ranged in length from forty-five minutes to six hours, although the norm was approximately two hours in length. Interviews were supplemented by frequent phone conversations or e-mail correspondences.[26] Additional field research—in New York and its suburbs, Chicago, Los Angeles, and San Francisco—was conducted through 2005.

Rather than following a classical ethnographic model, this book belongs more to the tradition of "retrospective ethnography" explored by sociologists Patricia and Peter Adler and Charles Tilly. Embedded in the temporal anchor of the late 1990s, a period in which a confluence of factors—the ascendance of the Internet, the Israeli airlifts of Ethiopian Jews, the multiracial movement, and the concomitant staking of new identities—brought a new visibility to individuals of both Jewish and African descent, this book combines macrolevel historical analysis with microlevel oral histories in order to "reconstruct actors' dispositions from the historical record" (Tilly 2007). This period, marked by an all-time low in black-Jewish relations, also saw the beginnings of mobilization among black Jews themselves. The strategies they used to refine and assert their collective identities and interests—be it as black Jews, multiracial Jews, or Black Hebrews and Israelites—can be more fully appreciated with the triangulation of interview data, historical records, and retrospective ethnographic observation. These strategies also shed light on larger dynamics between race and faith and how historically situated subjects use race as a meaningful descriptor of both religious experience and meaning. While numerous scholars have recognized various "construction sites" for making racial and ethnic identities, including labor markets, residential spaces, and social institutions, this is the first volume to detail racial projects emerging within the context of religion. Unlike the conventional use of the term, in which actors engage in racial projects to access tangible goods and resources, this book illumines how racial projects can also serve as a vehicle for claiming resources that are far less tangible, such as social recognition, religious legitimacy, or a new narrative framework.

This is also the first sociological study to explore the full complexity and diversity of black Jews, thus providing insight into their commonalities and differences, as well as the broad range of projects with which they counter white hegemony. Over the next pages, the reader will encounter biracial Jews of both matrilineal and patrilineal descent; black converts to Orthodox, Reform, and Conservative Judaism; and a former acolyte of the Black Jews of Dimona, Israel. We'll meet an elder of the Israelite tabernacle of the Church of God and Saints of Christ, which infuses Christian and Jewish teachings; a self-ordained rabbi from a Philadelphia-based congregation; and a Hebrew Israelite rabbi in Brooklyn who holds to the belief that European Jews are "Edomites." As readers engage with their voices, they will be poised to explore anew the dialogue between blacks and Jews that began in the late nineteenth and early twentieth centuries, as the meaning of blackness and Jewishness underwent profound changes, and which continues to this day. In so doing, they will also glean insights into the ways in which racial projects operate on the ground.

While most of my interviews took place more than a decade ago, one key aspect of the story is still very much evolving. In the course of writing this book—in which years were spent delving into the complexities of Judaism, black religious movements, and identity construction—I have myself become drawn towards Judaism and, in a sense, become part of the story.

Critical to the success of this book has been my relationship with the Institute for Jewish and Community Research in San Francisco. I met Dr. Gary Tobin, the institute's founder and president, in the late 1990s, just as I was completing initial interviews in New York, Chicago, and Los Angeles. He and his wife, Diane, were generous in providing me with access to their extensive network of black/Black Jews and included me in their annual think tanks held at the Fairmont Hotel in San Francisco, which brought together black Jews and Hebrews from the United States, African Jews, Latin Jews, Asian Jews, and gay and lesbian Jews. Through these conferences, I met people like Baruch A. Yehudah, a towering Israelite who then served as executive secretary of the International Israelite Board of Rabbis. His colorful Israelite garb, combined with his Fu Manchu mustache and gold loop earrings, made him one of the more memorable characters I would encounter along my journey. I also met Jack Zeller, an Ashkenazi Jew and the founder of Kulanu.[27] Zeller had been one of the key organizers in the conversion of the Abayudaya people of Uganda. The Abayudaya had adopted Jewish practices as early as 1917, but in 2002, under the stewardship of Kulanu, four Conservative rabbis from the United States and one rabbi from Israel oversaw the *halakhic* conversion of most of the remaining six hundred practicing Jews. (Some, who already believed they were Jewish, opted not to undergo conversion.) I made acquaintance with Gershom Sizomu, the spiritual leader of the Abayudaya and a regular participant in the forums. When I first met him, he had been attending the Zeigler School of Rabbinic Studies at the American Jewish University (formerly the University of Judaism) in Los Angeles. In 2008, he was ordained and returned to Uganda to establish a *yeshiva*. Sizomu is widely recognized as the first black rabbi from sub-Saharan Africa to be ordained at an American rabbinical school. Today he is a senior rabbinic associate at Be'chol Lashon and receives support for projects like the Tobin Health Center in eastern Uganda.

Along with Abayudaya and Lemba Jews, I came to know Rwandan Tutsi, like Yochanan (Jean) Bwejeri, who was living in exile in Belgium. According to Bwejeri, the Tutsi are descendants of a pre-Talmudic Hebraic tribe and the remaining royal branches of the Solomonic House of Ethiopia. He claimed to be a descendent of the Bene-(Za)gwe (Benengwe) clan of Ethiopia and heir of the title of Prince of Nkoronko, and he carried around a short, elaborately carved wooden staff that symbolized his royal lineage. As a friendship developed between us, he engaged my wife's services to translate, from French to English, an article he wrote on the Jewish roots of the Tutsi people.

Also participating in the annual think tank was Rabbi Rigoberto Emmanuel Viñas, a thirty-three-year-old Sephardi rabbi of *converso* background. His family, Cuban exiles, rediscovered their Jewish roots when they immigrated to Miami. Rabbi Manny, as he is known, founded El

Centro de Estudios Judíos Torat Emet, which serves not only as a center for Jewish learning and prayer but as a resource for those of *converso* background (former Jews who had been forced to convert to Christianity) who seek to return to their roots (Kagen and Morgan 2009).[28] At the time of our acquaintance, he had 180 families in his congregation, about a quarter of whom had gone through formal conversion.

I also had the honor of meeting the late Rabbi Hailu Paris, a revered patriarch of the Ethiopian Hebrew community who mentored a generation of Hebrew Israelite rabbis through the Commandment Keepers in Harlem, the Mount Horeb Congregation in the Bronx, and the Israelite Rabbinical Academy in Queens. Although his claim that he was born in Ethiopia and adopted by Eudora Paris, a member of Arnold Josiah Ford's delegation to Ethiopia, has been publically disputed, many Jews and Israelites have continued to see him as a crucial bridge between African American and European Jewry (Kestenbaum 2014). My greatest honor was to have met Ephraim Isaac, the preeminent Ethiopian-Yemenite scholar of ancient Semitic languages and civilizations and director of the Institute of Semitic Studies in Princeton, New Jersey.

During the conferences, we discussed everything from how to promote outreach, diversity, and growth among the Jewish people to anti-Israelism and anti-Semitism. Yet some of the greatest contention arose during Shabbat services. With groups ranging from self-identified Israelites, who veered towards traditional practices, to more secular but *halakhic* Jews (those born to a Jewish mother), fundamental differences emerged, especially when it came to the role of women. Should there be separate seating? Could women read from the Torah? Yet even these lively debates captured the passionate, argumentative spirit of Judaism. If there is any merit to the old adage "Two Jews, three opinions," one can only imagine the layers and nuances that are added to the mix when race, continents, and varying ancestral traditions and claims are introduced.

As I conducted interviews and explored the historical record, it became clear that scholars of religion had not looked closely at the impact of Jews and Judaism on black American identities. Blacks and Jews, the prevailing narrative went, were two distinct groups that first encountered one another during the late nineteenth century. My investigation revealed that the notions scholars held about the historical relations between Africans and Jews were simplistic, naive, and incomplete. The questions I have tackled throughout my journey, and which I address in this book, concern the intersection and negotiation of race, religion, ethnicity, and culture, and the ways in which these categories continue to serve as a basis for group difference in the modern world. This book explores how individuals assert their dual identities and find acceptance within their respective communities. How do they respond to the public conflicts waged between blacks and Jews? How do they view provocateurs like Minister Louis Farrakhan of the Nation of Islam? To what extent do they feel connected to Israel or identify with Zionism? How do they negotiate both racism and anti-Semitism, while learning to synthesize two socially stigmatized group identities that have been shaped by discrimination, segregation, and biological notions of group difference? Do Hebrews and Israelites observe traditional Jewish holidays and the dietary laws of *kashrut*? To what extent do they incorporate the Talmud and Mishnah into their religious practice? And how do they identify with the broader Jewish community in the United States and overseas? In short, how do Hebrews and Israelites consider themselves to be a part of the Jewish people as it has come to be defined in the modern era?

This book argues that their assertions of Jewish identity illuminate the fluidity of the relationship between race and ethnicity. Both East/West and black/white binaries shaped the racial morphing of Ashkenazi Jews throughout the nineteenth and twentieth centuries until their newly imagined whiteness became inextricable from their Jewishness. Today, scholars agree that Jews have become white folks (Brodkin 1998; Jacobson 1999; Roediger 2007; E. L. Goldstein 2008; Glenn 2010). But blacks who identify as Jews have had to create counterhegemonic projects to challenge these essentialist notions, some choosing to claim that only *they* are the true descendants of the children of Israel and that white Jews are imposters. Meanwhile, mainstream black Jews (those recognized within rabbinic Judaism) carry the burden of continually asserting their legitimacy; without a counternarrative of their own, they struggle to fit within a Western narrative of Jewishness that precludes their very existence.

Chapter 1, "Jews, Blacks, and the Color Line," moves across continents and decades to outline the evolving social scientific discourse on race regarding both blacks and Jews. It explores the shifting categories of the

US census and its role in solidifying race difference by deploying narrow conceptions rooted in color and phenotype—that is, the biological, inheritable, aspects of race—while redefining ideas about culture, religion, language, nation, and history as malleable, changeable constructs that only "ethnic" immigrants possessed. Finally, it examines how the "whitening" of Jewish identity continues to limit the claims of black Jews and Black Hebrews.

Since the nineteenth century, Western scholars have selectively made use of racial taxonomies to draw boundaries between Africans and Europeans, as well as among Africans themselves. Chapter 2, "B(l)ack to Israel," focuses on the Beta Israel, a small band of Ethiopians from the mountains of Gondar who claimed to be the descendants of the ancient Israelites. It traces how racial logic was used to argue, first, that these people could not possibly be Jews because they were black and, later, that they could not possibly be black because they were Jews.

If most Jews in the US trace their direct lineage to eastern Europe, many Black Hebrews and Israelites trace their lineage to Ethiopia or the Caribbean. For at least some individuals, there is likely historical merit to their claims. While chapter 2 focuses on the Ethiopian line, chapter 3, "Black-Jewish Encounters in the New World," examines the brief intersection of the African and Jewish diasporas in the Caribbean and the earliest Black Hebrew and Israelite communities in the United States.

Chapter 4, "Back to Black," explores the major dividing lines among Black Hebrews and Israelites today and how identity terms like "Jew," "Hebrew," and "Israelite" can serve as rhetorical constructs to map out territory and reify boundaries. It argues that the challenges of Black Hebrews to rabbinic hegemony—through biblical exegesis and the reinterpretation of key terms, verses, and passages—serve as competing racial projects to redefine the role of African peoples in world history and lay claim to a chosen status.

Chapter 5, "Your People Shall Be My People," focuses on black converts to normative Judaism. This group includes those who identify with mainstream Judaism as well as members of Black Hebrew groups who seek a connection with the broader Jewish world. While few studies of religious conversion focus specifically on converts to Judaism, the scant research available suggests that, unlike the case of conversion to Christianity, in which a life-changing experience often sets individuals on a new spiritual path, marriage and family play a significant role in conversion to Judaism. Yet the research suggests that in the case of blacks who convert to Judaism, other factors are at play. Many feel a spiritual connection to Judaism or believe that they had Jewish ancestors, and they long to formalize and strengthen these bonds to the larger Jewish world.

Scholars have explored identity formation among individuals with one black parent and one white parent, but the processes become ever more complex when the dimensions of ethnic culture and religion are inserted. Chapter 6, "Two Drops," examines the identity options of biracial Jews and the various strategies they employ to publically signify membership in one or the other community. The chapter also sheds light on the larger dynamics of how individuals selectively articulate and assert identities and broaden the boundaries and meanings of groups.

Chapter 7, "When Worlds Collide," examines the cleavages in black-Jewish relations in the United States and the degree to which insider/outsider status shapes the perceptions and responses of biracial Jews, black converts, and Hebrews/Israelites to black anti-Semitism and Jewish racism. The interviews, which were largely conducted during a period in which relations between blacks and Jews were at a historic low, shed light on the strategies these groups use to negotiate conflicting interests and to synthesize two socially stigmatized group identities.

The concluding chapter considers the significance of the growing population of self-identified black Jews and its implications for world Judaism in the twenty-first century. It also returns to the concept of racial projects, discussing how blacks have engaged in competing projects (both "racist" and "antiracist") to assert their identities as Jews and their place within the global Jewish narrative. Finally, it considers an expanded notion of racial projects, suggesting that they need not translate into tangible goods and resources. Rather, they can serve the psychological and social needs for acceptance, legitimacy, and self-affirmation.

1

Jews, Blacks, and the Color Line

It's so obvious for me. Some people, historians and even scientists, turn a blind eye to the truth. Once, to say Jews were
a race was anti-Semitic, now to say they're not a race is anti-
Semitic. It's crazy how history plays with us.
—Shlomo Sand, history professor at Tel Aviv University and
author of *The Invention of the Jewish People*[1]

If men define situations as real, they are real in their
consequences.
—W. I. Thomas, The Thomas Theorem[2]

During the late nineteenth century, just as concepts of race were being
solidified by racial statistics (the quantification of perceived racial difference using objective methodologies), eastern European Jewish immigrants
and Negro migrants from the South converged in Philadelphia, New York
City, and other dense urban areas.[3] Between 1900 and 1940, Jews and
blacks frequently lived in overlapping neighborhoods (Zunz 2000; Diner
2006). Jews ultimately benefited from the solidification of the color line,
which allowed for fluid, hyphenated identities—expressed as ethnicities—
and helped to justify the distribution of resources along a white/black
binary. On the other hand, all peoples of African descent, regardless of
culture or ancestry, were collapsed into one fixed category. Black Jews
thus represent the merging of two dichotomous categories—one fluid,
the other fixed—within a bifurcated system. Indeed, their very presence
forces us to reconcile two negating forces, the transcendent and the immutable, into a single new construct. Exploring the historical processes that
shaped the formation of racial and ethnic categories in the United States
allows us to see how these processes continue to shape the ways in which
we perceive Jews of African descent and helps us understand the broader
dynamics between race and ethnicity.

Racial Categories and the US Census

The system of white privilege in the United States relied on the formalization and maintenance of racial categories, adopted early by the US census, and the establishment of the one-drop rule, a uniquely American framework for understanding the meanings of particular ancestries and of our own imagined origins. The census helped to shape the formation of contemporary racial and ethnic boundaries; the segregated spaces that resulted from these envisioned boundaries in turn reinforced the census categories and were used as evidence of biological differences. Race made place, and place made race (Haynes 2006).

Between the end of Reconstruction and the 1920s, American society adopted the idea that a single drop of "African blood" was sufficient to warrant classifying someone as "Negro." Called the hypodescent rule by anthropologists and the traceable amount rule by the US courts, the one-drop rule determined civic, social, political, educational, residential, labor, and cultural boundaries. It was policed by an array of government agencies, market practices, and social norms and was ultimately internalized by individuals of mixed European and African lineage (F. J. Davis 2001; Haynes 2006). Hypodescent treated blackness as a contaminant of whiteness. In contrast, the classification of Native Americans was more benign: the Bureau of Indian Affairs, along with the courts and the census, used the concept of blood quantum, which attempted to quantify the ratio of "Indian blood" to "white blood" within an individual (Snipp 1989). Having a little Indian blood made one a little bit Indian, but having a trace of African blood rendered a person all black.

The social category "Negro" first emerged during the early period of colonial slavery. It was used to homogenize a variety of West African cultural identities—Igbo, Ewe, Serer, Biafada, Arada, Bakongo, Wolof, Bambara, Ibibio, and Oyo Yoruba—through a system of labor exploitation, political domination, and social exclusion (Blassingame 1979). While neither "Negro" nor "black" appears in the US Constitution, African slaves were referred to as "other Persons" in the Three-Fifths Compromise and as such were formally excluded from the social contract (Mills 1999). In 1790, Congress limited naturalization to "free white persons," and Negroes were barred from immigration until the Naturalization Act of 1870. The Fugitive Slave Act of 1793, signed into law by George Washington, further bolstered the institution of slavery.

The first census, taken in 1790, was limited to five social categories: free white males of sixteen years and upward; free white males under sixteen years; free white females; all other free persons (by sex and color); and slaves (Gauthie 2002). In the 1800 and 1810 censuses, the US Census Bureau tracked the number of all other free persons "except Indians not taxed" (Gauthie 2002). Between 1840 and 1860, the census added a "mulatto" category to distinguish among slaves. The designation was based purely on visible color differences. One noteworthy heading was entitled "Color" and instructed census takers to "insert in all cases when the slave is black, the letter B; when he or she is mulatto, insert M. The color of all slaves should be noted" (DeBow 1853; Nobles 2000).

In 1840, 1850, and 1860, the term "mulatto" was used but not defined for enumerators. But by 1870, "mulatto" had become imbued with biological import, defined as including "quadroons, octoroons, and all persons having any perceptible trace of African blood" (F. J. Davis 2001). By 1890, the term "race" was officially added to the color category, reflecting the new scientific discourse of the day, and census takers were instructed to assess the exact portion of African blood: "Be particularly careful to distinguish between blacks, mulattos, quadroons, and octoroons. The word 'black' should be used to describe those persons who have three-fourths or more black blood; 'mulatto,' those persons who have from three-eighths to five-eighths black blood; 'quadroon,' those persons who have one-fourth black blood; and 'octoroon,' those persons who have one-eight or any trace of black blood" (Beveridge 2001). That year, some 63 million Americans were designated as white, Negro, mulatto, quadroon, octoroon, Chinese, or Japanese. The mulatto category was finally abandoned in 1900, only to return briefly in 1910. By the 1920s, the term "Negro" was applied to any person with any African ancestry (F. J. Davis 2001). The shifting boundaries that solidified the one-drop rule challenge the notion that clear-cut boundaries ever existed between whites and blacks in America. Census takers ascribed race based on their own assessments until the 1960s and 1970s, when mail-in questionnaires and the self-reporting of race replaced door-to-door interviews (Perez and Hirschman 2009).

The one-drop rule was enforced as recently as 1982, when the Louisiana Bureau of Vital Statistics refused to change the racial designation of Susie Guillory Phipps from "Negro" to "white," ruling that one thirty-second of "Negro blood" made a person Negro (Omi and Winant 1994). Unlike European immigrants, who were deemed as possessing cultures, or even the Jews, who were seen as being imbued with biologies that could change over time, Africans were thus viewed through an immutable racial lens.

Segregated together in employment and housing, those with any visible "negroid" traits or known African ancestry were increasingly viewed, and viewed themselves, as one group (Haynes 2006). Both mixed and "pure" Negroes became one political category and social group, and the physiological, cultural, religious, and even class differences within the developing black community were overshadowed by the concept of a Negro race (Green and Wilson 1991; F. J. Davis 2001).

The census helped to solidify race difference by deploying narrow conceptions rooted in color and phenotype—that is, the biological, inheritable aspects of race—while redefining ideas about culture, religion, language, nation, and history as malleable, changeable constructs that only "ethnic" immigrants possessed (Hattam 2007).

Jews as Ethnic White Folks: The Evolution of an Idea

While the role of phenotype in marking the Negro/black social category has been well documented, less attention has been paid to the racialization of Jews. Well into the twentieth century, scholars of ethnology and social science employed new photographic technologies and anthropometrical measurements to establish whether Jews were a pure biological race. Eighteenth- and nineteenth-century social Darwinists considered Jewish difference to be manifested in the Jewish body, and Jewish physicality represented the antithesis of Christian civil society. The Jewish male's circumcised penis, the "Jewish foot," and the "Jewish nose" were all considered the physiological manifestations of Jewishness (Gilman 1991). The nose was considered the single most distinctive anthropological characteristic of the Jew, longer and narrower than that of any of the other people (Gilman 1991). It was just a few years following the defeat of the Nazi regime that the international scientific community finally concluded that, despite popular notions of Jewish physicality, Jews were not a biological race (Shapiro 1960). Sociologists have applied the concept of racialization most often to African Americans (Gotham 2000; Haynes 2006; Bridges 2011). Yet we can expand the concept to include the racialization of Jews in the sixteenth century. The nature of anti-Jewish prejudice has evolved from anti-Judaism—the belief that Jews were collectively responsible for the death of Jesus Christ—to anti-Semitism, which laid the basis for their racialization and the notion that the Jewish body was intrinsically evil (Fredrickson 2002). It is this shift, from Judaism as a source of social stigma to the Jewish body as a source of evil, that marked the new racial thinking of the early modern era.

The early modern era proved to be an especially important period because it developed the foundational logic that guides racial thinking in the modern world. It was during this period that the physical body first came to signify the permanent difference setting Jews apart from Christians—not religiously as Christ Killers but physically as possessing polluted bodies (Hutchison and Haynes 2008; Haynes and Hutchison 2012). Since antiquity, the Jewish body had been viewed as a "body of concealment," and by the Renaissance, the rite of circumcision was widely considered a secret practice and representative of other secret and ignominious practices of a supposed sexual nature (Sennett 1996). This was the period that ushered in four hundred years of transatlantic slavery and produced ideas about moral worth, skin color, and physical characteristics that intertwined with images of Africans as blacks, Jews as Africans, and blacks as Jews in the consciousness of Westerners.

By 1262, a "Jewish district" was thriving in Prague, and Frankfurt-am-Main, the most famous of the German ghettos, was well established in the 1460s (R. C. Davis 2001). Yet it was in sixteenth-century Venice, which had become a dynamic and cosmopolitan commercial center, that the Jewish ghetto took on a distinctly racial character. Sociologist Richard Sennett details how the Venetian ghetto acted like a social and political condom to shield Venetians from the polluting qualities of the Jewish body (Sennett 1996). It fostered a very different "ethos of isolation" from that of Renaissance Rome, where the objective was to transform the culture of the Jews (Sennett 1996). In fact, the Venetian ghetto can be viewed as a manifestation of early Orientalist thinking, which viewed the Jewish body as sensual and alluring, as well as the beginning of racialization in the New World (Sennett 1996). Orientalism is said to have begun in the early thirteenth century, when a field of study emerged that framed the Orient in juxtaposition to the Occident (Said 1977). The Orient was characterized as premodern, primitive, and backwards, yet it was also viewed as exotic, foreign, mysterious, and profound (Said 1978). Thus, the West had both contempt for and fascination with the Orient (Said 1977).

In Venice, Jews were Orientalized as a type, and the Jewish body—at once seductive and defiling—contained the "lure of the Oriental" and became a signifier of a stigmatized master status, that is, the manifestation or outward appearance of an inner deficiency that results or would result in infamy and dishonor, from which everything else about a person is interpreted (Goffman 1986; Sennett 1996). As Sennett makes clear, Europeans believed that by cloistering Jews behind ghetto walls, they were "isolating a disease" in their midst: "Christians were afraid of touching Jews: Jewish bodies were thought to carry venereal diseases as well as to contain more mysterious polluting powers" (Sennett 1996).

Jews were viewed as a "pariah" people and were increasingly associated with the leper's touch and filth; they were blamed for the spread of leprosy itself, which was often conflated with syphilis (Sennett 1996). By the time that Shakespeare's *Merchant of Venice* (1596–1597) opened in England, even the most prominent English Jews were held in contempt and treated little better than animals (Sennett 1996).

The practice of confining Jews behind ghetto walls developed over the course of centuries. In 1179, the Church's Third Council of the Lateran issued a vaguely defined decree that Christians should no longer live amongst Jews. Secular authorities throughout Christendom chose different interpretations of the papal policy (R. C. Davis 2001). And in 1215, Pope Innocent III hoped to prevent illicit sexual intercourse between Christians and Jews by imposing clothing distinctions on them. Already, artists had adopted the funnel-shaped hat sometimes worn by Jews to signify all Jews, and by 1220, the same hat was being used to depict Jews and heretics alike. By the 1260s, the pointed *Judenhut* was imposed by church authorities on all Jews of Germany and Bohemia (Vincent 1994; Malkiel 2001).

In Venice, by 1221, Jews were required by edict to wear distinguishing markers of material culture, while they were also forbidden from owning land within the ghetto and obligated to rent (at rates one-third above the norm) from absentee owners (Ravid 2001). Each morning they would don their yellow hats (men) and scarves (women) and leave the ghetto to work or shop among Christians (Calimani 1988). By 1424, the Venetian Republic had issued a decree banning marriage between Jewish men and Christian women. In 1443, relations between Christian men and Jewish women were prohibited, and all Jews were required to wear badges with yellow circles. The badge was replaced by a yellow *beretta* in 1496 (Ravid 2001; Horowitz 2006). In exchange for a special tax levied against them, Jews were allowed to direct the Università, a colonial-like structure of self-governance under the auspices of Venetian Republic (Calimani 1988; Malkiel 2001).

Venice, a trading economy, was desperately in need of a source of credit (Sennett 1996). As in other Christian societies, the Jews of Venice were prohibited from becoming nobles or serfs and were cast into an intermediary role, serving as merchants, peddlers, and moneylenders. Moneylending, or usury, which typically charged interest rates of up to 20 percent, was considered corrupt and a "theft of time" by Christians (Sennett 1996). Over a period of some one hundred years, three distinct Jewish ghettos emerged in Venice: the Ghetto Nuovo (New Ghetto) in 1516, the Ghetto Vecchio (Old Ghetto) in 1541, and the Ghetto Nuovissimo (Very New Ghetto) in 1633.

These ghettos came on the heels of a century of rising anti-Semitism. As early as 1378, Archdeacon Ferrand Martinez vilified the Jews not only for the murder of Christ but also for their outmoded practices, which doomed them to eternity. Over the next thirteen years, his fiery sermons in Seville incited violence against Jews, which culminated with the ravaging of Seville's Jewish quarter on June 6, 1391. Yet for the first time, a few Jews who agreed to be baptized were allowed to remain (Roth 1996, 21). The Spanish Inquisition was well under way before it was officially declared by papal bull in 1478. Christian leaders in Italy and Spain had already been spreading rumors that the Passover matzot were prepared with Christian blood and that Jews drank the blood of Christians to remove the stench associated with their diabolic nature (Baum 2008, 32). Even after they fled Spain (1492) and later Portugal (1540), Jews were treated as a permanently alien presence.

In Venice, the practice of usury and the outbreak of the bubonic plague (as well as syphilis) further stigmatized Jews and the Jewish body

(Sennett 1996, 225) and prompted the building of the first Venetian ghetto. Unlike the Roman Ghetto (1555), which was built by Pope Paul IV to convert Jews to Christianity, the Venetian ghettos were created to contain Jews (Sennett 1996, 236). By 1589, they contained some 1,700 Jews, who were organized as an administrative unit governed first by a leader and later by a council of elders. By 1642, 2,414 individuals were housed in the three increasingly overcrowded spaces (Calabi 2001). Five synagogues were eventually established to accommodate Jews emigrating from France, Italy, Germany, the Levant, Spain, and Portugal (Ravid 2001). Despite the Jewish cultural renaissance that evolved with each successive wave of newcomers, Jews were unable to obtain formal citizenship rights and were collectively taxed as a corporate entity in return for sovereignty in matters of religion and justice (Malkiel 2001).

Jews as Black

Descriptions of Jewish and black physicality converge in the scholarship of the late nineteenth century. Consensus held that Jews were black or swarthy and that Jewish blackness "was not only a mark of racial inferiority but also an indicator of the diseased nature of the Jew" (Gilman 1991; Brodkin 1998). Indeed, this theme would later be exploited in the art propaganda of the German National Socialist Party. *Entartete Kunst* (Degenerative Art) opened in Munich in July 1937 (Barron 1991, 15). The exhibit, which singled out the Josephine Bakers, Bix Beiderbeckes, Duke Ellingtons, and Benny Goodmans of the Jazz Age, advanced a Nazi conception of racial degeneracy that linked blacks and Jews in "an Afro-Jewish plot to subvert Aryan culture." Jews and blacks were framed as "degenerates" marked by abnormal bodily deformities, feebleness, and behavioral and sexual excesses (Barron 1991, 26). Between 1937 and 1941, an *Entartete Kunst* exhibit toured thirteen German cities and exposed more than two million visitors to the idea that avant-garde art was subversive and associated with Bolshevism, Americanism, and Jews (Barron 1991). In 1938, the Nazis staged an exhibition of degenerative music, called *Entartete Musik*.[4] The poster created for the exhibit morphed blacks and Jews into a grotesque composite.

As their numbers increased in the 1880s, eastern European Jews in America were viewed as a potentially foreign element, along with other non-Protestant immigrant groups, such as the Irish and Italians. The eighteenth-century image of the Jew as backward and parasitic became countered by new images of modern Jews as a natural part of the urbanized, capitalist order of the civilized world (E. L. Goldstein 2006, 2). Between 1885 and 1913, ethnologists, sociologists and anthropologists deliberated over whether Jews were a preindustrial "race" (Hattam 2007). Lamarckian science competed with the social Darwinism of the nineteenth century. Jean-Baptiste Lamarck was a French zoologist and early evolutionary theorist, perhaps best known for championing the theory of the inheritance of acquired characteristics, which was presented in 1801—a full fifty-eight years before Darwin's book on natural selection was published (Burkhardt 2013).[5] According to Lamarck, if an organism changes during its life in order to adapt to a new environment, those changes will be passed on to its offspring. Unlike Darwin, who argued that we inherit our genetic codes wholesale from our parents, Lamarck believed we also inherit the traits and adaptations that our parents acquired during their lifetimes (Burkhardt 2013). Lamarckian thought impacted the way nineteenth-century scientists came to view social differentiation. They believed that history, climate, and geography could transform a group's social practices, such as language or religion, into an inheritable biological trait like temperament or a particularly shaped nose. Repetition became habit, habit became instinct, and instinct was inheritable. Lamarckians distinguished between "historic" races, that is, groups whose heterogeneous origins crystalized into a common bloodline over time, and "natural" racial groups, which corresponded to broad geographic regions and were symbolized by skin color: black, white, red, and yellow (Hattam 2007, 3). Africans were collectively seen as a natural race, unchanged by time, while Jews and Mexicans were understood to be historic races, groups whose genetic makeup had been transformed over time by climate and geography (Hattam 2007, 24–25). Interestingly, late nineteenth-century Jewish racial scientists embraced Lamarckian notions of historic races to counter anti-Semitic notions of Jews as an unhealthy race or nation (Hart 2011, xxvi).

In 1897, the MIT economist William Z. Ripley wrote a series of essays on the "Racial Geography of Europe" that were published in *Popular Science Monthly* and later compiled in *The Races of Europe: A Sociological Study*. Rejecting his earlier ideas that historical races were shaped by environment, he argued that nationality often followed language but that *race* bore no relationship to either. In chapter 14, entitled "The Jews and Semites," he struggled to find a term for Jews that transcended religion while avoiding the stigma of "race" and opted for the vague construct of "people" (Ripley 1940; Hollinger 2006; Hattam 2007). The object of racialized discourses themselves, Jews appropriated the idioms of race to claim inclusion (Hart 2011). The decoupling of Jews (and the Jewish body) from ideas about geography would set the stage for their transformation into a fluid, hyphenated American identity anchored in whiteness, ethnicity, and cultural pluralism.

A Hyphenated Whiteness

Roughly two million eastern European Jews immigrated to the United States between 1870 and 1920 (Lederhendler 2009), a period in which modern racial classifications were solidifying and a new *herrenvolk* (master race) republicanism was pushing nonwhite groups outside the margins of civil society (Loewen 2005; Roediger 2007).[6] Historian James W. Loewen refers to the strategic withdrawal of African Americans from northern and western towns and rural areas during this period as the "Great Retreat" (Loewen 2005). Realtors, banks, police chiefs, chambers of commerce, local white citizens, and the state "openly favored white supremacy and helped to create and maintain all-white communities" (Loewen 2005). Whites reconstructed notions of civil society by using mob violence and intimidation to drive out first the Chinese and soon after black Americans, from small, street-car, and industrial working-class towns, suburbs, and assorted counties across the nation (Muhammad 2011, 9).

Negro migrants from the South encountered thousands of towns and local jurisdictions that had been established as "sundown towns," places where the predominantly white population barred blacks and other racialized residents from settling (Loewen 2005). Jews were sometimes excluded from these white-only spaces as well, forcing many to abandon their religious practice and pass as "parvenus," Hannah Arendt's term for people who pass into Anglo-gentile society (Arendt 1978; Loewen 2005).

The courts reinforced white privilege, ruling in numerous cases— spanning from 1878 to 1928—that various persons from the Philippines,

Burma, and Hawaii, as well as those classified as "mixed race," should be denied classification as white. Still they were unclear about the status of Semitic peoples like the Syrians and "Arabians" (Baum 2008). The myth of a Caucasian race had existed since the 1790s, when the German naturalist Johann Friedrich Blumenbach (1752–1840) co-opted the term from the popular philosopher Christoph Meiners. Yet the link between Caucasian origins and whiteness was rejected in 1923, when the Supreme Court denied naturalization to a "high-caste Hindu" in the *US v. Bhagat Singh Thind* case (Baum 2008). The court reasoned that while the children of European parentage lost their "distinctive hallmarks" and quickly "merged into the mass of our population," Hindus did not. Meanwhile, beginning in the 1930s, the Home Owners' Loan Corporation and the Federal Housing Administration permitted the redlining of Jewish inner-city neighborhoods, contributing to their concentration into suburban "gilded ghettos" (Phillips 2016).

Heated debates arose in academic journals over which groups could blend easily into an evolving American nation, one that defined itself increasingly as native, Protestant, and white (Hattam 2007). Could Jews become part of this *herrenvolk*, which reassured the emerging white working class that one might lose everything but one's whiteness (Roediger 2007)? Could they still maintain their religious practices and distinct identities as Jews? Cultural pluralism—an idea first articulated by Jews—provided the answer. By representing the nation as a culturally pluralistic society, a nation of hyphenated identities, Jews could be both white and Jewish.

The vision of America as a culturally pluralistic society countered the narrative of a melting pot, in which divergent groups come together to form a new culture, losing their own cultural distinctions in the process. Both of these concepts were introduced by Jews in the first decade of the twentieth century: the former by Horace M. Kallen, a Jewish immigrant from Germany; the latter by Israel Zangwill, a Jewish novelist and playwright from England, whose play *The Melting Pot* introduced a powerful metaphor of racial and cultural amalgamation that would be linked with American identity for the next century. In Zangwill's play, the hero proclaims, "America is God's Crucible, the great Melting Pot where all the races of Europe are melting and reforming!" (Ratner 1984). Zangwill's play, which was first staged in 1908, affirmed the classic assimilation model in its purest form, while Kallen's cultural pluralism stood as a direct challenge. Kallen concluded that American vitality lay not in adopting an Anglo-Saxon culture but in allowing individuals to retain their ethnicity while adopting common democratic principles and politics as their own (Ratner 1984). Cultural pluralism could save the Jews from extinction in America while protecting them from racial marginalization. Contrary to what classic assimilation models argue, rather than disappearing into whiteness, Jews tried to inhabit a position between whiteness and otherness. Many immigrant Jews found these ideas an acceptable compromise between racial exclusion and total group annihilation (Hattam 2001).

It was Kallen, along with the Jewish scholars Julius Drachsler and Isaac Berkson, who would use the term "ethnic group" to assert social difference—plurality over singularity, malleability over fixity, culture over biology, and language and religion over blood and ancestry (Hattam 2007). Groups that were defined as "ethnic" were deemed culturally compatible with whiteness, in contrast to those that were racialized as other. Cultural pluralism eventually found its way into sociological scholarship through the work of Georg Simmel and Robert Park, who adopted the term "ethnic" to describe religious, national, and cultural difference.

Scholars have shown that early twentieth-century America used the institutionalization of racial classifications on official census documents as a way to distinguish social and political differences between groups considered morally fit for absorption into American civic and political life and those held apart from the body politic as permanent racial outsiders (Hattam 2007; Loveman 2014). Kallen's cultural pluralism model helped Jews to transcend the national census categories by creating an ethnic identity within a pluralist framework that was neither racial nor religious in character, yet still identifiably Jewish. Ethnicity increasingly became an alternative scheme for signifying social differences among non-Protestant immigrants, especially Jews.

During the 1920s and 1930s, the concept of ethnicity was adopted by urban sociologists from the Chicago school, under the leadership of Robert E. Park, but did not come into widespread use until the 1930s (Hochschild 2005). Preoccupied with the cultural contact between groups in the bustling Chicago metropolis and with the processes of social disorganization and assimilation in the urban milieu, Park posited a "race relations cycle," consisting of four stages in the development of group relations: competition, conflict, accommodation, and assimilation. The cycle, which presumed a natural progression of group contact, treated both racial and ethnic groups as equivalent, organic groups (Haynes 2006). According to this theory, Negroes, like the immigrants of Europe, would lose their historical attachments to race and become absorbed into the industrial city. While Chicago scholars emphasized ethnic difference as uniquely American, racialization regulated the distribution of societal rewards and punishments; the allocations of goods; the performance of services; the organization of residential communities, neighborhoods, and schools; and even who one married and where one was buried (Haynes 2006; Omi and Winant 2014).

Racial difference was treated as fixed and immutable in biology. Racial stigma was perceived as an essential characteristic of individuals ascribed as black, in contrast to ethnic peoples, who were understood as being only loosely tied to ancestry and strongly linked to culture and, consequently, subject to individual and societal change. As noted earlier, Jews and Mexicans were deemed special kinds of groups: heterogeneous, plural, malleable, and defined by culture, language, and religion. Most considered Jews a race in 1880. Struggles over the nature of "Jewish difference" and identification as white "produced debates and ideological instabilities that made it difficult, even undesirable, for white Jews to accept Black Jews as authentic" (Gold 2003). By 1935, for census, immigration, and naturalization purposes, Jews were widely accepted as being on the white side of the color line, in contrast to blacks (Africans), who were defined as racially other and politically second class (Hattam 2007).

By 1910, Jews were divided between those who argued for ancestral and cultural continuity and those who defined themselves as assimilated, secular "white Americans." Reform Jews, who had immigrated from Germany before the nineteenth century, along with a handful of Sephardi Jews, such as the Cardozos and Lopezes, had become well entrenched in American society and entered elite, largely Christian circles in both business and politics (Sarna 2005). The arrival of a new, ostentatiously Jewish wave of immigrants from eastern Europe—pious *shtetl* Jews, secular socialist Jews, cultural Yiddishists, and Zionists— undermined their sense of security. It was in fact Zionists, like the German immigrant Kallen, who held most firmly to the idea that "ethnic groups," "ethnic types," and "ethnic loyalties" existed and that Jews were the ideal representation of the "ethnic" (Hattam 2007). The Zionist scholar, Hannah Arendt, built on the insights of sociologist Max Weber in her classic 1944 essay, "The Jew as Pariah: A Hidden Tradition," to claim that the transformation of Judaism (writ religion) into "Jewishness" (writ culture) was the central question facing Jews in the modern world. Could the socially ostracized religious Jews of eastern Europe simply be like other peoples and blend into an increasingly secular modern world, or would doing so condemn them to historical annihilation? For Arendt, the only answer was to reject their "exceptional" status as assimilated individuals and reaffirm their individual and collective claims as human beings, becoming "conscious pariahs" (self-conscious Jews) rather than aping gentiles (Arendt 1978).

Sociologist Aziza Khazzoom, an expert in ethnic inequality and categorization in Israeli society, makes the case for an expanded and historicized account of Orientalism in the Jewish world and frames the last two centuries as a series of Orientalizations: "Through this history, Jews came to view Jewish tradition as oriental, developed intense commitments to westernization as a form of self-improvement, and became threatened by elements of Jewish culture that represented the Jewish past. Self-classification then drove how others were classified" (Khazzoom 2003). In "The Great Chain of Orientalism: Jewish Identity, Stigma Management, and Ethnic Exclusion in Israel," Khazzoom argues that the Jewish need to manage a spoiled identity encouraged Jewish immigrants to redraw group boundaries in their host hierarchies (Khazzoom 2003).

"Arabs are simply Jews on horseback, and all are Orientals at heart," wrote Benjamin Disraeli in his novel *Tancred*. The literary critic Edward Said reconceptualized the term "Orientalism" to characterize the set of power relations and hegemonic ideas that framed Europe as "Occidental" and its cultures and peoples as superior to those of the backwards, unchanging Orient: "An Oriental man was first an Oriental and only second a man" (Said 1978). As we entered the twentieth century, notions of civilized and savage, East and West, gave way to categorical differences between white and colored (or nonwhite) (Said 1978).

Orientalism informed early twentieth-century Jewish identity formation in the United States, as scientific racism rekindled old anxieties regarding the Jewish body. As scholar Janice Fernheimer writes, "For

Christian Americans *all* Jews were Eastern and Oriental, and thus 'raced' as Hebrew or Israelite" (Fernheimer 2014). As Orientalism gave way to the processes of racialization, Jews used notions of a hyphenated American identity to position themselves as Western and white while protecting their unique cultural identity and way of life.

During the same period that eastern European Jewish immigrants were struggling to overcome their Oriental stigma and reinvent themselves as Westerners, many native- and West Indian-born blacks were embracing the Oriental framework, claiming to be descended from the ancient Israelites and thus the true heirs of Judaism. By recasting themselves as Hebrews or Israelites, they seized upon a new racial paradigm that transcended the stigma of blackness and elevated them from marginalized to chosen. For European Jews, however, these terms yanked them back into the "very particularity that they were trying to escape" (Fernheimer 2014).

Jewish historian David Biale has suggested that during the nineteenth century at least some eastern European Jewish immigrants arrived "with a kind of double consciousness" that was reflective of both a "tribal stigma of race" and a "quasi-messianic" view of America as the land where they might escape their "pariah status" (Goffman 1986; Biale 1998, 18; Salamon 2006). W. E. B. Du Bois coined the term "double consciousness" to refer to the psychological "two-ness" that blacks experience from being both Negro (black) and American (white) (Du Bois 2015). As pointed out by observers over the years, Jewish hopes to escape the limitations of Western history often paralleled the aspirations of Negroes. But by the 1920s, Jews sometimes resorted to racial language to "justify and legitimize their perceived racial difference," often highlighting unique group attributes that distinguished them from blacks (E. L. Goldstein 2008).

In the decades leading up to World War II, Jews were seen not only as religiously and ethnically alien but also as racially distinct—a view reinforced by Zionists and Nazis alike (Biale 1998; E. L. Goldstein 2008; Sand 2010). The postwar era brought an end to overt discussions of Jews as a race, and in 1963, the United Nations Educational, Scientific, and Cultural Organization (UNESCO) declared that Jews were not a race and that few peoples in modern times possess "so varied a biological history" (Shapiro 1960; Sand 2010).

Ironically, new advances in genetic research have refueled debates on race and biology among Jews and non-Jews alike (El-Haj 2012; Osterer 2012). Sociologist Shelly Reuter shows how Tay-Sachs disease has been framed as an exclusively Jewish disease, much like sickle cell anemia is framed as a black disease (Reuter 2006). Meanwhile, cystic fibrosis continues to be seen as a Caucasian disease, despite scientific evidence that greater genetic variation exists within commonly used racial categories than between them (Wailoo and Pemberton 2006). By 1995, a "Revised UNESCO Statement on Race" declared that "race" had no legitimate place within the biological sciences (Duster 2003a). The elusive search for a Jewish gene or an identifiable set of genetic markers is testament to how we continue to reproduce our understanding of Jews as a biological group. Scholars have shown that the growing popularity, acceptance, and use of a genetic approach to health and disease have reinvigorated long-discredited ideas about race (Duster 2003a; El-Haj 2012; Nelson 2016).

While contemporary social scientists call for a postethnic/postracial America in which Jews and other groups become "communities of choice," many Jews view themselves as ethnics and linked by ancestry (Lazerwitz, Winter, et al. 1997). Furthermore, religious and secular institutions continue to invoke blood logic as a way of defining and maintaining Jewish identity (Glenn 2002). The very terms that have entered modern parlance—"Jewdar," which refers to the supposed innate ability of Jews to detect another Jew in their midst, and "Jewhooing," the practice of private or public naming and claiming of Jews by other Jews—captures the essentialist notions of Jewishness that many secular Jewish institutions still entertain (Glenn 2002; Glenn 2010). Sociologists Shelly Tenenbaum and Lynn Davidman found that the trend towards a biological understanding of Jewish identity was more pronounced among nonreligious, unsynagogued Jews (i.e., those not affiliated with a synagogue) and the adult children of intermarried (Jewish and non-Jewish) parents:

> Despite their minimal ritual practice and lack of religious belief, respondents claimed that their biology was enough to make them feel essentially Jewish for life. In fact, the genetic essentialism of their Jewish identities led some to question whether or not a person could convert and become "really" Jewish. (Tenenbaum and Davidman 2007)

Moreover, *Yiddishkeit*—a Jewish way of life based in a somewhat romanticized eastern-European *shtetl* ideal—and the Holocaust have become cornerstones of an American Jewish identity. Some Jews have gone so far as to define *Yiddishkeit* as "Jewishness" (Schaefer 1996). Given this framework, black Jews constitute a contradiction in terms. In my interviews with biracial Jews, black converts to Judaism, and Black Hebrews and Israelites, many participants expressed feelings of alienation from their Ashkenazi brethren. Rabbi Capers Funnye, the spiritual leader of Beth Shalom B'nai Zaken Ethiopian Hebrew Congregation in Chicago, shared a story that exemplifies the Yiddish-centrism confronting black Jews attending "white synagogues, where people say, 'Well we just don't know about, you know, black Jews, where do they come from . . . and how can they directly prove that?'"[7] Rabbi Funnye recounted,

> Then I give them one of Dr. Ephraim Isaac's comments, from Princeton, who was here lecturing and talking to about six hundred women from Hadassah, a large organization of Jewish women. And after his lecture, one woman said, "Well, you know, Dr. Isaac, I'm just astounded and amazed about Jews in Ethiopia, and Jews in Africa." And the doctor said, "I'm amazed that you're amazed." And she said, "Well, why?" He said, "Where are you from?" She said, "Well, I'm from Poland, my mother and my grandmother were from Poland and the Ukraine." And he said, "You know Ethiopia is mentioned in the Bible over forty times. I've yet to find Poland. So I'm amazed that you're amazed."

The oppositional framing of racial ascription and ethnic fluidity not only allowed millions of eastern European Jewish immigrants and their descendants to "become" white but also reinforced the notion that all Jews are of European descent, and thus white, thereby limiting the ability of black Jews and Hebrew Israelites to assert their claims as Jews. In the next chapter, we will explore the roots of the Beta Israel—the Jews of Ethiopia—and the transformative feats in both language and racial logic that were performed on them before they could be fully accepted as Jews.

2

B(l)ack to Israel

You see, Jews, the word "Jew" has no meaning. Hebrew, this is all I know, they call me when I was home. You see, where I come from they call me "Falasha." In other words, I don't belong there. "Falasha" means somebody that you brought in. Yes, foreigners just like you call a lot of people here alien, and it was supposedly my own country.
—First-generation Ethiopian Jewish immigrant, interview excerpt[1]

Since the nineteenth century, Western scholars have selectively used racial taxonomies to draw boundaries between Africans and Europeans, as well as among Africans themselves. These taxonomies were invoked when Europeans encountered advanced civilizations, as in Egypt, and have been used to polarize tribes, such as the Hutu and Tutsi of Rwanda, that had formerly lived in harmony. And they were also used to reconcile the seemingly irreconcilable claims of a small band of Ethiopians who claimed to be the descendants of the ancient Israelites. Known as the "Falasha," a derogatory term meaning "foreigner" or "exile," these Ethiopians would eventually be airlifted to Israel and recognized as the quintessential Black Jews of the modern world (Weil 1997; Isaac 2005).[2] But before that could happen, a jumbled logic was applied by Western scholars and activists alike to argue, first, that these people could not possibly be Jews because they were black and, later, that they could not possibly be black because they were Jews (Haynes 2009). Ironically, these newly embraced Jews, today known as the Beta Israel, have begun to adopt a Western-style racial consciousness since arriving in Israel and have come to define themselves as black. By tracing the transformation of the Beta Israel—from a persecuted religious minority group in Ethiopia to an Orientalized and then racialized group in the West, we can see how "fixed" racial categories are in fact continuously destabilized, renegotiated, and reimagined in the West.[3]

Halving Africa

When Muslim invaders arrived in northern Africa in 639 CE, seven years after the death of the Prophet Muhammad, they called that portion of the continent—north of the Sahara and west of Arabia—the "Maghreb," which means "west" in Arabic.[4] The Maghreb encompasses a large region that extends from Egypt west to the Atlantic Ocean and south to the Sahara and that traditionally includes the countries of Tunisia, Libya, Algeria, and Morocco. Scholars have often treated the Sahara Desert as a natural and nearly impassable barrier between the cultures of the predominantly lighter-skinned peoples of the Maghreb, whom scholars believe originated from eastern Africa, and their darker-skinned brethren, labeled "Negroes," in the continent's interior.

Well before the early modern era, the linking of region to racial and cultural variations was essential to the racial logic emerging in the West (Lewis and Wigen 1997). In his seminal work, *The Mismeasure of Man*, the paleontologist Stephen J. Gould suggests that the racial classification systems put forth by eighteenth- and nineteenth-century scientists stemmed from "shared social beliefs" rather than scientific deduction (Gould 1996). The first taxonomic approach to humankind was published in 1735 by the Swedish botanist Carl Linnaeus (1707–1778) (Jordan 1974; Gould 1996). In the first edition of *Systema Naturae*, Linnaeus subdivided the human species into four varieties based on skin color and continent of origin: white European; red American; brown Asian; and black African. By the tenth edition, he had assigned characteristics to each variety—aboriginal Americans were described as "red, ill tempered, subjugated . . . and ruled by custom," while Europeans were defined as "white, serious, strong . . . and ruled by laws"—and had created a new group for "wild and monstrous humans, unknown groups, and more or less abnormal people" (Willoughby 2007). Georges-Louis Leclerc, Comte de Buffon (1707–1788) used the term "tawny" to describe the racial makeup of inhabitants from Egypt to the Canary Islands and divided the African continent into western and eastern regions, arguing that there were "two kinds of blacks" and that the distinctions between them resulted from the varying climates. "True Negroes," according to Buffon, were to be found in western Africa and the Sudan, which were considered the hottest places on Earth, and those from Senegal and Nubia were "perfectly black," "the blackest of men" (Leclerc 1997, 22). The scholar Johann Gottfried von Herder (1744–1803) reasoned that the highly evolved civilizations and cultures of North Africa could not have originated in Africa because indigenous Africans were by definition lacking in reason and self-consciousness. Thus, he reasoned, the Ethiopians and Moors were of "Arabian descent," while the indigenous North African Berbers were "of the Asiatic form, though in the midst of Africa" (Herder 1997, 72). Not only did Herder distinguish the pure "Negroes" of Guinea, Loango (Congo), and Angola from groups like the Wolof-speaking peoples of Senegambia, he reasoned that some groups, such as the "Hottentots" and "Caffres," were "retrogradations" of pure "Negroes" (Herder 1997, 73).[5]

In 1776, Johann Friedrich Blumenbach, a German physician, anatomist, and anthropologist, published *On the Natural Variety of Mankind*, which systematized much of the racial logic of the day and made him the central authority on the topic. Building on Linnaeus's taxonomy, Blumenbach subdivided the entire species of mankind into five principal varieties—Caucasian, Mongolian, Ethiopian, American, and Malay—and associated different skin tones with each of them: Caucasian was white; Mongolian, yellow; Ethiopian, black; American, copper (red); and Malay, tawny (brown). In contrast to the "knotty" forehead of the "bandy-legged" Africans, Caucasians were characterized by their "smooth" forehead and "symmetry" and were deemed the "most handsome and becoming" (Blumenbach 1997). Blumenbach traced the ancestral origins of all Europeans, save for the "Lapps" (Sami) and descendants of the Finns, to the Caucasus Mountains in southern Georgia. By the mid-nineteenth century, the essentially folk basis of racial ideology had become fully legitimated in science (Smedley and Smedley 2012).

Unlike Buffon and Herder, Blumenbach made only one distinction among Africans: he placed peoples in northern Africa in a wholly separate category. Despite evidence of biological mixing between Africans, Asians, and Europeans, the concept of racial purity was paramount to maintaining a black/white racial dichotomy (Smedley and Smedley 2012). By aggregating all Africans south of the Sahara into one racial designation, "black Africa" was created and the hunt for the elusive pure Negro abandoned. Blumenbach's categories left an indelible imprint on the Western world and confined all future association of the "black" variety to the sub-Saharan region.

Scholars have focused on the term "white" as central to contemporary understandings of the race concept, but it is the linked scientific term "Caucasian" that lies at the heart of racial logic and permits phenotype to be used selectively in dividing the African continent into racial types. Selectively chosen African populations have been separated from Africa and assigned to the non-African (nonblack) racial category. By using the geographic and racial category of Caucasian to imply kinship and biological continuity across vast regions, scholars have obscured the social history of various North African peoples, "blackening" the southern Africans and "whitening" the northern ones. To complicate matters, linguists have used the term "Caucasian" to refer to a wide variety of languages that have been classified into different language families but that nevertheless come from the Caucasus region.

The Myth of Ham: An Evolving Exegesis on Sin and Race

Napoleon's invasion of Egypt in 1798 sparked further interest in human origins, cultural production, and African civilization. How could Africans have created such an advanced civilization? How could Egyptians be African yet not *of* Africa? The whitening of the Egyptians, as well as other northern African populations, begins with the retelling of the biblical story of Ham, referred to in modern times as "the curse of Ham." In Genesis 9:20–27, Ham's father, Noah, places a curse upon Ham's son Canaan after Ham sees his father drunk and naked in his tent.

The interpretation of Hebrew scripture became part of "the common heritage" of all Near Eastern cultures during the first centuries of the Common Era (Goldenberg 2003). Although Hebrew sources had long associated Canaan with Africa and blackness, it is through the Ham myth that ideas about blackness and slavery became merged in fifteenth-century Christendom. As historian David M. Goldenberg observes in *The Curse of Ham: Race and Slavery in Early Judaism, Christianity, and Islam* (2003), the tendency of Christian scholars to mistranslate the Hebrew word *ham* as "dark," "black," "brown," or "hot" linked the figure of Ham with black Africa (Goldenberg 2003). And by the mid-nineteenth century, ministers both black and white proclaimed the blackness of Ham as fact.

The classical Greek conception of a threefold division of the earth into the continents of Europe, Africa, and Asia was fused with religious conceptions of mankind as early Christian writers mapped onto it the story of Noah's curse (Wood 1992; Lewis and Wigen 1997). By the early fifteenth century, this continental paradigm incorporated a racial framework; Noah's three sons—Ham, Japheth, and Shem—now corresponded to racial differences among the continents of Africa, Europe, and Asia, respectively. In the art and literature of the period, Ham was increasingly depicted as a dark-skinned African, thus solidifying the link between blackness and cursedness. This characterization of Africans as the descendants of the cursed sinner Ham found resonance in Western cultures, especially in societies increasingly dependent on racial slavery. But as rational, scientific explanations became more widely accepted in the 1700s, scholars began to challenge the hegemony of the Hamitic myth, which was no longer seen as providing an adequate explanation for human variation.

The place of Africans in nature was central to early ecclesiastical debates concerning the unity of mankind. In the new scientific discourse, monogenism developed a preevolutionary explanation that supported the traditional biblical interpretation that a unified humankind descended from a single Adam. Human races, it was argued, were the product of "degeneration" from the original Adam and Eve (Gould 1996). By the time of Buffon, climate was often identified as the root cause of racial difference, with temperate climates producing better, more handsome, and more intelligent racial types. A more radical view emerged during the late eighteenth century that rejected Buffon's notion of one interbreeding human family; polygenists argued that races were distinct biological species that evolved from different Adams and that the African Negro was actually subhuman (Sanders 1969; Gould 1996). These ideas filtered into scientific inquiry through the American school of anthropology (Sanders 1969). While polygenism was a more attractive defense of racial slavery (Rogoff 1997), both polygenists and monogenists agreed with the conclusion that the Negro was inferior; their differences lay only in the cause of this inferiority.

All of these carefully crafted arguments would be called into question with Napoleon's conquest of Egypt. How could the descendants of Ham create a great civilization? Scholars speculated that only one of Ham's sons, Canaan, was cursed by God (Sanders 1969). Under the new Hamitic hypothesis, Egypt, along with northern Africa, was whitened. The theory became especially popular in the American South, where science often deferred to scriptural interpretation (Rogoff 1997). The Hamitic theory was further solidified in the work of C. G. Seligman, the British ethnologist and author of *Races of Africa*. First published in 1930, the book attributed the civilizations of Africa to a foreign, mainly Hamitic element, described as "pastoral Caucasians" and "quicker witted than the dark agricultural Negroes" (Seligman 1930; Sanders 1969). The argument would remain intact over the next three reprintings of the book, which reached well into the 1960s.

Paralleling the development of the Hamitic hypothesis was the myth of Semitic descent. During the nineteenth century, archeologists, anthropologists, journalists, and missionaries, as well as fiction writers and journalists, resurrected the Solomonic myth, which attributed the building of a great stone fortress in southern Africa to King Solomon and a lost Jewish kingdom (Kaufman 2005). The theory had first gained currency three centuries earlier, when amateur historians and chroniclers of the day linked the apocryphal fortress to the fabled golden Ophir, where the Queen of Sheba procured gold for the Temple of Solomon (Tyson 2000).[6] The discovery in 1871 of the Great Zimbabwe, the largest stone structure south of the Sahara, gave legitimacy to the biblical account but also evidence that a great civilization had once existed in black Africa.[7] Given the unfathomability of indigenous black Africans constructing such a feat of engineering (Kaufman 2005), it was resolved that the Great Zimbabwe had been built by Semites from the north.

Through the myth of Semitic descent, the whiteness of Jews became normative. Jews were vastly different from other Caucasians, it was argued, yet they remained within the white family. The English novelist Sir Henry Rider Haggard, author of the acclaimed *King Solomon's Mines* (1885), popularized this notion by depicting King Solomon as a white but sexually immoral, diamond-hoarding Jew (Kaufman 2005). Interestingly, the Solomonic myth allowed Jews to be presented as both other (because they were Jewish) and same (because they were white).

Whitening the "Black" Jews of Abyssinia

The rise of evangelical Christianity infused Western ideas regarding biblical ancestry and race into the social fabric of colonial Africa. Beginning in 1830, the French travelers Combes and Tamisier wrote about the Falasha, an Ethiopian group that identified as Jews and traced their origins to Menelik I, the rumored son of Solomon and Sheba. By 1860, missionaries from the revived London Society for Promoting Christianity amongst the Jews set off for Ethiopia—the sole Christian state on the African continent—to establish it as a Levantine outpost and convert the Falasha to Christianity (Kaplan 1987; Seeman 2000). Soon the Falasha began attracting the attention of a small number of Jewish scholars and activists, and in 1867, the Alliance Israélite Universelle financed the expedition of Joseph Halévy, the French Orientalist, to Ethiopia (Kaplan 1992b, 128; Weil 2011). Halévy confirmed the rumors, igniting a Jewish countercampaign to reunite the Falasha with their modern Jewish brethren and bring them international recognition as Jews (Kaplan 1987; Weil 2011). He cited their fair complexion and religious practices as proof of their "ancient Mosaic" origins (Seeman 2000). Over the next decades, Halévy's student, Jacques Faitlovitch, would bring 256 young Falasha to Europe, the Middle East, and America, introducing them to rabbinic Judaism and preparing them to one day return to and reeducate their Ethiopian brethren (Weil 2011).

In 1911, Faitlovitch arrived in New York to establish a branch of the International Society for the Promotion of Judaism among the Falasha; he reported some fifty thousand Ethiopian Jews and contended that "a greater number, though converted by Christian missionaries in former days, still retain consciousness of their Jewish affinity much as did the Maranos of Spain" (*New York Times* 1911).[8] Like his mentor Halévy, Faitlovitch resorted to racial language to explain their presence, emphasizing the intelligence and refined physical features that distinguished them from other Ethiopians. (Similar arguments were used to distinguish the Christian Abyssinians from other dark-skinned animist Africans [Seeman 2000].) He also argued that they were foreign to the African continent and therefore racially distinct from indigenous black Africans.

Still, the very presence of the Falasha challenged the whiteness of Jews. Their assimilation in America was contingent upon removing the stain of blackness from their history. While European-descent Jews were seen as a historical race, they were also regarded as the embodiment of modernity and of "progressive business techniques" and were considered a subset of the "Great Caucasian Family" (E. L. Goldstein 2008). As historian Eric L. Goldstein (2008) writes in his introduction to *The Price of Whiteness: Jews, Race, and American Identity*, "Unlike African Americans, who were seen by whites of the nineteenth and early twentieth centuries as the epitome of a backward, preindustrial race, Jews appeared to be implicated in the urban, industrial capitalist order that characterized the modern 'civilized' world." At the same time, the secret rituals and language of the Jews further set them apart. They were depicted as the embodiment of antimodern tribalism and unbridled personal ambition that posed a threat to Western civilization. Jewish whiteness was tenuous, even contextual, and Jews were often met with a mix of identification and repulsion. Within the context of rising anti-Semitism and the preoccupation with racial hygiene in the United States and Europe, as well as a surging xenophobic backlash against new immigrants, American Jews took pains to de-emphasize their Eastern origins and distance themselves from any association with the African continent. Some scholars posited that the religious practices of the Falasha revealed the corrosive influence of African genes and culture, thus undermining their claims to kinship with European-descent Jews. While many individual rabbis embraced the Falasha as coreligionists, mainstream Jewish institutions were far more measured in their support.[9]

By the mid-1920s, Faitlovitch's Pro-Falasha Society had begun to build momentum. At the 1925 convention of the Central Conference of American Rabbis, Rabbi J. Max Weiss, secretary of the American Pro-Falasha committee, announced an expedition to Africa in order to study the Falasha.[10] Throughout the next decade, the committee continued to provide religious instruction, establish synagogues, develop educational literature, and introduce modern techniques of medicine and hygiene to an estimated fifty thousand to seventy thousand Abyssinian Jews who "remain faithful" to Judaism and Jewish identity.

Noble Lost Tribe

The rise in media coverage of "Abyssinia's Lost Tribe" during the 1920s coincided with an increased interest in diasporic Jews, like those in China and India. Yet reports of the Ethiopian Jews were fraught with contradictions; they were portrayed as black and primitive but also as Jewish and thus heirs to an ancient, noble lineage. One *New York Times* (1931) article portrayed the director of the new Jewish school in Addis Ababa as "a linguist, a scholar, and a graduate of institutions in several European countries," as well as "gentle and cultured," but who looked "more like a North African chieftain, a man of the sword and lance, than the man of peace and refinement that he is." Although the accompanying photograph captures a bearded man who is indistinguishable from many African Americans in color, hair texture, and facial features, he was described as looking Semitic and of descending from "men of Israel." Indeed, "looking Semitic" was a euphemism denoting the physical characteristics that ethnologists had ascribed to Jews and that singled them out as a unique race. (The term "Semitic" is a strictly linguistic designation that encompasses several Near Eastern languages, including Arabic, Hebrew, and Amharic, the official language of Ethiopia. Ethiopians are Semites not because of color or race but because of language [E. L. Goldstein 2008].) In fact, Ephraim Isaac, the noted scholar of Semitic languages and religions, asserts that "most scholars" agree that Hebrew and Ge'ez, or Old Ethiopic, are not only two closely related Semitic languages but that Oromifa, Amharic, and all the other languages known as Semitic and Cushitic derive from one single Proto-Afroasiatic language that existed in Ethiopia, Eritrea, and the Horn of Africa some ten thousand years ago (Isaac 2013).

Public perception of Ethiopian Jews had begun to solidify by the 1930s, when Italy invaded Ethiopia. In one article typical of the period, entitled "Future of the Ethiopian Jews," they were described both as black and as a "distinct racial and religious unit," a "racial entity," and "a tribe of Hamitic stock" who held a language "closely related to Hebrew" (*New York Times* 1936). The conflation of linguistic and racial concepts not so subtly linked the Hamitic Jews to their Caucasian ancestors and distinguished them from other dark-skinned Ethiopians. Others simply called them "the most gifted of Africans" due to their Caucasian/Arabian origins. In fact, according to contemporary historians, while "there is clear evidence of Jewish influence" on the Solomonic Dynasty of Ethiopia, historical evidence suggests that the emergence of the Beta Israel as a distinct people is actually the product of political, economic, and cultural factors that coalesced the distinct and formerly dispersed *ayhud* during the fourteenth and fifteenth centuries.[11] The term *ayhud* has been linked to the Ethiopian religious term for Jews, as well as to rebels against King Solomon and heretics to the Christian church. Some historians believe the terms "Jew" and "Christian" may in fact obscure the history of world religions in Africa (Kaplan 1992a, 210).

During the 1940s, when the Semitic language scholar Wolf Leslau began conducting research in Ethiopia, he found that the Beta Israel, who were then still referred to as the Falasha, spoke a variety of Afro-Asiatic (Semitic) languages, ranging from Amharic, the national language in the central region, to Tigrinya in the north, as well as the Agau dialects Quarenya and Khamir (sometimes called Cushitic languages) in the southeast. Yet their religious texts were written in Ge'ez, which is closely related to Aramaic and Hebrew (Leslau 1951). They still followed both lunar and solar calendars and did not have knowledge of postexilic Jewish holidays, such as Purim. They followed biblical laws concerning animals, cleanliness, and circumcision and observed the Sabbath, as well as Yom Kippur, the Fast of Esther, and Passover. (At the time, they still offered a sacrificial lamb on the eve of Passover [Leslau 1951; Ullendorff 1967]. Their Judaism revolved around the "cult of the Sabbath" and the distinction between the "clean" and the "unclean," two cornerstones of modern-day rabbinic Judaism (Leslau 1951).[12] They adhered to male circumcision on the eighth day, like other Jews, but like other Africans also practiced a form of female circumcision called "excision" and considered girls marriageable at age nine (Leslau 1951).

Leslau found that the Beta Israel community made no racial or physical distinctions between themselves and other Ethiopians, although other Amhara Ethiopians claimed to identify the Beta Israel by their smell, since the rituals that required frequent bathing left them with the distinct smell of water (Leslau 1951). Still, Leslau contended that the two groups were physically distinct, and he resorted to popular stereotypes of Jewish physicality to describe them. Some Falasha in the north, he observed, "possess the facial traits of what is generally called the 'oriental Jew'" (Leslau 1951). He distinguished the shorter, cropped hair of Falasha women from the longer hair of the Amhara, noting that their short hair "gives these women a particularly refined look" (Leslau 1951).

Later scholars contested the authenticity of the Beta Israel. The French sociologist and historian Maxime Rodinson concluded in the early 1960s that Ethiopian Judaism was at best an imitation and veneration of the Hebrew Bible (Isaac 2005). Edward Ullendorff, the British emeritus professor of Semitic languages and Ethiopian studies, argued that the "Judaized elements" of their "so-called Judaism" stemmed from Old Testament influences that had entered through South Arabia (Ullendorff 1967). Yet at the same time, he acknowledged that Jews from established colonies in the region could have been part of the waves of migration that crossed the Red Sea into Abyssinia (Ullendorff 1967). Most contemporary scholars, such as Steven Kaplan, Stephen Spector, and James Quirin, view the Falasha as "Judaized" *ayhud*, whose "Jewish" identities formed within Christian-dominated Ethiopia, rather than as direct descendants of Jews (Kaplan 1992a; Quirin 1992; Spector 2005). The British historian Tudor Parfitt explains that the Falasha are a distinct group of the Agau people who adopted Judaism in the fifth century BCE, when the religion first arrived in Ethiopia (Kessler and Parfitt 1985; Karadawi 1991). Parfitt sees no sign of "Jewish blood" and suggests that the Judaism of both black Africans and African Americans might really be an "adopted—or perhaps rediscovered" religious identity (Parfitt 1987; Parfitt and Semi 2002; Bruder and Parfitt 2012). Historian Joseph C. Miller builds on this premise, maintaining that African politicians and intellectuals created African tribes and contemporary notions of ethnicity by manipulating supple collective identities to meet new historical circumstances (Miller 2001). Indeed, evidence from population genetics reveals no direct genetic link between the Beta Israel and modern Jewish populations. Still, both the genetic and historical records are, at best, fractured, murky, and incomplete, allowing for multiple interpretations of uncertain scientific and historical "facts." As the anthropologist John L. Jackson Jr. suggests, a rich, rigorous, and full social knowing of claims is next to impossible (Jackson 2013).

The development of an Israelite identity among a number of African populations, such as the Igbo (Ibo), Maasai, Yoruba, Xhosa, Ashanti, Khoikhoi, Fulani, Zulu, Lemba, Shona, and, more recently, the Tutsi, could stem from missionary activities and the flood of Bibles brought into Africa during the nineteenth century, coupled with existing indigenous monotheistic religious practices (Zianga 2013, 184). Alternatively, Israelite identity might have evolved through the spread of Islam in the sub-Sahara between 800 and 1600 CE, which brought biblical knowledge and practices to the eastern and western coasts, or possibly from contact between ancient *ayhud* and Israelites (Robinson 2004).

Jack Zeller, the founder of Kulanu, maintains that Ethiopian Jewry is ancient: "In the Bible, Moses marries a Cushite, which is the ancient term for Ethiopian" (Zeller and Zeller 1998). Indeed, Falasha identity appears to be rooted in early Christian Ethiopia; the national epic the *Kebra Negast* (The Book of the Glory of Kings) places the origins of the Ethiopian royal house with Menelik I, the son of Solomon and Sheba. Throughout their transition from *ayhud* to Falasha and, more recently, to the Beta Israel, the historical origins of the group remain unclear. Despite the overlap between their practices and those of Ethiopian Orthodox Christians, the evidence bears that they have maintained a distinct Jewish identity since at least the fourth century.

Out of Africa

The postwar era ushered in a period in which Jews from Asia, Africa, and South America were incorporated into mainstream Jewish historiography. In 1947, Wolf Leslau conducted a comprehensive study of the language, folklore, and history of Ethiopia under the auspices of the Guggenheim Foundation and the Viking Fund. The resulting publication in the Yale Judaica series, *Falasha Anthology* (1951), made Beta Israel texts available to English-speaking audiences for the first time and brought academic legitimacy to the group's claims. Since then, the Beta Israel community has been increasingly integrated into Jewish history, although almost always through a racial prism that suggests their premodern condition (Leslau 1951; Salamon 2006). At least as early as October 1962, the *New York Times* ran advertisements boasting that one could learn about the "black Falasha Jews of Ethiopia . . . the yellow Jews of China and the . . . great modern communities of America, Europe, and Israel."

The United Nations' charter to partition Palestine and create the State of Israel triggered an onslaught of retribution against Mizrahi Jews living in Arab countries. After 1948, some eight hundred thousand Jews were expelled from North Africa and the Middle East (Shulewitz 2000). In Yemen, violent attacks against Jews, reported as *pogroms* by the media, rallied Jewish activists and led to the first secret airlift operation to Israel, known as Operation Magic Carpet. Despite widespread disorganization on the part of the Israeli government and the American Jewish Joint Distribution Committee, the mission was touted as a successful rescue of persecuted Jews in the wake of Nazi atrocities, portraying the Israeli state as beneficent deliverer of Mizrahi Jews from squalor and victimhood from hostile Arabs (Meir-Glitzenstein 2011). Between December 1948 and late 1951, more than fifty thousand Yemenite Jews were brought to Israel via secret Alaska Airlines flights from Yemen (Meir-Glitzenstein 2011, 150).[13]

By the 1970s, the Beta Israel's plight became a rallying point for American Jews and mainstream Jewish organizations. War and famine had exacted their toll on the Falasha, especially those living in the provinces of Gondar and Tigre, where drought and political unrest had resulted in more than two hundred thousand deaths (Onolemhemhen and Gessesse 1998).[14] In 1973, as the Yom Kippur War between Israel and Egypt unfolded thousands of miles away, Ethiopia severed diplomatic ties with Israel and took the side of its Arab neighbors. Now on the verge of starvation, many Beta Israel from Tigre Province headed for the Sudanese border. Others followed from as far as Gondar, some walking hundreds of miles for nearly a month (Onolemhemhen and Gessesse 1998). The plan to transport the Falasha to Israel began on a small scale in 1979. In 1984, the first official airlift, which was carried out quietly, brought some eight thousand Beta Israel to Israel, many carrying horrific stories of missing relatives and brushes with death (Wagaw 1991; Onolemhemhen and Gessesse 1998). A year later, news broke that the US Central Intelligence Agency and the Israeli Mossad, in collaboration with Sudanese state security, were carrying out secret operations to smuggle the Falasha through Sudan (Karadawi 1991).

While the popular narrative of the Beta Israel is one of exile, loss, and return, formal recognition of their Jewishness was gradual. It came first from the Sephardi authorities, who resolved in 1973 that the Ethiopians were descended from the tribe of Dan and had been taken into captivity by the ancient Assyrians.[15] Ashkenazi rabbis did not join in the ruling for another two years, raising questions of racial bias and drawing criticism from the Beta Israel and Afro-American Jews. At the same time, tensions were mounting between blacks and Jews in the United States, as well as between Israel and Arab states. In 1975, the United Nations passed a resolution equating Zionism with racism. The new Black Jews of Israel provided an opportunity for Israel to ease black-Jewish relations and improve its tarnished image abroad. As Dr. Ephraim Isaac, director of the Institute of Semitic Studies in Princeton, New Jersey, put it,

> The *aliyah* [immigration] of Ethiopian Jews to Israel was a most re-markable event in modern Jewish history that heightened the sense of ingathering and Jewish unity. The spectacle of pinkish-white-skinned Ashkenazim of post-industrial Jewish culture, light-brown-skinned Sep-hardim and Middle Eastern Jews of mediaeval culture, the varied but often medium brown-skinned Beta Israel Ethiopians of First Temple period culture all working together and sharing the burdens and exaltations of defending the Jewish homeland—all this deflated the pernicious international charge that Israel is racist. This extraordinary mosaic (or Mosaic!) was like some ancient prophecy coming true." (Isaac 2005)

Black to Israel

In 1977, Israeli Prime Minister Menachem Begin set the stage for the mass exodus of Ethiopian Jews. Over the next fourteen years, some 30,000 Ethiopian Jews were covertly airlifted "home" to Israel (BenEzer 2002). Today more than 120,000 Ethiopian Jews are living in Israel, and thousands more have immigrated to American cities such as New York and San Francisco (Sales 2015). While other African Jews—from North Africa, Uganda, southern Africa, and Nigeria—have immigrated to Israel as well as to the United States, it is only the Beta Israel who have become world-renowned as descended from the ancient tribe of Dan. Their Jewishness, along with their blackness, is accepted by most Jews, international agencies, and government bodies.

The new immigrants maintained identities that were centered on their exile as Jews, and many were baffled by the secular identities of their new Jewish brethren in Israel (Onolemhemhen and Gessesse 1998). And while Western notions of racial difference were foreign to the Beta Israel, they had once adhered to other stratifications that incorporated color distinctions. Hagar Salamon, an Ethiopian Jewish scholar of folklore and the author of *The Hyena People: Ethiopian Jews in Christian Ethiopia*, finds that prior to the abolition of slavery in Ethiopia in 1924, the Beta Israel were owners of other Africans. Ethiopian immigrants continue to draw a status distinction between the *barya* (descended from slaves and considered to be black) and the *chewa* (whose ancestors were free and who are considered red or brown in pigmentation), although no physical differences have been observed by scholars (Salamon 1999; Salamon 2003). In July 1999, I interviewed Joshua, an Ethiopian Jew who had settled in the Hasidic community of Crown Heights, Brooklyn. Joshua was born in 1950 in Gondar Province, in "a small village up in the mountains of Ethiopia." Although he had immigrated to Israel in his youth, he had spent much of his adult life in Brooklyn. During our discussion, he made reference to the class distinctions between Ethiopian Jews and non-Jews:

> You come to my father's compound where I come from. Again, our society is not like your society here. As I say, this is my home. I'm from Ethiopia. This is my house. And I have a big land. Alright, in that big land I have people to work for me. And a small little hut that belongs to them. They become a part of my family.

When recalling his childhood studies at the *yeshiva*, he explained that he found no resistance "because, as I said again, not the people that you are seeing today, that I associate with in my youth. There, we were brown skins. Most of us come from Israel. We were brown, curly hair." Although some Beta Israel immigrants prided their higher status as *chewa* and viewed themselves as red or brown rather than black, the process of absorbing and integrating nearly one hundred thousand Ethiopians into Israeli society has been shaped by Western notions of race and the belief that the Beta Israel are black (Parfitt 1987; Salamon 2003). Media accounts during the airlifts implied that these Jews were being lifted from squalor and backwardness into the modern world (Onolemhemhen and Gessesse 1998). Although the official Israeli policy of absorption emphasized learning and mastering Hebrew and the norms of urban Israeli society, the response to the Beta Israel was often anything but welcoming; their treatment was comparable to that received by "dark-skinned Yemenite Jews" (Onolemhemhen and Gessesse 1998). In the summer of 1991, the Society for the Study of Ethiopian Jewry was founded in Israel to provide a forum for scholars to discuss Ethiopian Jewish culture, history, and religion, and their way of life in Israel.

A 1992 survey of Ethiopian immigrants revealed that the group encountered ethnocentrism and discrimination, particularly in housing, and that most had settled in development towns, rural areas, and small cities (Onolemhemhen and Gessesse 1998). Ethiopian immigrants who had lived in Israel for five or more years had fewer than five non-Ethiopian friends—the majority of whom were Jews from Morocco, Yemen, and Iraq—and they identified Israeli ethnocentrism as a major obstacle to their assimilation (Onolemhemhen and Gessesse 1998). When asked how African ancestry influenced their new lives in Israel, 27.6 percent answered that they were seen as "backward and uneducated," and 24.1 percent reported that their "black skin is problematic." However, the Hebrew language was most commonly cited as an obstacle (Onolemhemhen and Gessesse 1998). Numerous studies since the airlifts indicate that both ethnic and color differences, as well as racism and discrimination, have played a significant role in the Ethiopian incorporation process (Ringel, Ronell, et al. 2005). To complicate matters, thousands of Falasha Mura (Falasha who years earlier had left their traditional villages for the opportunities of the city and who no longer practice Judaism and/or were Christianized) have immigrated to Israel in recent years. Unlike the *conversos* from Spain, who had converted to Christianity while secretly maintaining their distinct identities as Jews, these new immigrants jeopardize the already precarious status of the Beta Israel and threaten to undermine their legitimate claims to Judaism.

The first Beta Israel were required to undergo symbolic immersion in a ritual purification bath called a *mikveh*. The rabbis claimed that this was a necessary rite because of the historical separation of the Beta Israel from rabbinic Judaism. Yet some of the more educated immigrants refused to undergo the ritual cleansing and regarded the act as an insult to their piety and loyalty to Judaism. Many cited "white" Russian Jews, who had also been isolated from Judaic practices but exempt from such requirements, as proof of racial bias. The belief that the *mikveh* requirement for Ethiopians was racially motivated has become widely accepted as fact by many Beta Israel and Jews of African descent in the United States.

Joshua described the three conversion ceremonies he has had to undergo since leaving Ethiopia. On each occasion, he was required to submit to a *bris* (in Hebrew, a *brit milah*, or covenant of circumcision, which is usually conducted on the eighth day of a newborn male's life):

> I've done conversion now three times, three times. When I'm talking about conversion I am going back to telling you, the *bris*? You know what a *bris* means? Each time they say you have to do that, your conversion, you have to go through the process of being *bris*, again and again. . . . Because one did not believe in the other. That's why I say it is a hypocrite society. . . . One in Israel, two here. The last one was done at the Hasidic Jewish Center. As a matter of fact, they had to come here to give me a *bris*. And they took us to somewhere in Long Island to do our *mikveh*. . . . But still, to some so-called super Orthodox, it may not even be Orthodox enough. But, being an Orthodox or not being an Orthodox or being a Jew or not being a Jew, it depends on the man upstairs to decide who is who. Who is clean, who is not clean. Who can be accepted in his minions of soldiers. But for an individual to tell you that you're not clean enough to be part of earth, this sets up a discrimination that I don't like. . . . Now a Russian who has never seen Torah in his entire life, if he comes to this country or if he comes to Israel, they will automatically take him in as a Jew. Why? They consider him a pest. A Jew from Ethiopia, if he did not come with a group or airlifted by some miracle, he's still an outcast, and he has to go through the process of conversion, even in Israel.

Aviva, a black American convert to Orthodox Judaism, had spent time with the Beta Israel shortly after they had arrived in Israel.[16] Her assessment was more equivocal: "Well, I went in '79. I was there from '79 to '80. And then I came back in '85 and was [there until] '88. And they were demonstrating. And we'd go down, another African American Jewish friend of mine, we walked amongst them and talked to them because it feels like . . . I'm not going to say their battle was my battle. But I understood what their battle was about." Still, she did not believe that the conversions were racially motivated:

> A lot of people talk about the Ethiopians, and they made a lot of fuss about it because they were a very strong religious group that had suffered an awful lot being Jews in Ethiopia. They were not allowed to own land. They were very discriminated against and treated absolutely horri-

bly about by the Ethiopian Christians. And so, they knew that they were Jews. They felt this for a very, very long time, for thousands of years. . . . They're a religious people. . . . On the other hand, I understood what rabbinic law says.

Russian immigrants were subject to the same law, she insisted: "A high percent of them were not Jewish, and they are undergoing conversions, and they're just doing fine. No big [deal], you know." Those that didn't convert were not accepted as Jews, she explained, "and if they die, they will not be buried in the Jewish cemetery." She told the story of a Russian family who had immigrated to Israel and whose son had been serving in the Israeli army:

Unfortunately for him though, he got killed. . . . And [the family] thought they were Jews because they were discriminated against as Jews. . . . The father was Jewish. They were not Jews, and that boy could not be buried in a Jewish cemetery.

Another factor that had complicated the immigration process for the Beta Israel, Aviva pointed out, was the high incidence of AIDS: "And so they unfortunately had . . . a higher rate than any other group that was in Israel. . . . And then, of course, they're black too. You know, it's a double whammy." Aviva stayed in contact with the immigrants and visited them whenever she returned to Israel. While she defended some of the more controversial policies implemented by the Israeli government, she was critical of the behavior of many (white) American Jews, which she deemed patronizing:

I've met a lot of American Jews, and what they love the Ethiopians [for], they like to help them. . . . I always thought that was extremely paternalistic. Not that they didn't need a lot of help. I always thought a lot of the do-gooders and liberal Jews needed a black cause. And they got them in the Ethiopian. Because, see, African Americans don't tend to be receptive to that, not since the '60s. . . . But Ethiopians, they didn't know any better. And they just felt that this was a fellow Jew helping them. They didn't know that maybe someone else was saying, "You poor thing," and looking down on them or taking them as a group that's just so backwards. And people were always telling me how backward they were. How backward they were. And I met some. Yes, it's true. A lot of them came from provinces, and they didn't have any running water.

Since 1977, the Israeli Health Ministry has barred most residents from African countries from donating blood, including those born in Ethiopia. In 1996, thousands descended upon Prime Minister Peres's office when word spread that Ethiopian blood was being routinely discarded by the national blood bank. In December 2013, during a routine blood drive at the Israeli Parliament, Pnina Tamano-Shata, a member of the Yesh Atid party and the first Ethiopian-born Jew elected to Parliament, offered to donate blood, only to have it rejected.[17]

According to Steven Kaplan, a professor of comparative religion and African studies at Hebrew University in Jerusalem and the author of *The Beta Israel (Falasha) in Ethiopia: From Earliest Times to the Twentieth Century*, Beta Israel immigrants in Israel are in the process of "becoming black," that is, taking on a new black racial identity (Kaplan 1999). Foreign films in Israel routinely translate the disparate terms "black," "Moor," "black man," "Negro," and even "nigger" as *kushi*, which means an inhabitant of the ancient kingdom of Cush (Kaplan 1999).[18] While it seems most Israelis regard all Africans as descendants of Cush and therefore *kushim*, the Beta Israel distinguish themselves from other Africans; to them, only non-Jewish Africans are *kushim*.[19] The group has attempted to negotiate two intersecting notions of racial membership: one in Israel and one globally. While rejecting the *kushi* label and claiming a full Jewish identity, the Beta Israel have also embraced a global racial identity as "black" Jews and have turned to American civil rights language to claim their rights in Israel. Meanwhile, Beta Israel youth have grown alienated from both mainstream Israeli society and the culture of their parents' generation (Ringel, Ronell, et al. 2005). Forging new hybrid identities, many have adopted elements of Afro-Caribbean and Afro-American cultures as their own. By the late 1990s, many had embraced an international "Rasta" image that combined dreadlocks, hip-hop and reggae club music, and black liberation colors (red, gold, black, and green). Global artists who spin reggae songs on a Jewish axis, such Alpha Blondy from the Ivory Coast or Matisyahu, a Hasidic Jew from the United States, have become popular.

In 2005, Israel officially incorporated the Beta Israel into the national narrative, creating Hazkarah (memory), a holiday that commemorates those Ethiopian Jews who perished before and during Operation Moses.[20] The remembrance day is held in conjunction with Jerusalem Day, which celebrates the reunification of Jerusalem and the establishment of Israeli control over the Old City after the 1967 Six Day War (Semi 2005). In 2011, Hagit Yaso became the first Ethiopian Israeli to win the Israeli version of *American Idol*. One year later, Belaynesh Zevadia was appointed the first Ethiopian Israeli ambassador to go to Addis Ababa. In 2013, the twenty-two-year-old Ethiopian-born Yityish Titi Aynaw was crowned Miss Israel, becoming the first black woman to win the title. One of several Ethiopian immigrants who have risen to fame in Israel, she aimed to use her new celebrity as a way to highlight Israel's growing diversity. In a 2013 interview with the *Jewish Daily Forward* she said, "Israel really accepts everybody. That I was chosen proves it."[21]

Despite these inroads, many of the 120,000 Ethiopian immigrants and their children still fare significantly worse than the general Jewish population on most socioeconomic measures. According to the 2012 report, *The Ethiopian-Israeli Community: Facts and Figures*, by the Myers-JDC-Brookdale Institute, poverty rates are much higher among Ethiopian Israeli families (41 percent) and children (49 percent) than among the general Jewish population (15 percent and 24 percent, respectively).[22] Gaps in education are strongest between Ethiopian children born in Israel and those born in Ethiopia: 13.2 percent of students in the former group attend special education schools, compared with 8.4 percent of students in the latter group (and 8.9 percent of the general population). A full quarter of the men and slightly less than half of the women are employed as unskilled workers, compared to insignificant percentages among the general Jewish population (Myers-JDC-Brookdale Institute 2012). Another study found that among Ethiopians who had immigrated to Israel between 1979 and 1991 and who were under forty-five years old at the time that they had immigrated, 31 percent experienced negative attitudes from other Israelis, 39 percent experienced housing problems, and 35 percent had financial difficulties (King, Fischman, et al. 2012). By international standards, the Ethiopian Israelis appear to have been ghettoized (Myers-JDC-Brookdale Institute 2012).

And like their African brethren in the United States, Ethiopian Israelis are more likely to experience discrimination from the police, and their youth are disproportionately incarcerated. While Jews of Ethiopian descent comprise a mere 2 percent of the total Israeli population, they represent a staggering 30 percent of juveniles who are serving sentences (Leifer 2015). According to one study cited in a 2015 article for *Dissent*, 41 percent of Ethiopian immigrants reported being stopped by police for no justifiable reason. Fear of the police is higher among Ethiopian Jews than any other demographic group, including Israeli Arabs (Leifer 2015). Indeed, Israel experienced its own Black Lives Matter moment in spring 2015, when a video—capturing the assault of an Ethiopian Israeli soldier, in uniform, by police—circulated. Thousands of protesters in Tel Aviv and across the country took to the streets (Kershner 2015; Leifer 2015).

When the Beta Israel first arrived in Israel, their identities were shaped by religious persecution and inherited social status rooted in Ethiopian society. Their association with color had led them to contrast themselves with their darker, non-Jewish neighbors in Ethiopia and with the *barya* (former slaves), who were deemed "black." As Hagar Salamon writes, "Central to the Beta Israel's changing racial perceptions are the Ethiopian racial cosmology and hierarchies. As in many other systems of racial distinctions, skin color assumes the dimension of an entire spectrum, in which the Beta Israel did not perceive the color of their skin as black. Probing even further, beneath the skin, deeper layers become visible" (Salamon 2003). Through interactions with just a few Christian missionaries and Jewish Zionists, a small group of young Falasha attained status as the true lost Jews of Ethiopia (Kaplan 1992a; Haynes 2009). Yet since their arrival in Israel, they have been subject to a binary black/white racial framework, which in turn has led them to form new social identities. Once religious others, the Beta Israel have been transmogrified into racial others among their fellow Jews (Haynes 2009).

Black-Jewish Encounters in the New World

The Hebrew Bible narrates the quintessential story of exile and return, of bondage, deliverance, and the promise of redemption. It is the story of a chosen people that has long served as a powerful metaphor for the black experience in America. For at least some Black Jews, laying claim to this ancestral line is a strategy for inserting themselves back into history. In some cases, the knowledge of a Jewish ancestor may serve as a catalyst for exploring one's Jewish roots or may provide justification for claiming Jewish identity; in other cases, the links are more allegorical. Yet the presence of "real" Jews in the histories of even a few African American families has contributed to the general belief that at least some blacks are, by definition, Jews.

First Encounters

If most Jews in the US trace their direct lineage to eastern Europe, many Black Hebrew and Israelite groups that emerged in the early twentieth century trace their lineage to Ethiopia or the Caribbean. For at least some individuals, there is historical merit to their claims. Jews had been active in the Ottoman slave trade from antiquity through the nineteenth century, and there is strong evidence that they owned sub-Saharan African and Ethiopian slaves, as well as Muslims in Egypt (Schorsch 2009). While slavery was widespread in Europe throughout the Middle Ages, certain groups, including Moors, heretics, and Jews, were at times forbidden to own Christian slaves. The Siete Partidas of Alfonso X, in 1261, forbade Jews, Moors, and heretics from converting their non-Christian slaves, although we know that many African slaves were converted to Judaism (Schorsch 2009). In the 1400s, legislation in Castile banned Christian women from nursing or raising Jewish children and forbade live-in Christian servants (Schorsch 2009).

The first modern-day black African or Negro to undergo a formal conversion to Judaism was discovered in the record of the Inquisition of 1474. According to the record, Xalonio di Castro Iohanni, from the house of Xaguala di Castro Iohanni, underwent a circumcision "at the hands of some Jews from the city of Marsala" (Schorsch 2009). During the sixteenth century, a rather large contingency of African-descent Jews—both converted Africans and Euro-Africans—was incorporated into the Jewish community of Amsterdam (Schorsch 2009). While there is no basis on which to calculate the exact percentage of African slaves who formally converted to Judaism in Europe or the Americas, the practice clearly worried authorities. Pope Gregory IX complained about it, and Christian legislation in the fourteenth century routinely made reference to banning the circumcision of non-Christian slaves (Schorsch 2009). Responsa, or rabbinic writings on biblical law, from the early modern Mediterranean show Jews seeking legal clarification of practices (Schorsch 2009).[1]

Scholars have identified the importance of the Atlantic in shaping the African and Jewish diasporas, which intersected in colonial society. After Portugal and Spain joined under a single monarch in 1580, many Jews and *conversos* fled, first to the Netherlands, where they could openly practice their Judaism, and later to Dutch- and British-controlled areas in the New World—such as Curaçao (arriving in 1651), Suriname (Dutch Guiana) (1651), Jamaica (1677), and Barbados (1654)—which offered them varying degrees of religious and national freedom (Faber 1998). (Studies of rabbinic responsa reveal that many Jews fleeing the Inquisition took their maidservants and slaves with them [Schorsch 2009].) Curaçao and Suriname became the two largest Jewish communities in the New World (Sutcliffe 2009).

The largely Sephardi communities that sprouted across the black Atlantic continued to practice Old World Judaism, which recognized slavery in biblical terms. Slaves of Jewish owners were often immersed in a *mikveh* to legitimate their bondage, a practice that stems back to Egypt (Schorsch 2009). Household slaves were often converted via circumcision—in accordance with the Torah, which mandates that all male slaves be circumcised (Genesis 17:12–13)—or immersion to render them ritually proper to prepare kosher food (Schorsch 2009, 219).

Renowned historian and slavery expert Hugh Thomas reports that Spanish merchants of the early 1600s often accused Portuguese *conversos* of continuing to practice Judaism in secret and filling the Americas with Africans who held heretical (Jewish) beliefs (Thomas 1997). Between 1636 and 1654, northeastern Brazil was one of the few havens in the Western Hemisphere where Jews could openly practice their religion. They were also granted rights to residence and to trade in retail, which included slavery.[2] Sephardi Jews transformed their New World communities by formally converting numerous African servants and slaves, in accordance with biblical law, and producing Euro-African offspring (Faber 1998; Schorsch 2009).[3] Rabbi Funnye described to me one Afro-Jewish community in Brazil:

> I've been in touch with a community in Brazil, in São Paulo, where I'm told that there are nearly two hundred thousand Brazilians who the father is Jewish and the mother is African, of African descent, black Brazilian. . . . And they're interested in converting to Judaism, but the Reform and the Conservative rabbis down there are telling them it would cost them $3,000 an individual to convert. Making it very prohibitive. So, I'm gonna try to find me a couple of rabbis from the community here, the white community, who would be willing to go to Brazil with me. The community members would pay the way, start up some classes, make trips down there every three months or so forth, and tell people to join with the classes and with their studies.

While formal recognition of sexual relations between Jews and Africans, along with their inclusion as coreligionists, was discouraged in early colonial communities, it was not forbidden. Two particularly important places of contact between Africans and Jews were the Jewish village (quarter) of Jodensavanne and the capital city of Paramaribo, which lay forty kilometers to the north along the banks of the Suriname River (Ben-Ur and Frankel 2012). Earning the nationalistic sobriquet "Jerusalem by the Riverside," Jodensavanne was arguably the most politically independent Jewish community in the New World, complete with its own synagogue, school, and militia. While the militia searched for Maroons (runaway slaves), some 210,000 African slaves were traded at the colony between 1667 and the 1820s. Jewish and slave children grew up together in the same household, speaking the Portuguese-based creole Dju-tongo and sharing Anansitori (West African Spider stories) (Ben-Ur and Frankel 2010, 40).

The children of Jewish men and African slaves were frequently given Jewish names and Jewish upbringings (Levine 2007, 103; Davis 2010, 84; Vink 2010, 3; Ben-Ur and Frankel 2010, 43). Cultural transmission between Jews and Africans seems widespread. One prominent eighteenth-century observer reported four villages and plantations of "Jewish Maroons" among the Djuka tribe (Ben-Ur and Frankel 2010, 70). In fact, even the Saramaccan Maroon clan names come from the Jewish owners of the plantations from which their ancestors escaped centuries earlier (Vink 2010, 4).

In the Paramaribo, one can find traditional Jewish tombstones marked with African symbolism. Frequently, Jewish men converted female African slaves so they could marry them as Jews. In some cases, slaves were emancipated following their conversion to Judaism. While community leaders often defended traditional Jewish identities and practices, "color" and "freemen" status eventually superseded *halakha* in determining who was a part of the community (Vink 2010, 6). In Brazil, between 1630 and 1654, Jewish purchasers dominated slave auctions, buying and selling slaves to plantation owners and others on credit (Faber 1998, 17). The Jewish community imposed a tax on its members for each slave purchased from the Dutch West India Company, and freedom was automatically granted to any slave who converted to Judaism. According to its congregational minutes, "A slave shall not be circumcised without first having been freed by his master, so that the master shall not be able to sell him from the moment the slave will have bound himself [to Judaism]."[4]

Still, conversion did not guarantee manumission, and in Curaçao, individuals of both pure and mixed African descent served as slaves to other, often non-Jewish owners (Schorsch 2009). Nor did conversion guarantee *halakhic* status to their descendants, even though Sephardi Jews subscribed to the ancient practice of patrilineal descent (Ben-Ur 2009). Emancipations remained a private matter, negotiated between Jewish master and African slave, until 1733, when the Court of Policy and Criminal Justice began regulating manumissions to include instruction in Christianity (Schorsch 2009).

By the early eighteenth century, Jews were increasingly wedged between Jewish law, which governed the treatment of slaves, and the racial hierarchies that held sway in colonial settlements. In rural Jodensavanne, Suriname, the male descendants of female house slaves were often manumitted and then ritually immersed and incorporated into the Jewish community (Schorsch 2009). However, by the seventeenth century, those descended from Jewish fathers and African mothers were increasingly denied community membership; the logic of Jewish descent—based on traditional Orthodox notions of matrilineal kinship and blood—became intertwined with the logic of racial descent, which established the low status of the African as permanent.

This shift paralleled what was occurring back in Europe. Historian Jonathan Schorsch details how, following the passage of legislative restrictions in 1627, the Portuguese Jewish community of Amsterdam adopted new attitudes about whiteness and the conversion, circumcision, and burial of blacks, mulattos, and slaves (Schorsch 2009). In accordance with a 1647 *haskama* (approbation), a separate cemetery was constructed for black and mulatto Jews; while the justification used for the special burial space was *halakhic*, the language of the ordinance was explicitly racial (Schorsch 2009).

In the center of the village of Jodensavanne, the newly built brick synagogue was consecrated as Kahal Kados Beraha VeSalom (Holy Congregation Blessing and Peace) in 1685, but by that time, Africans outnumbered Jews at least six to one (Ben-Ur and Frankel 2010, 123). To delineate the Sephardim from their Jewish African offspring, the Jewish community erected a two-tier status structure that distinguished *jehidim*—full-fledged members by virtue of birth and race—from those who married people with African ancestry (Ben-Ur and Frankel 2010, 15). The latter were to be "discharged from their status as Jehidim, and immediately recorded as Congregantes" (Ben-Ur 2009). Converted slaves also received the intermediate status of *congregante*. This bifurcation remained in place for almost two hundred years. Death records maintained by the Surinamese cantor David Baruh Louzada between 1779 and 1824 show that, of the 1,371 people assigned to the non-*jehidim* status, 99 were identified as *congregantes* (Ben-Ur 2009). Moreover, while both the fathers' and mothers' names were cited for *jehidim*, only the (non-Jewish) mothers' names were included in the death records of mulatto Jews or *congregantes*, thus expunging any link to the Jewish ancestry of the deceased (Ben-Ur 2009). By 1841, distinctions between *congregantes* and *jehidim* had officially ended (Ben-Ur and Frankel 2010, 125).

Once the Surinamese community migrated from Jodensavanne to the urbanized and largely white Christian world of Paramaribo, laws regarding Jewish membership, along with manumission practices, shifted (Ben-Ur 2009, 164–166). By 1825, with the dissolution of the *Mahamad* (assembly), Jewish communal autonomy in Suriname ended (Ben-Ur 2009). By the 1840s, slaves were no longer permitted to convert to Judaism (Ben-Ur 2009).

Vestiges of old Caribbean communities of mixed Africans and Jews have long been noted but largely discounted as insignificant (Brotz 1970; Parfitt 2013). The long-held rumors of "Negro" Jews were finally corroborated in 1974, when the American Jewish Archives published the first English translation of a document that detailed the Paramaribo community of Suriname. Written by David de Ishak Cohen Nassy, a descendent of a Portuguese *converso*, the document not only revealed the presence of an ongoing battle between the Jewish community and neighboring Maroon communities of escaped African slaves, but it detailed the splintering of the Jewish community when 1,311 "white" Jews became engaged in a dispute over burial customs. Ultimately 650 "Mulatto" and African Jews were relegated to the status of *congregantes* and restricted from participation in community governance (Parfitt 2013).[5]

Historian Tudor Parfitt, the founding director of the Center for Jewish Studies at the University of London, who has been described as the "British Indiana Jones,"[6] recognizes that there existed a "significant population of black Jews in colonial contexts as well as in Amsterdam" during the eighteenth century (Parfitt 2013). By the nineteenth century, not only were Jews thought to have African blood, but the supposed Jewish origins of some African communities were used by travelers, missionaries, ethnographers, ethnologists, and civil servants to explain a wide variety of African customs, rituals, and languages (Parfitt 2013).

The story of Josef Nassy (1904–1976) reveals the paradoxes of hybrid identity in the early twentieth century. Born in Paramaribo, Suriname, to the illustrious Nassy family and a descendant of the prominent Sephardi Jew David Nassy, Nassy immigrated to New York in 1919 to live with his father and study applied art. Ten years later, Nassy immigrated to Europe and installed sound systems for a film company while continuing his art training. In 1939, he married a Belgian woman and began earning his living as a portrait artist in Brussels. In April 1942, just four months after the United States entered the war, Nassy was detained as an enemy national in German-occupied Belgium. (He was still holding an American passport.) He was later transported to the Laufen and Tittmoning internment camps in Upper Bavaria, near the Austrian border (Gamerman 1997). Writing to his wife from the camps, he reported, "There are about 500 of us here, supposedly Americans, but they are really Poles, Czechs, and all kinds." He was one of fifty Jews interned as enemy nationals rather than as Jews, and although he remained secretive about his religious background, he wrote that he warmly whispered "shalom" to his fellow Jews (Gamerman 1997).

Nassy remained an obscure figure until 1989, when some 115 of his drawings, paintings, and ink washes made a tour of New York, Jerusalem, Hamburg, Brussels, and Chicago. The first American public showing of his work, entitled *In the Shadow of the Tower*, was held at Congregation Rodeph Shalom in its Philadelphia Museum of Judaica (Boasberg 1989). In 1997, the US Holocaust Museum presented his work in an exhibit, entitled *Josef Nassy: Images of Internment* (Gamerman 1997). His haunting sketches of black musicians and Jewish men, along with solitary figures set against bleak contexts of prison guards, watchtowers, and barbed wire fences, captured the gross ironies and physicality of confinement.[7] Interestingly, Nassy was never adopted into the canon of Afro-American or even Afro-European artists. A search for his name on the websites of the Studio Museum in Harlem and the Schomburg Center for Research in Black Culture turns up nothing. The fact that Nassy painted Jews and was known as someone who painted Holocaust imagery may have marginalized him as a Jewish artist and prevented blacks from claiming him as one of their own. Yet his status as a Jew is treated as ambiguous among Jews as well. The United States Holocaust Memorial Museum describes him as a "black expatriate artist of Jewish descent" rather than as a Jew of African descent.[8] His blackness is presented as a transcendent category.

African and Jewish Diasporas in America

We have seen how the African and Jewish diasporas briefly intersected in the Caribbean. These intersections extended into colonial America as well. The colony of Charles Town was one of three leading seaport colonies in the United States. (The colony of Charles Town became the town of Charleston, South Carolina, in 1783, following the American Revolution.) By the seventeenth century, Charles Town was the site of a burgeoning slave society, where race relations still remained flexible. During its early days, deerskin trade with local Indians, along with the cultivation and export of rice, dominated commerce. Only a small number of Indians and Negroes were in involuntary servitude, while a far larger number of white indentured servants satisfied the demand for labor (Reznikoff 1950). At first, the Jews of Charles Town did not have the right to vote or hold office. Not until 1740 did the British Parliament grant naturalization to Jews throughout the colonies; the act strengthened their investment in whiteness as a means to citizenship and social inclusion (Reznikoff 1950).

Charles Town was a small colony that aimed to become a plantation economy (Morgan 1998). Englishmen and African slaves from Barbados were among the first to settle Charles Town, and Barbadian law, which defined slaves as real estate or "freehold property" rather than chattel (Sirmans 1962), held sway. While chattel slavery endowed the master with absolute ownership of his slaves, freehold property was attached to the landed estate of its owner, granting the holder of the property the right to use, rather than own, the slave. In the Low Country and in Barbados, it was customary to transfer slaves by indenture along with land passed between owners. Slave codes enacted in Charles Town were similar to those in Barbados; they were cryptic and relied more on custom than on a clear legal definition of slavery (Sirmans 1962). The law stated, "All Negroes, Mollatoes, and Indians which at any time heretofore have been bought and Sold or now are and taken to be or hereafter Shall be Bought and Sold are hereby made and declared they and their Children Slaves to all Intents and purposes" (Sirmans 1962). Interestingly, the colonial assembly enacted legislation in 1696 whose aim was to eliminate potentially dangerous gatherings of slaves on the Sabbath and directed the constables of Charles Town to break them up (Sirmans 1962).

Relations between groups were fluid. The Barbadian-influenced settlement was in fact much like a West Indian hamlet, where contacts between native peoples, white servants, and Negro slaves were unpredictable and unregulated, a quality lost after the 1840s (Morgan 1998). In the Low Country of Carolina, cattle ranching was common, and most slaves were engaged in frontier work: clearing land, cutting wood, and growing food. And much like in the Chesapeake region, Africans, Indians, and whites frequently worked together, and marriages occurred between free Negroes and white indentured servants (Morgan 1998). Today, on the margins of villages, towns, or isolated rural areas, there are a few hundred small communities, called "triracial isolates," that are home to folks of European, African, and Native American ancestry (Daniel 2001). Family names include Brass Ankles, Buckheads, Creels, Chavises, Redbones, Redlegs, and Yellowhammers (Daniel 2001).

The colony of Charles Town, with its robust slave economy, became a natural conduit for Sephardi Jews who had previously settled in the Netherlands, Curaçao, and Barbados. Not only did the new Jewish immigrants own Negro slaves in Charles Town and the surrounding Low Country, but some served as merchants or auctioneers (Reznikoff 1950). Others brought Negroes from the Caribbean as household servants and field hands. It was not unusual for Jews to bequeath freedom to their "family servants" upon death, though there are few records of formal conversion (Reznikoff 1950). Still, the liberal culture of early South Carolina allowed some Jews to wed blacks. During the antebellum period, Anna Cohen of Georgetown wed John Mitchell, a founder of the black mutual-aid Brown Fellowship Society. Isaac Cardozo, son of Aaron and Sarah Cardozo and vice president of the Reformed Society of Israelites in Charles Town, cohabited with Lydia Williams, a free woman of color, and they had three children, one of whom was founder of the Avery Institute, a black Reconstruction-era school (Melnick 1980; Kaufman 1998).

In the autumn of 1749, the Charles Town community founded Congregation Beth Elohim Unveh Shallom—House of God and Mansion of Peace (Reznikoff 1950). By 1800, Charleston had become the largest community of Jews in the nation; approximately 500 out of an estimated 2,500 nationwide lived there (Reznikoff 1950). By the early nineteenth century, an influx of Jewish immigrants from Germany brought significant changes to the Jewish community of Charles Town. Practices shifted from Sephardi Orthodoxy towards a unique, homebred Reform Judaism, and Spanish and Portuguese were removed from the liturgy.

In 1820, the threat of colored converts led to the synagogue's leadership to establish Rule Number 23, a special provision stipulating that "this congregation shall not encourage or interfere with making proselytes under any pretense whatsoever, nor shall any such be admitted under the jurisdiction of their congregation, until he or she produce legal and satisfactory credentials, from some other congregation, where a regular Chief [Rabbi] or Rabbi and Hebrew Consistory is established; and provided, he, she, or they are not people of color" (Melnick 1980).

It is to this place and time that the first recognized black Jew in the United States can be traced. Billy Simonds, otherwise known as "Uncle Billy" or "The Black Jew of Charleston," was a newspaper carrier for several Charleston papers. He claimed to be descended from Rechabites—an ascetic biblical sect descended from Rechab through Jehonadab that had lived among the Israelites in the Holy Land (Jeremiah 35)—and that he had settled in Africa and was then purchased and brought to America by a Jewish owner (Melnick 1980). Simonds attended Beth Elohim and was regularly called a "coreligionist." Despite the creation of Rule 23, accounts report that Simonds was "universally respected by his coreligionists" and "the managers of the Hazel Street synagogue very commendably honored the old man with one of the most respectable front seats." Rabbi Maurice Mayer, a radical reformer of the day, noted that Simonds was "the most observant of those who go to the synagogue" (Melnick 1980). Before Simonds's death in 1857, Rabbi Mayer wrote, "Although in the South, as well as in the free North, blacks and colored persons sit apart from the whites in all public places, churches, theatres, and the like, Uncle Billy sits in the nave of the temple among his white coreligionists" (Melnick 1980).

Whether Simonds was a born Jew, descending from Jews who had settled in Africa, as he maintained, or whether he had been converted to Judaism by one of his Jewish former masters, we may never know for sure. And while no burial record for Simonds exists in the Return of Deaths in the City of Charleston, Judaic history scholar Ralph Melnick speculates that he may have been secretly buried in the Jewish cemetery (Melnick 1980).

It is not surprising that many Jews of African descent in the United States know the story of Uncle Billy and make reference to him when tracing their history. Some point to the Sephardi Cardozo family, whose name is prominent in the annals of African American history. What if a Cardozo descendant wished to revert back to the Jewish fold of their great-great-great-grandfather? Rabbinic rules would require a formal conversion, and this is where Israelites and *halakhic* Jews generally part company.

Early Black Jewish Sects in America

Most Jews had come to the Atlantic colonies seeking economic autonomy and freedom from religious persecution. Formal recognition of persons of mixed descent, including their own progeny, would bring attention to their own marginality; after all, they themselves were just beginning to be incorporated as full citizens. By the end of the nineteenth century, descendants of Jews and Afro-Americans were categorized based on their black ancestry alone. By 1920, the color line had been solidified in civic life, and by 1930, the US Census Bureau had issued new instructions that clearly supported the notion that Americans may belong to only one racial category (Domínguez 1993; F. J. Davis 2001; Haynes 2006). The logic of racial purity and presumptions of racial endogamy mutually reinforced the normative categories. Persons of mixed African ancestry were now officially designated as monoracial by the government. As racial ancestry trumped other signifiers of peoplehood, the Jewish roots of mixed-race Americans were rarely taken into account. Scholars concluded that Judaism had little or no impact on the lives or religious practices of Afro-Americans. Moreover, when scholars retell the saga of the Jews of Ethiopia, most begin with the Israeli rescue missions of Operations Moses, Sheba, and Solomon. This abridged story leaves the false impression that the Jews of Abyssinia remained isolated until the end of the twentieth century (Shelemay 1986; Kaplan 1987; Kaplan 1992a; Kaplan 1992b; Kaplan 1999; Seeman 2000; Summerfield 2003). In fact, a few Ethiopian Jews did migrate to America and interact with African Americans, West Indians, and American Jews on the streets of New York during the early part of the century. But only those who became immersed within mainstream Jewish communities were able to maintain their status as "real" Jews. Those who moved across the color line were relegated to the black-only category.

The notion that black Jews could have lived in Harlem during the early twentieth century has been routinely dismissed by scholars. The Jewish educator, social worker, and professional Jewish organizer/activist Graenum Berger describes his surprise—and later skepticism—upon meeting an Ethiopian Jew:

> One Friday night—the year was 1913—a black man appeared at the synagogue wearing a robe, a *tallit* [prayer shawl], and a *kippah* [skullcap]. He

claimed to be a Falasha, an Ethiopian Jew. He spoke Yiddish. He had come to the city like many itinerants, collecting money for Falasha relief. He walked home with us, had dinner, and occupied my bed. He remained over the Sabbath, went to shul [synagogue] with my father and me on that day, and in the evening he was given money for both the relief fund and his carfare, so that he could reach Utica, the next Jewish-settled city. This was my first contact with a black person. There were a dozen black families residing in town, who belonged to the A.M.E. Zion church, which was a block east of the synagogue. Some of their children attended school, but none were ever in my classes. Many decades later, when I became involved with Ethiopian Jews, this flashback came to mind. My studies have revealed that the visitor could not have been an Ethiopian Jew. (Berger 1987)

As noted earlier, the ethnologist Joseph Faitlovitch first brought national attention to the "black Jews of Abyssinia" when he began visiting them in 1904. Faitlovitch wanted to connect the Ethiopian Jews to the global Jewish community and brought a few students to New York City. Given the norm of racial segregation during the era, these visitors lived among the Black community of Harlem. Many remained, some marrying Jews, others finding black American or Caribbean mates. During the 1950s, another small group of Ethiopian Jews immigrated to Israel to study, and a number of them eventually returned to Ethiopia as teachers. While most scholars ignored them, the Jewish social worker Graenum Berger championed their cause and, in 1974, formed the American Association for Ethiopian Jewry.

The mixture of Negroes from all across the globe was fertile ground for new religious movements. Some were syncretic, others more inventive, with roots shrouded in mystery and mythology. Between 1919 and 1930, at least eight black factions laid claims to Judaism. Some Black Jews claimed to have direct lineage to Ethiopia, while others claimed more indirect routes through the Caribbean. Still others probably made it up. Many were West Indians who had ties to Marcus Garvey, a young Jamaican radical who advocated black imperialism. In 1918, Garvey incorporated the Universal Negro Improvement Association (UNIA), proclaiming "One God, One Aim, One Destiny."

Arnold Josiah Ford, a Barbadian Freemason and Garveyite who traced his ancestry back to the ancient Israelites, served as musical director of the UNIA. Reportedly fluent in Hebrew and Yiddish, he established and served as rabbi for Congregation Beth B'nai Abraham in Harlem (Dorman 2013; Fernheimer 2014). While Ford studied Talmud with liberal white Jews, he asserted that "'real' Jews were black and that white Jews of European descent were 'merely "offshoots" of the original lineage of black Jews or converts who had received the religion secondhand from Africans'" (Chireau 2000; Fernheimer 2014).

Ford was influenced by the Ethiopian movement, which was popular during the period, and advocated for the establishment of a homeland for Black Jews in Ethiopia (Könighofer 2008). At the heart of Ethiopianism is the belief that blacks are the chosen people and that Africans (Ethiopians) are uniquely a part of God's plan for redemption (Chireau 2000). Historian Jacob S. Dorman describes Ford as representative of the kind of Pentecostal Ethiopianism that characterized the second generation of Black Israelite thinking (Dorman 2013). Ford left the UNIA after unsuccessfully attempting to convince Garvey to adopt Judaism. He had learned Hebrew from European Jews in the Garment District, although he often claimed to have studied Hebrew and Talmud in Egypt (Dorman 2013). In 1923, he teamed up with Samuel Valentine, a Jamaican immigrant and Freemason, and formed Congregation Beth B'nai Abraham (Könighofer 2008; Dorman 2013). They attracted many of the new Afro-Caribbean immigrants who were flocking to New York in search of work (Dorman 2013). Ford was reportedly a member of an official delegation that traveled to Ethiopia for the coronation of Emperor Haile Selassie. Some sixty members of Beth B'nai Abraham later joined him on an unsuccessful mission to create a Jewish colony on eight hundred acres in a province north of Lake Tana, which was inhabited by the Beta Israel (Chireau 2000, 26). Ford died in Ethiopia in 1934, although many early scholars speculated that he had returned to the United States under the name of Fard and established the Nation of Islam (Brotz 1970; Gerber 1977; Berger 1978; Wolfson 2000; Könighofer 2008). Dorman further posits that some of Ford's ideas made their way to Jamaica, where they found fertile ground among the Rastafarians (Dorman 2013).

Another UNIA member, Rabbi Mordechai Herman, endorsed the establishment of a shared homeland for Black Jews in Palestine (Chireau 2000). In 1924, Herman took over the Moorish Zionist Temple of the Moorish Jews on West 127th Street in Harlem (Chireau and Deutsch

2000; Gold 2003; Könighofer 2008). Both Herman and Ford recruited Garveyites into their congregations and had strong West Indian representation amongst their flocks.

Black Muslim groups emerged during this period as well. In fact, it was during this time that Elijah Poole (soon-to-be Elijah Muhammad) met W. D. Fard, or Master Fard Muhammad, who identified himself as God incarnate, a belief that would become one of the cornerstones of the Nation of Islam. One key element unifying the Black Jews and Black Muslims of this era was that both used theology as a political tool to create community and challenge the racist representation of black people in the dominant culture (Weisenfeld 2016). As such, they both served as vehicles for racial projects that fostered pride and promoted new understandings of history and identity.

Afro-Americans have long had a strong metaphorical identification with the Israelites of the Old Testament. Many slave revolts were led by messianic leaders (Dorman 2013). Some identified so strongly with the story of exodus that they themselves "became Jews." Their world, embedded in the Old Testament, transcended space and time; past and present became one. In the quest for liberation, Afro-American cultural traditions have embraced dramatic reenactments of the exodus story, while black leaders have often been envisioned as "approximate types of Moses" (Smith 1995).

A number of factors contributed to the Negro's identification with ancient Israel. The majority of Africans in North America were brought from West African societies, which regularly practiced ritual circumcision, the ritual slaughter of animals, and the separation of women during menstruation. These so called "Hebrewisms," invoked by Black Hebrew groups such as the Harlem-based Commandment Keepers and other "Judaizing" Africans and African Americans, have been frequently dismissed as inauthentic cults (Brotz 1952; Landes 1967; Brotz 1970; Gerber 1977; Fauset 2002; Landing 2002; Bruder 2008; Rubel 2009; Bruder and Parfitt 2012; Dorman 2013). A number of scholars have described early Black Judaism as a fusion of messianic salvation and black nationalism (Brotz 1970; Baer and Singer 1992; Fauset 2002; Rubel 2009). A few have even framed African Jews within the context of new or emerging Jewish communities that have either converted or merely identified as Jews (Brettschneider 2015; Parfitt and Fisher 2016). While the Hamitic hypothesis has shaped thinking about civilization in Africa since the

nineteenth century by tracing all significant African cultural develop-
ments to Asia, we know that since the Middle Ages Arabic writers such
as al-Idrissi have spoken of Jews living south of the kingdom of Ghana
(Bruder 2008). According to historian Hugh Thomas, during the fourteenth century, Jewish traders from Spain traveled across northern Africa and into the Sahara, establishing colonies and marrying local blacks,
such as the Fulani. Eventually, they traveled as far south as Senegambia,
which later, during the transatlantic slave trade, would serve as a strategic route into the Sudan (Thomas 1997; Gossett 1997). And since 1000
BCE, the central Arab trade route across the Sahara, linking Timbuktu
to Sijilmasa, had been traveled by dark-skinned African merchants, as
well as by Jewish merchants from North African ports (Thomas 1997).
Yet Thomas falls victim to the Hamitic myth, positing that the racial
mixture of western Africa was made up of "Hamites—called Libyans or
barbari by the Romans, and Berbers by the Arabs, a word actually deriv-
ing from *barbari*—and black people to the south of the desert" (Thomas
1997). Whether a real ancestral connection to the Israelites existed or
was merely imagined, African slaves in North America were uniquely
predisposed to identifying with and as the children of Israel.

While history has characterized the Negro slave in America as un-
questionably Christian, most Africans slaves did not adopt Christianity
until the Second Great Awakening, beginning at the dawn of the nineteenth century. It is not surprising that the sacred world of slave society
continued to hold on to many traditional African religious practices,
which were drawn from both Islam and the Old Testament (Raboteau
2004). The rich biblical imagery often found in the spirituals of slave society—in melodies such as "Steal Away" and "Swing Low"—spoke to the
strong identification with the children of Israel (Chireau 2000; Levine
2007). This hybrid form of American musical culture was reproduced in
the religious sphere of slave society as well.

Historian Lawrence W. Levine shows that African American slave
religion interpreted the Christian Bible through an Old Testament lens
that rejected white Christianity's focus on obedience to the father in
favor of a radical messianic message of deliverance:

> Thus, it was not uncommon for whites to have sung of Jesus: "Oh when
> shall I see Jesus / And reign with him above," while to a markedly similar

tune blacks sang of the Hebrew people: "Oh my Lord deliver'd Daniel, / O Why not deliver me too?" Where whites sang "Lord I believe a rest remains, / To all thy people known," blacks used the same tune to sing of Moses leading his people out of Egypt. (Levine 2007)

Slaves envisioned a connection between the captivity of the ancient Israelites and their own. Exile, captivity, freedom, and the promised land all became central metaphorical ideas in black religious life. According to Levine, "The most persistent single image the slaves' songs contain is that of the chosen people" (Levine 2007, 33). Such phrases as "I am born of God," "We are the people of God," and "To the promised land I'm bound to go" were commonly invoked, as were references to biblical heroes, such as David, Jonah, Moses, and Daniel (Levine 2007). Levine shows that African American religion "extended the boundaries of their restrictive universe backward until it fused with the world of the Old Testament, and upward until it became one with the world beyond" (Levine 2007). In this world where past, present, and future merged, there ever remains the continual "possibility of imminent rebirth" (Levine 2007).

Black Judaism was shaped by memory, allegory, metaphor, exegesis, and, of course, a bit of myth making. Some Black Jews even articulated what has been labeled "Black Zion," that is, the chosenness of the black people as the true descendants of Abraham. While black-run newspapers, such as the *Chicago Defender*, the *New York Sun*, and the *Afro-American*, tended to present a "tolerant forum" or even celebrated black claims to Jewishness, the mainstream Jewish press was largely dismissive and viewed them as exotic curiosities (Gold 2003; Rubel 2009). So too did most scholars of the period. E. Franklin Frazier dismissed them as urban cults in his classic *The Negro Church in America* (1964), as did the cultural anthropologist Ruth Landes, who readily lumped them with the followers of Marcus Garvey, Father Divine, and Big Daddy Grace (Landes 1967). Judaism represented, in her view, yet another manifestation of a nationalist search for group identity among a rootless postemancipation people, a psychological salve for a troubled turn-of-the-century Negro psyche (Landes 1967).

Arthur Huff Fauset, one of the earliest black Americans to earn a doctoral degree in anthropology, examined early Black Hebrew groups in

1942. Like Landes, he associated Black Jews with other religious groups led by charismatic figures like Father Divine, Big Daddy Grace, Elijah Muhammad, and Noble Drew Ali. In *Black Gods of the Metropolis* (1944), which emerged out of his dissertation, he characterized the Church of the Living God—Pillar and Ground of Truth for All Nations, an Israelite group founded by Prophet F. S. Cherry that merged Jewish and Christian teachings, as representative of "the most important and best-known cults." Likening the group to the Moorish Science Temple, Fauset saw the Church of the Living God as part of a constellation of nationalist, Islamic "cults," despite the preservation among its members of Christian hymns and the book of Revelation from the New Testament (Rubel 2009).

Still, individuals from the mainstream Jewish community, especially in New York City, continued to take interest in these exotic Jews. One of the first extensive scholarly studies to evaluate the claims of Black Jews was a 1947 master's thesis entitled "The Black Jews of Harlem" by sociologist Howard Brotz, then a young scholar at the University of Chicago. More than a decade later, Brotz concluded, in his full-length study *The Black Jews of Harlem: Negro Nationalism and the Dilemma of Negro Leadership*, that the "Black Jews may be accurately regarded as sects of Christians who pressed their identification with the figures of the Old Testament to the extreme belief that they themselves are Jews" (Brotz 1970). Later he argued that Black Judaism was a unique twentieth-century manifestation of Booker T. Washington's self-help orientation filtered through Ethiopianism and that it was doomed to fail (Brotz 1970). Brotz's explanation did not anticipate the steady growth of black Jews during and after the civil rights era of the 1960s.

Religion scholar Nora L. Rubel used Prophet Cherry's Church of the Living God—Pillar and Ground of Truth for All Nations to explore early Black Judaism in the United States (Rubel 2009). The group, which is the oldest-known organized Black Jewish congregation, was first established in 1886 in Chattanooga, Tennessee, but moved to Philadelphia, Pennsylvania, at the turn of the century. Today, the congregation maintains its own "office of rabbinate," and while it celebrates Passover and observes the Sabbath, it also includes teachings about Jesus Christ, whom members claim was a black man. Echoing earlier scholars, Rubel argues that Cherry and other black proponents of Jewish identities emerged from a "backdrop" of racial nationalism and were at the same time "indistinguishable from black Christians" (Rubel 2009). However, since early black Christians did not emerge from a context of nationalism, something else must explain the growth of Judaic practices among blacks in such specific locales. None of these theories account for groups like Congregation Temple Beth'El, founded in Philadelphia in 1951.

Temple Beth'El represents an independent tradition of Black Jews. Unlike the Church of God and the Commandment Keepers, which were early syncretic groups that evolved from Christian origins, the group chose from the outset to practice their understanding of Judaism. The group's founder, Louise Elizabeth Dailey, was born into a strict Baptist family and later worked as a domestic in an Ashkenazi home, where she noted that many practices observed by the family—such as the salting of meat, the prohibition of work on the Sabbath, the covering of mirrors after a death in the family, and the practice of "sitting *shiva*" for seven days—coincided with those observed by her own family. According to community lore, after praying to be guided in "the ways of the Hebrews," she began a journey into Judaism and brought hundreds of followers along with her.[9] While worshipers observe the Sabbath, *kashrut* (i.e., religious dietary laws), immersion in the *mikveh*, and circumcision on the eighth day, they have not undergone conversion. And while claiming to be "descendants of Abraham," they make no claim of exclusivity.

Dailey's daughter, Rabbi Debra Bowen, is the congregation's current religious leader, or "Overseer," as well as a fellow at the Institute for Jewish and Community Research in San Francisco and a student in rabbinical training at a Reconstructionist academy in Philadelphia. Bowen is also an accountant and manager, while her husband is a certified functional family therapist and adjunct professor of African American studies and social administration at Temple University. Both, it could be said, engage in what Evelyn Brooks Higginbotham calls a "politics of respectability." They live in a middle-class suburban development equipped with private airport runways and large homes.

While, like many Israelites, her group believes that they are merely taking back a history that whites stole from them, their religious practices and beliefs have little in common with those of the Israelites, who are largely embedded in urban ghetto environments and are prone to reject so-called "white" Jews or even the term "Jew" altogether. In fact, members of Congregation Temple Beth'El have adopted Talmudic study and embrace Ashkenazi Jews as coreligionists. In 2006, the congregation was reported to hold joint services with its neighbor, Congregation Tiferes B'nai Israel, an unaffiliated synagogue that has served the predominantly Ashkenazi Jews from Bucks-Montgomery counties since 1924 (Holmes 2006). Congregation Temple Beth'El defies easy classification; it espouses an Afrocentric perspective, claiming that the origins of Judaism are black, yet it also embraces Ashkenazi Jews as coreligionists and engages in rabbinic Judaism and Talmudic study. In 2009, the congregation received its first Torah from Israel, an important step in its evolution. While prior attempts to secure a Torah had been stymied, it was Rabbi Rigoberto Emmanuel "Manny" Viñas, who ultimately delivered. As noted earlier, Rabbi Manny is a Cuban Jew who directs El Centro de Estudios Judíos Torat Emet, a synagogue in Yonkers, New York, that is dedicated to the return of *converso* and secret Jews to Judaism.[10]

Rabbi Capers Funnye captures the rich complexity and diversity of groups that stake claims as Black Hebrews or Israelites and shows that single explanations, definitions, or reductions are useless:

> And this community is so disparate until it is almost hard to call it a community. But yet at the same time, there are certain tenets that tend to galvanize brothers and sisters from all over the country with a sense of self. But beyond that, when you get into the theological practices, as dark as I am, my Judaism is considered very white by many in the Black Jewish community, who . . . don't even use the terminology of "Jew."

Documentation of colonial-era marriages between Jews and Africans in both the Caribbean and America, as well as of conversions and burials of African slaves by Jewish owners, lends credence to the collective memories of Black American Jews, who trace their Jewish lineage through their paternal line. We also know that myth, metaphor, and a strong identification with the Israelites of the Old Testament shaped the beginnings of Black Judaism in the United States, so that many early sects believed that they were the true heirs to this heritage and that Jews of European descent had stolen their history. The rhetorical devices and essentialist constructs that they have employed to stake their claim in history can be best understood as a manifestation of racial projects, which we explore in the next chapter.

4

Back to Black

Hebrews, Israelites, and Lost Jews

They go back to the histories of their people. To Israel, far, far
back, they go back, because if they continue to go back they are
going back into black. They are not going back into white. They
are going back into black, and that was the original, and that is
why I told you . . . there are two religions, Islamic and Judaism,
black people religions.
—Elder William Williamson, Church of God and Saints of
Christ[1]

With the exception of the Falashas, whose claim to Jewish identity was, according to rabbinic sources, predicated upon a claim
to descent from the tribe of Dan and who, in any event, are not
known to have been of definite gentile genealogical origin, all
contemporary black Jews are acknowledged to have been *behe-
zket akum*, i.e., to have been descended from progenitors known
to have conducted and identified themselves as non-Jews. . . . In
view of their earlier known identification with Christianity, any
claims advanced by, or on behalf of, these groups to descent from
the ten lost tribes of Israel or by the only authentic descendants
of the original ethnic Jewish community must be dismissed as
sheer fabrication.
—J. David Bleich, "Black Jews: A Halakhic Perspective" (1975)

Hebrews—sometimes known as Israelites, Hebrew Israelites, or Ethiopian
Hebrews—comprise a loosely defined movement and include sects that
are unaffiliated with one another and that significantly diverge in religious
practices and political views. The term has been invoked by religiously
observant congregations—including Congregation Temple Beth'El in

Philadelphia, the Commandment Keepers in Harlem, and Beth Shalom B'nai Zaken Ethiopian Hebrew Congregation in Chicago—as well as by both "Christian-influenced Israelite" congregations, such as the Church of God and Saints of Christ, and "Islamic Judaic" groups, such as the Nubian Islamic Hebrews. It has been used by movements that claim direct lineage to the lost tribes of Israel, such as the Original African Hebrew Israelite Nation of Jerusalem, as well as by black supremacist groups, such as the Nation of Yahweh or the Israelite School of Universal Practical Knowledge. As Rabbi Capers Funnye put it to me, "The only broad stroke that you can probably say of all Hebrews, Hebrew Israelites, and Black Jews is that somewhere in the context of their literature and their thinking and their psyche, they feel that Judaism is an African-born religion and faith and that the matriarchs and the patriarchs were people of color."

Funnye, who in 1985 formally converted to Judaism under a Conservative rabbinical court, is cousin to the former first lady Michelle Obama and has been sometimes affectionately dubbed "Obama's Rabbi" (Chafets 2009). As noted earlier, in addition to serving as the spiritual leader of Beth Shalom B'nai Zaken Ethiopian Hebrew Congregation on Chicago's South Side, Funnye serves on the Chicago Board of Rabbis and on the boards of the American Jewish Congress and the Jewish Council on Urban Affairs. When I first interviewed him, in March 1999 in Chicago, he shared that he views Black Judaism as a "returning to the faith of our forefathers . . . that we are returning to what we are, the inherent bred stock of many of the Africans that were brought to the western hemisphere, during the period of chattel slavery."

The diaspora of the Jews, he explained, extended beyond "North Africa above the Sahara and into the Mediterranean Basin, and eventually into Europe." It also meant Central, South, and West Africa. Still, he found value in a formal conversion process:

> And this is where I differ from a lot of other Black Jews, a lot of other Hebrews, who say, . . . "The right was ours, and so we're returning and so we don't need to go through no process." And I'm a person that says "Yeah, but you were torn from this."

He compared the journey to that of a homeless person, who had been lost sleeping on the street:

You pass by this beautiful house every day, but you sleep on a cardboard box. One day someone finds you, and they say to you, "John, this is the deed to that house. It's yours. You are actually a long-lost relative of the person who was there, and they commissioned me to find you. Here is your deed. Everything in the house is yours, all of the servants, everything. You just get up out of your box, you take the key, and you walk in your house." What is the first thing that you're going to do? I would hope, the first thing you would do is clean the stench of the street, of the box, of the homelessness from you. You're going to bathe. If this is ours, organically, there's still stench relative to dietary laws that were not observed. There's process.

At the same time, Funnye defended the right of the Beta Israel immigrants to resist forced conversion in Israel:

And the Beta Israel said we'll walk back to Ethiopia first and starve. Excuse me, no. But they were doing that when the Ethiopians were coming in few in number. They were almost forcing them to undergo conversion, or symbolic *mikveh*. And so, the Ethiopian Jews refused when they got there and amassed large numbers. And I'm extremely happy that they did. Many in the Ethiopian Hebrew community have refused on those same grounds.

While Funnye and his entire family had converted to Conservative Judaism, he placed no such demands on his congregants. He recalled a time when the regional director of the Conservative movement approached him and proposed that his members undergo a symbolic *mikveh*:

I said, "Excuse me. I have people in this congregation in their eighties, people in this congregation in their seventies, people in this congregation in their sixties, who have been Jews for forty years, fifty years, sixty years. I am not going to ask them to go through a process so that you will be happy. If it is not sufficient for you to know that any person that has come into the congregation in the last five years has undergone a *halakhic* conversion, has a standing membership in this congregation, [and] has lived their life as a Jew, I'm not going to ask them to re-Jew-up to satisfy you."

On the other hand, he found the Reform movement, which was ready to embrace his congregation "with open arms," too liberal:

> And Black Jews, by and large, are very conservative in their thinking. . . . And almost Republican, just as most Black Christians are very conservative in their thinking. This is black people, period. . . . Our being leftist and all this kind of stuff was trying to get rights to vote, to shop, to sit in the bus, and all those types of things. So, black radicalism is not where black folks are, by and large. And so, for us, the Reform's position on the gay and lesbian community was an issue for many of our members.

Another issue for Funnye's congregants was the nontraditional role of women in the Reform movement, including their opportunity to read from the Torah and become rabbis. Funnye recalled one attempt to integrate women into the Torah service: "The elder women primarily . . . and some of the younger women said, 'Leave the tradition alone!' Some of the men were vehemently against it and [said], 'Well, I might have to leave.' One or two people said that."

Funnye had been raised in the African Methodist Church. He first became interested in Black Judaism in the early 1970s, after graduating from Howard University. He had just returned to Chicago and was working at the accounting firm of Arthur Anderson, where he met "three or four young brothers, and they had these little, I called them, beanies on their heads," which they explained weren't beanies but *kippot*. "You know, we're Jews . . . we're Hebrews. . . . You're probably one too," they told him.

That next year, Funnye began studying with the black rabbi, Robert Devine, of the House of Israel.[2] Devine embraced a syncretic form of Judaism, one based on both observance of the Torah and recognition of Jesus as the Lord and savior (Wolfson 2000). Through his studies with Devine, Funnye rediscovered the Bible through a new lens. He saw himself and his people's history reflected in Deuteronomy 28:68: "[I found] a statement that no preacher had ever drawn to my attention before in the Bible. It said, 'And God will take you into Egypt again, in ships. In a manner whereof I have spoken unto you, and there you shall be sold, for male and female slaves to your enemies. And no man shall buy you,' meaning that that servitude, you're not going to be able to be redeemed out of. And I found it extremely powerful."

He also found himself in Genesis 50:11, where Jacob is brought from Egypt to Canaan for his burial, and the Canaanites mistake the Hebrews for Egyptians, who are of Africa. But it was the book of Ezekiel that most resonated with him. As a child, Funnye had sung the little ditty of the dry bones,

> but the songs never get to the part of Ezekiel [37:11–12] that said, "These bones are the whole house of Israel, they are scattered, cut off, and like dust. But they shall be drawn together, and they will stand up and [receive a great honor]." And then he said something astounding: "Say to these bones, once they have stood up. Once they have the breath of life breathed in to them, I will open up your graves and bring you out of your graves of my people. And bring you again to this place of the nativity of your forefathers." And that really struck home with me. Of the plight of people of African descent in America. . . . Certainly, this whole piece with slavery. So, these were my starting points.

After several years of study with Devine, Funnye underwent conversion as an Israelite. Still, he "wasn't necessarily quite comfortable with this Jesus pitch" and found himself yearning for a more faithful rendering of Judaism. In 1979, he discovered the Commandment Keepers of Harlem and Congregation Beth Shalom, an Ethiopian Hebrew synagogue founded by Rabbi Levi Ben Levy located in Bedford-Stuyvesant, Brooklyn. Funnye was immediately struck by how radically Levy's Judaism departed from what he had been practicing until then:

> I looked at their Bibles, and they didn't have King James Version Bibles that we did. I looked at their prayer books, and they didn't have one side of the page with the Hebrew typed out in English phonetics, so one could read along. Their Hebrew was so fluid and so fluent. The Torah service that we were doing here at the House of Israel wasn't true Torah service. You know, we were making the prayer, the *brachot* [blessings], but we weren't really reading from the Torah.

Levy encouraged Funnye to study with Rabbi Abihu Ben Reuben, the spiritual leader of the Ethiopian Hebrew Congregation.[3] Rabbi Reuben had been leading the congregation since 1951, when he was ordained under Wentworth Matthew (Landing 2002). He was now approaching seventy, and Levy was concerned that the congregation would die when he did. "He was very blunt about it," Funnye said. Over the next six years, Funnye studied with both rabbis and attended the Spertus Institute of Jewish Studies in Chicago, completing both a bachelor's and master's degree in Jewish Studies.

In 1985, he was ordained by Levy, who served as chief rabbi of the International Israelite Board of Rabbis, and at the same time underwent a second conversion with his family, this time under both Conservative and Orthodox rabbis. After Rabbi Reuben died in 1991, Funnye became the sole spiritual leader of Beth Shalom B'nai Zaken Ethiopian Hebrew Congregation—a new name reflecting the merging of Reuben's Congregation of Ethiopian Hebrews and Funnye's own Congregation Beth Shalom (Landing 2002). Reflecting back on the choices he's made and the ways in which he's sought to reconcile the tensions between his Jewish and Israelite identities, Funnye said, "It took me a while but I had to move to a place where I had to ask myself on a very personal level, do I want Black Judaism to survive or do I want Judaism to survive?" Ultimately, he's come to realize that the future of Judaism, of a Jewish way of life, is more important.

* * *

The late Rabbi Bill Tate, spiritual leader of the Beth Shalom Congregation in Brooklyn, had taken a similar path to Judaism as Funnye: from Christianity to a hybrid of Judeo-Christian practice and finally to a vision of Judaism lived through the *ba'al teshuva* status of his grandchildren. Unlike Funnye, however, who had normalized his Jewish status through *halakhic* conversion, Tate remained squarely in the Israelite world. He had been raised as a Christian but remembered seeing a photograph of his great-granduncle—his grandmother's uncle—that dated back to the early 1800s: "He had a *tallit* and *yarmulke* [skullcap]."[4] When Tate was about eighteen, he met an Israelite named Ishmael Cohen, a gospel singer at the Tabernacle of Israel, a Judeo-Christian temple in Bedford-Stuyvesant, Brooklyn. Cohen described God as a spirit that works through people, "and we as men and women on this earth are the instruments of the most-high God to carry and fulfill whatever he wants done on this earth." Tate believed Cohen was a manifestation of God who opened his eyes to Judaism. Reflecting back to his beginnings, he acknowledged that he had once held a limited view of Jews and Judaism:

> We considered ourselves Israelites. Don't forget, I'm speaking now from a background of full knowledge and telling you a story about when I didn't have the full knowledge. So, my vocabulary may throw you off a little bit. But now I'm reverting back to when I was not as fortunate as I am now to be a qualified rabbi. . . . And I was not called a "rabbi" at that time. . . . I believe they put a title on me of *nabi* [prophet].

As an Israelite, he kept the Sabbath, adhered to all the dietary laws of *kashrut*, and celebrated "all the feasts." A proud man and fervently devout, he expressed frustration with white Jews—whom he described as "Edomites," ancient enemies of the Israelites—and their reluctance to fully embrace him as a fellow Jew. Rabbi Tate later explained that the term "Edomite" derived from "Edom," another name for Jacob's brother, Esau: "And Edom is a white man. They call him an Edomite . . . and the enemy of Israel because the Bible said Edom will always hate, hate Yakov [Jacob] in an expression of guilt. The Black Israelite community says they're from Yakov, and they say the white folks is from Edom; even though they're Jewish, they're from the same father." Yakov was one of the twelve tribes, but Edom wasn't, he explained. Prior to our meeting, he had prepared a statement, which he read to me:

> We, as Israelites, pray to the God of Israel. We keep the Shabbat, all the Jewish holy days, or Jewish festivals. We establish our synagogues. We have our hearts and minds set on studying and fulfilling the *mitzvah* of the Torah. And we are going to forever remain faithful to the Torah. However, it is extremely disconcerting that we are always questioned, and there is a question as to whether we should be considered as Jews or a part of the nation of Israel by the white Jews.

Tate defended the religiosity of his black brethren and claimed that it was unfair to be held to the same measures of piety as other Jews when they had unequal resources:

Our lives was in accordance with keeping with the Torah. Our method is what makes us questionable. We didn't have access to the knowledge of our Hasidic brothers. We didn't have the books. This is no different than the Ethiopian Hebrews that are in Israel now.

Despite his indignation at white Jews, he took great pride in the acceptance that his children had won, "to the point where . . . not one of them, no one could claim that they were not born Jews. Practicing, living, that's all they know is Torah. They don't know nothing about Christianity. They know nothing about J. C. [Jesus Christ]. They don't know nothing about worshipping no other God but the God of Israel. My children!" In fact, he proudly noted, his oldest daughter was now married to a Lubavitcher Jew and completely immersed in the Hasidic community: "If you close the door and put a Hasid in that room, put a Lubavitcher in that room, put a Satmar, yeah put a Satmar in the next room . . . and my granddaughter in that room, and they all begin to speak, you wouldn't know the difference."[5]

For Tate, there was nothing more crucial for building a strong Israelite community than knowledge of Hebrew: "If we're going to call ourselves a people, how are we going to be a people without a language?" Although he regretted that his own Hebrew had not advanced further, he was proud of the foundation he had built for future generations:

We're just beginning. . . . We're nowhere near where we should be. . . . But it's a growing process with us. I'm going to give you the prime example of my life. I'm not fluent in *Ivrit* [Hebrew]. I read the Hebrew prayer book, but my dialogue is limited. Grammar is limited. But my grandchildren are fluent. That's all you're going to find in the Israelite community now, Hebrew.

While there is tremendous variance among individual groups, the major dividing lines in the theology of Black Hebrews and Israelites can be traced back to two men: William Saunders Crowdy, who founded the Church of God and Saints of Christ, and Wentworth Arthur Matthew, founder of the Commandment Keepers.

Church of God and Saints of Christ

Founded in 1896, the Church of God and Saints of Christ is one of the earliest Israelite congregations in the United States and has its roots in post-Reconstruction America. The notorious Black Codes of the South restricted the movement of newly emancipated Negroes and kept them working in the fields. Following waves of violence in the late 1870s, scores of Negroes from Mississippi and Louisiana fled west in pursuit of land that had recently become available through the Homestead Act. Many found work as laborers on farms or in the railroad and mining industries; women found work as domestics and washerwomen (Haynes 1923). All-black towns, such as Nicodemus, Kansas, and Boley, Oklahoma, were founded during this time. Black communities also sprouted in the unincorporated outskirts of many sundown areas across the nation (Loewen 2005). Some of the migrants were recently converted Christians motivated by a millenarian belief that God would deliver them into the promised land, just as he had delivered the children of Israel (Levine 2007; Wilkerson 2011). William Saunders Crowdy—a former slave, Civil War veteran, and the founder of the Church of God and Saints of Christ—emerged from this tradition.

Crowdy believed that blacks descended from one of the ten lost tribes and that Jesus was black. He was not the first to introduce this idea. William Christian, a pastor from Arkansas and founder of the Church of God (later renamed the Church of the Living God), had drawn on scripture to argue that many biblical characters, including Adam, King David, Job, Jeremiah, and Jesus, were "of the Black race" (Dorman 2013). Crowdy's teachings incorporated the Old Testament, Hebrew dietary laws, and observance of the Sabbath and the Jewish calendar, especially Passover, but they also included New Testament practices, such as "repentance for sin, baptism by immersion, confession of faith in Christ, the reception of unleavened bread and water at the sacrament of the Lord's Supper, the washing of the feet by an elder, and the pledge of the holy kiss."[6] In 1896, the Crowdys founded their first three tabernacles: in Lawrence, Topeka, and Emporia, Kansas. While Crowdy embraced a multiracial membership (as Father Divine and his Peace Mission would do some thirty years later) and preached for racial equality, he also asserted the radical idea that Jesus, the Jew, was black (Dorman 2013; Weisenfeld 2016).

During the 1930s, when Howard Z. Plummer assumed leadership and pushed towards a stricter, more rabbinic practice of Judaism, the group split into two factions (Landing 2002). Although both retained the name of Church of God and Saints of Christ, each developed very different ideologies and practices (Könighofer 2008; Dorman 2013). One group, which maintains a website at www.churchofgod1931.org and has its international offices in Cleveland, Ohio, identifies itself as "first and foremost . . . a determinedly Christian church . . . built upon the person of Jesus Christ, the son of God." The second group, COGASOC, also referred to as Temple of Beth El, is headquartered in Belleville, Virginia. Despite the name, members do not believe that Jesus was the son of God but rather a prophet, much like their founder, Crowdy. Led by Rabbi Phillip E. McNeil, the group uses the terms "Israelite," "Hebrew," and "Hebrew Israelite" interchangeably, follows "Abrahamic customs," and strictly adheres to the "tenets of Judaism" (Landing 2002). Today it has tabernacles throughout the Midwest, Northeast, and South, as well as in Jamaica, according to its website at www.cogasoc.org.

William Samuel Williamson was "born and raised" in the latter Church of God and Saints of Christ and served as an elder in his tabernacle in Stratford, Connecticut. When I spoke with him in 1999, he was 73 years old. Elder Williamson had worked as a maintenance man, or what he jokingly called a "floorologist": "I specialized in floors, you know, cleaning them all around." His parents had been raised as Christians, "but when they heard the preaching on the streets, they heard it, and it sounded good to them, and they joined." He explained that his role as elder derived back to biblical times: "So here you read in the Bible, Moses is called for all the elders of Israel, that was each family, the elder, not the whole family, just the head." The use of the term "tabernacle" was also based on the Old Testament: "You don't hear the word 'synagogue' until the New Testament. . . . You hear of 'tabernacle.'" When I asked about the use of the term "Christ" in the church's name, he focused on the word's meaning:

A lot of people will ask you, "If you practice Judaism, how can you have the word Christ in your name?" Ah, "Christ" means "to be anointed"; it is a Greek word. And if you read in the Bible, you'll find out who else has been anointed, other Greek men have been anointed, and that David was anointed. Saul, the first king, was anointed. You can go down the line of those that have been anointed. There is a ceremony, they put the oil on their head and go through a different ceremony, all right. And they are anointed, and that goes right on into the word "Christ." There is a difference in the word "Jesus," and there is a difference in the word "Christ," Jesus the man and Christ the spirit. He never called himself "Jesus Christ." Man put that title on him, "Christ," because he did have the spirit. All right. But he was never anointed, he was baptized by John the Baptist, but as far as being anointed, those projects of political foretimes, he was not anointed, by that ceremonial means, but that spiritual, powerful feeling made him such a great figure in the world that automatically praise and glory came upon him.

Elder Williamson recited all twenty tenets of the Church of God and Saints of Christ. The first several tenets attested to its break with Christianity:

We believe that there is a creator. He is both creator and ruler of everything, terrestrial and celestial. We believe that the creator is one, and that there is no unity like his. We believe that the creator alone must be worshiped, he is God. His Lord should not give to another nor his praise to graven images. We believe that the creator is eternal, he was, he is, and he always shall be.

Prophets, both past and present, he explained, were central to the group's theology:

We believe that God's prophets are true and that by a prophet God delivered our forefathers from Egyptian bondage, and by a prophet we shall always be preserved. God is always going to have someone down here to lead you on. We believe that the prophesy of Moses, our foremost prophet, is true and that God has raised up to us a prophet like unto him. And that is, that prophet is William Saunders Crowdy. That is the reestablishment of our religion here in America.

Two tenets are solely devoted to the Ten Commandments, which are central to the group's core belief system: "We believe that the Ten

Commandments are divinely given to Moses. We believe that the Ten Commandments are immutable."

Despite the many fundamentally Jewish beliefs he shared, Elder Williamson made a clear distinction between the identification with Jews and the practice of Judaism: "No! I don't never tell nobody I am a Jew. I never tell nobody I am a Jew. They ask me my religion, I tell them we practice Judaism; it is a way of life." The Jewish way of life, and one of its most important distinctions from Christianity, he explained, was the focus on the here and now:

Judaism is how you live here on earth. Christianity will tell you about the hereafter. It is like one of the songs our forefathers would sing: [*sings*] "You got shoes, I got shoes, all God's children got shoes." Blacks will say, "When I get to heaven." No, you should have your shoes down here. When you get to heaven, how do you know how to put them on if you don't have them down here? This here is our dressing room. This will teach us how to live daily, a good life, you can't live, ignore here, and waiting for the hereafter, you have to start here. The starting point from here to there is your first step. If you aren't going to make that first step here, how are you going to get over there? A lot of people will say, "I am going to do it Thursday and Friday." Well, you got today, Wednesday, before you get to Thursday or Friday. So, you have to take each day at a time. And when you take each day at a time, you might not be alive Thursday, God knows, or Friday. But you got to live this moment, a good life in this moment. The Judaic way of living.

Jacob, a young Israelite and frequent attendant of the New Haven chapter of the Church of God and Saints of Christ, echoed this view: "I think what binds all Jews together is a certain struggle to understand what God is through the Torah, or even who God isn't through the Torah. . . . I don't care what you believe. To be a Jewish person has nothing to do with what you believe. It has to do with tell us how you live your life." His stance is not too different from that of many secular Jews, who emphasize action before faith and an ongoing and dynamic wrestling with God through the Torah.

While Torah was the code for living a Jewish life, Shabbat was what made living possible for Jacob:

Oh, man . . . Shabbat is *the* day of the week. Okay, it's the epitome of the week. There's nothing, no other day of the week comes close to Shabbat. Without Shabbat, I would not be able to function, period. I would break down. In a lot of ways, it keeps me whole, keeps me sane. That's one thing. I think the best part of Shabbat for me is the time to socialize and fellowship with other [*pause*] Israelites. . . . Fellowship with other Jews is wonderful, but . . . I don't get as much of a feeling of solidarity and appreciation and joy as I do spending with Israelites.

Jacob had long dreadlocks, which he adorned with a colorful knit *kippah*. One could easily take him for a Rastafarian, and although he had been born and raised in a small town near Jacksonville, Florida, about ten minutes from the Georgia line, he spoke with a distinct West Indian lilt. Both grandparents on his father's side had been Israelites, and their ancestors had come from East Africa, unlike the vast majority of slaves to the New World. From East Africa, they were brought to the West Indies: "So, I made logical assumptions that there they had to have encountered some Sephardi Jews. But my father never told me anything about conversion. It may or may not have played a part." Although he wasn't raised in the faith, he became interested in his family's history in his early teens: "By the time I was in high school, it was safe to say that I wanted to be a rabbi." By that, he meant an Israelite rabbi.

Jacob was pursuing a master's degree in theology and had a sophisticated understanding of the tensions between normative and Black Judaism and the political context in which Israelites "have cultivated a space for Jesus":

Do I consider Jesus a prophet? No. But there is space made in the Israelite's community for that assertion. Now that's scandalous to our fellow European Jews. But you have to remember European Jews come out of an experience with Christianity, an historical experience with Christianity, which is devastating and traumatic and proceeds from the foundation of the movement, which Jesus set in motion. Israelites don't have that historical experience. Israelites, in sub-Saharan Africa, don't have that historical experience. So it's not just black folk in America who are saying, "Well, you know, make room for Jesus as a Jew." . . . I think those concerns of my white Jewish friends are due, in fact, to a genealogy of suffering.

He noted that while his white Jewish contemporaries would readily agree that there were Jews of all creeds and colors and nationalities, "within the paradigm of American academic discourse, 'Jew' has all too often been a referent to western or eastern European Jewry." His attraction to the Church of God, as opposed to more observant congregations such as the Commandment Keepers, was more political than spiritual. He characterized the division between Israelites and Commandment Keepers (or Ethiopian Hebrews, as they also are known) as one of class:

> There's a tendency, I found, in the Commandment Keepers . . . to shun certain elements. . . . And I think that's potentially problematic. What's the extent to which the Ethiopian Hebrews can address some of those spiritual, economic concerns of the African Americans who are Israelites that may not reside in that, you know, lower-middle-class, if there is such a thing, upper-working-class, you know, economic bracket that other Israelites are not in. It's no secret the Israelites that like to incorporate racial consciousness into their theological understanding do not tend to be in the same class. . . . So my question is, okay, what were the tools that are being cultivated in Ethiopian Hebrews to address the concerns of Israelites who are part of the black working class? . . . Most Israelites read race into scripture. And they have to, because racism is a part of their fundamental day-to-day reality. . . . If you're a black person and into the black middle class, it's still a part of your fundamental day-to-day reality. But at least you have the economic foundation to psychologically dislocate yourself from perpetual attention. You know, if you can deceive yourself, at least you can do that. Poor black folk can't do that. They just can't. No matter how much you want them to. So, on the one hand, . . . I'm admiring what the Ethiopian Hebrews are doing, and this is why I align myself with them. But on the other hand, . . . I retained a lot of the racial consciousness that people in our movement tend to [have]. . . . And I think, I believe, that's in keeping with the true spirit of Rabbi Matthew. Rabbi Matthew didn't take race out. His second- and third-generation followers did, but he didn't.

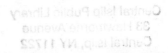

The Commandment Keepers

Much like the Church of God and Saints of Christ, the original Commandment Keepers Church of the Living God the Pillar and Ground of Truth and the Faith of Jesus Christ incorporated elements from both Judaism and Christianity (Dorman 2013, 153). The Harlem-based group, founded in 1919 by Rabbi Wentworth Arthur Matthew, began as a Christian church, although over two generations it has evolved into an observant congregation with its own ordained rabbis. Like William Christian and William Crowdy before him, Matthew placed blacks at the center of Judaism. The group traced its lineage through Ethiopia and preached that blacks in America were their descendants and one of the lost tribes.

Historian Jacob S. Dorman posits that for Matthew, blackness signified the covenant between God and the chosen people. Matthew viewed Jews of European descent as merely imitators, and even as he began integrating more Jewish rituals and practices into his services, his bitterness towards white Jews only increased:

> He taught that Black Jews were the real Jews, descended directly from Jacob, who was Black because the Bible says his skin was smooth. White Jews were descended from Esau, who was hairy, and like Esau, they had intermarried and assimilated Gentile ways. Furthermore, all Blacks were descended from the Ten Lost Tribes, of Israel, whom, he claimed, had been driven from Canaan and settled in Ethiopia. (Dorman 2013)

Interestingly, earlier Israelite leaders such as Elder Warren Roberson, founder of the Temple of the Gospel of the Kingdom of the Ever-Live-and-Never-Die Church, argued that it was black Americans, not white Jews, who descended from Esau, since it was Esau who was tricked out of his inheritance (Dorman 2013).

Although most of Matthew's initiates were women, they were relegated to the back of the sanctuary, a practice common among Orthodox Jewish congregations. Dorman attributes the diminished status of women to both patriarchy and "the discourse of civilization" (Dorman 2013, 174):

> To be civilized meant to segregate the sexes; the alternative religions of Harlem in the 1920s inscribed within themselves the patriarchy of their

times. . . . African Americans may have suffered the indignity of seg-regation in public spaces, but within the zone of their own alternative churches, Black Israelites asserted their respectability by creating separate spaces for men and women.

Despite their Afrocentric roots, the Commandment Keepers were the only Black Hebrew group to formally commit to treat Judaism as nonracial and to recognize rabbinic Jews as their brethren. Resolution 801A, adopted in 1981 under the auspices of the International Israelite Board of Rabbis,[7] "affirms the brotherhood of all people who worship the God of Abraham, Isaac, and Jacob without regard to race, tradition, or terminology (for ex-ample: Black Jews, Hebrews, Israelites, Jews, etc.)."[8] The Commandment Keepers might be understood as part of a wider Harlem-based Ethiopian Hebrew tradition, which included groups that did not survive the Great Depression, such as the Moorish Zionist Temple (not to be confused with the Black Muslim-based Moorish Science Temple), founded by Rabbi Mor-dechai Herman, and Beth B'nai Abraham, founded by Rabbi Arnold Ford.

Today, the Commandment Keepers have narrowed the gap with mainstream Jewish groups; in fact, joint services have been held in New York (Lyons 2012). Still, members maintain an identity distinct from "white," European-descent Jews and prefer to be known as Hebrews or Hebrew Israelites. Beth Elohim Hebrew Congregation, an offshoot of the Commandment Keepers, enumerates the reasons for this preference on its web page:

(A) These are the terms used in the Torah (Holy Scroll) to refer to the "children of Israel"; (B) these terms do not wrongly associate being Jewish with being white—which is the prevalent misconception of the term; and (C) they avoid the changing nomenclatures of terms like Negro, Black, Afro-American, and now, African American. Although some credible scholars have attempted to determine the racial classification of the an-cient Israelites, we believe that whatever the historical truth was, the pres-ent reality is that G-d is spirit and those who worship Him must "worship Him in spirit" rather than in pigmentation.

Beth Elohim was founded in 1983 by Chief Rabbi Levi Ben Levy, an early member of the Commandment Keepers who was ordained by

Rabbi Matthew in 1967. Since 1988, the congregation has been led by Levy's eldest son, Rabbi Sholomo Ben Levy. When I visited the temple in 1999, there were close to eighty members, most in their thirties and forties. Surrounded by other ministries and storefront churches, Beth Elohim was set apart by the two stars of David flanking its black awning. A sign in black with white lettering greeted visitors, "Everyone Welcomed," and announced Sabbath services on Saturdays at 10:30 a.m. "Shalom" was written in both English and Hebrew. The sanctuary was in repair when I visited. Benches were being refinished for Passover, and there was a leak in the middle of the room. I peeked through the bookcase and found the familiar Sabbath and festival prayer books, along with the Jerusalem Bible, the Holy Scriptures, and a newly revised edition of the Passover Haggadah by Rabbi Nathan Goldberg. I also spotted *The Art of Being a Jew* (1962) by Morris Norman Kertzer. One distinguishing item was a photograph of the Beta Israel, followed by an appeal for support to the community. I recalled seeing this same bulletin at Beth Shalom, Rabbi Tate's congregation in Bed-Stuy, Brooklyn. I would discover that the Ethiopian Hebrews in the United States strongly identified with the Ethiopian Jews, who had recently been embraced by Western Judaism, and drew on their success to claim legitimacy.

Rabbi Benyamin Levy, Sholomo's younger brother and the assistant rabbi of Beth Elohim, described the challenges of growing up in a strictly observant household and attending a public school:

> We were very observant. I would say more to the Orthodox style. Observed all the holidays, ate kosher foods, observed the Sabbath. Observed all the rituals that went along with that. So, coming up as a Hebrew, I mean, it was a balancing act because being in the public-school system, we didn't go to the *yeshiva*, you know, with the other kids who did. But we understood. . . . I always maintained that I was a Hebrew. So regardless of being in the public school, I wouldn't eat any of the food that they had in the school system. Which all my professors, all of the students, the teachers knew that I was Jewish, you know. One of the first questions that [they] would ask, my name, you know, Levy. "How did you get that name?" You know. And then all, all through my whole life, you know, I've always gotten that question.[9]

Like many Black Jews, Levy self-identified as a Hebew Israelite, which he argued was more historically accurate than the term "Jew":

> I mean, biblically speaking, we're talking about people in the Bible. . . . They were called . . . "Israelites," you know. So that would be the correct name if you will. All throughout the Torah, nowhere does it say anything about "Jewish," you know. See you have all the different tribes. . . . So that's why I say when you want to educate somebody on who you are . . . I would introduce myself as a Hebrew Israelite. And that also tells you, again from a biblical point of view, their lineage. You know, we know that Abraham was the first Hebrew. Abraham, Isaac, and then there was Jacob. Jacob's twelve sons become the children of Israel. So, from Abraham and the Hebrew to Jacob, Israelite, you're giving your whole history right there.

Language offers a window into the process of boundary making (Benor 2016). Identity terms like "Jew," "Hebrew," and "Israelite" can be seen as rhetorical constructs to map out territory and reify boundaries in which individuals are included or excluded (Star and Griesemer 1989). While providing the basis for determining one's legitimacy, the terms act as anchors yet are flexible enough to adapt to local usages and maintain a common identity across locales (Star and Griesemer 1989).

As sociologists Omi and Winant illustrate through their concept of racial projects, the ways in which race is articulated, interpreted, and represented translate into the organization and distribution of social resources along racial lines (Omi and Winant 1994). Winant distinguishes between racist and antiracist racial projects, defining the former as one that "creates or reproduces hierarchical social structures based on essentialized racial categories" (Winant 2004). Using this definition, the early Black Israelite and Hebrew movements—Cherry's Church of the Living God, Crowdy's Church of God and Saints of Christ, and Matthew's Commandment Keepers—can be viewed as engaging in racist projects. So too would modern sects on the fringe of today's Hebrew Israelite movement, such as the Israelite School of Universal Practical Knowledge, which has replaced one essentialist narrative (Jews are white) with another (blacks are the original Hebrews and white Jews are imposters). Such counterhegemonic black narratives—which philosopher Jean-Paul

Sartre termed as "anti-racist racism"—are closely related to an Afrocentric canon that emerged from segregated ghetto communities during the late nineteenth and early twentieth centuries; their persistence attests to the continued resonance of essentialist racial frames for black identities (Sartre and MacCombie 1964). Still, the views of some Black Hebrew groups have evolved over the years, as attested by the Commandment Keepers, who once claimed that Black Jews were the true Jews but now embrace a universal nonracial understanding of Judaism. Their journey gives credence to Sartre's description of Negritude as a historic mission that ends with its own transformation (Sartre and MacCombie 1964). While preserving a distinct cultural identity, the Commandment Keepers have deracialized claims to Jewish identity and Judaic practice (Santamaria 1987).

Black Zionism and Racial Projects

The Original African Hebrew Israelite Nation of Jerusalem attracted international attention in 1969, when some three hundred of its members immigrated to Israel. Also known as the Hebrew Israelite Community of Jerusalem—and often labeled in the media and by scholars as Black Hebrews or the Black Jews of Dimona (Landes 1967; Ben-Yehuda 1975; Gerber 1977; Lounds 1981; Baer and Singer 1992; HaGadol and Israel 1992; Markowitz 1996; Hare 1998; Singer 2000; Jackson 2013)—the group emerged in Chicago in the 1960s, under the leadership of Ben Ammi Ben-Israel (born Ben Carter) and Shaleah Ben-Israel. Carter had studied with Rabbi Levi Israel, a Garvey-influenced Israelite who embraced an "Afrocentric Israelite culture," before studying under the guidance of Rabbi Abihu Reuben, who had been ordained by Wentworth Matthew of the Commandment Keepers. Reuben reportedly gave Carter his Hebrew name, Ben Ammi, which means "son of my people" (Gerber 1977). Like many Hebrews, taking on a new name was part of reclaiming an authentic Hebrew identity. Ben Ammi perfected his theatrical preaching style amidst the bustling shoppers and street vendors of Chicago's Maxwell Street. By 1963, he was considering repatriation to Africa (Gerber 1977).

He joined the Abeta Hebrew Cultural Center, a group of like-minded Hebrews who talked frequently about immigration to Africa (Baer and Singer 1992). While the group sought a return to the promised land, exactly where that promised land was remained unclear at first. They curiously avoided any discussion of Israel, preferring instead to entertain repatriation to Ethiopia, due to its link to Solomon and Sheba. The impracticality of the venture led them to shift their interest to Liberia, an African nation founded on religious tolerance and a racial constitution that offered citizenship to "Negroes or persons of Negro descent" (Gerber 1977). By November 1967, Ben Ammi and some 160 members had made their way to Liberia, to land purchased in 1951 by a former Garveyite. The plan was doomed from the start. They had arrived during the country's rainy season and, just like the first American settlers, found themselves in primitive conditions and with no government support. They had no running water, lived out of tents, and had to clear land for agriculture. Yet Ben Ammi was quoted as saying, "We'd rather live in the jungle in Africa than in a house of Cicero." By year's end, however, a scant twenty members had secured meaningful employment, and dozens of disillusioned Hebrews returned to the United States (Gerber 1977).

As Ben Ammi assumed a leadership role, he continued to recruit new members and contemplated the next move for his Abeta group. By 1968, he and his closest confidant—fellow Hebrew Charles Blackwell—were discussing Israel as an alternative homeland. Blackwell traveled to the Israeli Embassy in Monrovia to investigate immigration and returned elated. "I found it! I found it!" Blackwell shouted. "I found our ticket into the country" (Gerber 1977). Under the Law of Return, any Jew could immigrate to Israel. While Ben Ammi and his followers—who claimed direct lineage to the tribe of Judah—fell outside the boundaries of normative Judaism, Blackwell had discerned a gray area in the law: if one claimed to be a Jew, the onus was placed on Israel to prove otherwise. After all, many Europeans had immigrated to Israel with little proof of their Judaism. Hebrew Israelites back in the United States engaged in a media campaign and suggested that the Israelis would be acting like the Nazis should they seek to deport Ben Ammi and his followers. To reject the claims of these Black Jews would seem arbitrary and prejudicial. And disproving their claims seemed near impossible, especially when they reached back to the ancient Israelites.

The group first entered Israel on tourist visas in 1969—in two contingents that arrived in July and December—and settled in the towns of Dimona, Arad, and Mitzpe Ramon in southern Israel (Singer 2000). (Ben Ammi would later rewrite their sojourn in Liberia, claiming it was but a stopping place to purify themselves for their trip to the promised land.) When the Israeli government required them to *halakhically* convert to Judaism in order to receive status as new Jewish immigrants, they responded that "they were already Israelites and thus Jews by ancestry," thereby invoking the same claims to direct, ancestral lineage that white, matrilineal-descent Jews make as a matter of course (Fernheimer 2014). Fernheimer writes:

> In making such claims, the Hebrew Israelites used a similar rhetorical strategy, but marshaled in a different set of evidence and different interpretations of other, familiar biblical passages to prove their identity claims. This series of discursive moves called attention to the ambivalences inherent in Jewishness and its blurred boundary between race and religion. (Fernheimer 2014)

While the Israeli government did not accept their claims and reasoning, neither did it expel them.

The Hebrew Israelites have remained in Israel since the 1970s and now comprise a closed society of some three thousand men, women, and children, yet their status in Israel has been tenuous at best.[10] In 1990, after a long battle with authorities, the group was granted temporary resident status, which allowed them to receive social benefits, including health care and housing. Permanent resident status finally came in August 2003, although only a handful of Hebrews have become naturalized citizens, and none have been accepted under the Law of Return (Fernheimer 2014). Meanwhile, members who remained in the United States operated a popular chain of juice bar/restaurants called Soul Vegetarian and Source of Life in Washington, DC, Chicago, Atlanta, Cleveland, Tallahassee, Charleston, St. Louis, and Largo, Maryland.[11]

Barbara, a Black Hebrew living on the South Side of Chicago, had gone to Dimona in the early 1970s.[12] Her husband and brother-in-law had first been recruited after the group settled in Israel; other male family members followed: "In my husband's family it was him, his brother-in-law, his father. And he had three younger brothers that went. . . . So that means you got six men in one family." That did not include the three wives—Barbara, her mother-in-law, and brother-in-law's wife. Within one year, all three wives would lose their husbands. From the start, Barbara had discouraged her husband from joining. The Hebrew Israelite group targeted young men like her husband, "twenty-five and under." Negative rumors about Ben Ammi had long circulated in their Chicago neighborhood, Barbara said, but

> I really didn't think too much of it until he came back and was recruiting people. . . . That's how my husband got involved. And Rabbi Reuben [of the Congregation of Ethiopian Hebrews in Chicago] tried to get him not to go. . . . And I tried to get him, if you're going to go, go on his own. I said, "Be your own man, don't follow nobody." They was telling the men that they didn't have to work, they didn't have to worry about what they was going to eat. And they didn't have to worry about where they were going to stay. . . . They was just painting this big picture, you know, this big beautiful picture.

The picture was quite different once they got to Israel: "After we got over there, all hell broke loose." She described a cult-like society in which deputies were named "princes," polygamy was common practice, and women's heads were shaved. Families were broken up: "They broke up me and my husband. They put me out on the street." Members who didn't fall in line were declared outcasts:

> They went behind closed doors and had this meeting on my brother-in-law. And the next thing we know, . . . he was in the park and a few brothers had accosted him. And I don't know if words were exchanged. I don't know what all went on. But they ganged him, and they hit him in the head with a hatchet and cut his throat. Now that was the murder that you probably heard about over there.

It was difficult to corroborate this story, but I did find several reports of criminal investigations into the community. The most recent was a *Jerusalem Post* article from December 2012, "Distrust in Dimona," which described numerous failed attempts by the Israeli government, in coordination with the Federal Bureau of Investigation, to prosecute leaders of the sect for insurance fraud, passport forgery, and child abuse (Katz

2012). One FBI informant described how members who faltered were brought back into line:

> There are cellars, he said, where followers who "stray from the path" are beaten with sticks until they once again "see the light" and return to the path of the righteous. Such allegations—in addition to suspicions about the cult-like behavior of the Black Hebrews—have concerned the Israeli authorities for years.

Similar abuses had been described twenty years earlier in the *New York Times Magazine*. The March 1981 article, "Strangers in the Holy Land," reported that members were discouraged from seeking professional medical care and were referred instead to "divine healers" within the community (Kurtis 1999). One couple, Thomas and Hazel Whitfield, "broke away" after two of their children died of malnutrition:

> Both were dedicated followers of the charismatic Ben-Ammi Carter. But Hazel Whitfield could not adjust to the practice of multiple wives. The group pressured her to accept her role and, when she refused, her children were taken away from her and placed with other families as punishment. In the course of the separation, one child developed symptoms of malnutrition that were ignored by the "divine healers" of the sect. (Kurtis 1999)

Other members lost children under similar circumstances. Writing about his experiences, Thomas Whitfield described how one member fell to pieces after his daughter died: "He couldn't take it any longer. I watched him going out of his mind. Other men in the settlement would beat him. They thought he was jiving them, that he was putting on" (Kurtis 1999). Neither the Israeli nor the American authorities have secured evidence of any abuse. Nor have all allegations been taken seriously. The *Post* cited Yoel Ashur, an Israeli official who had headed a special task force (now dissolved) on the Hebrew Israelite community. Ashur characterized most of the complaints as coming from former members who had "a tree they needed to bark up."

In 2003, Israel granted some three thousand members permanent resident status and offered members a five-year path to citizenship. In

February 2009, Ben Yehuda—a sixty-two-year-old resident of the settle-ment Village of Peace—became the first member of the community to gain full Israeli citizenship (Esenten 2009). The community has become much more integrated into Israeli society, and its youth now enlist in the Israeli Defense Forces. In a 2009 article posted by the *Jewish Chronicle*, reporter John Torode described how this once-authoritarian and close-knit group has "morphed into the law-abiding favorites of an Israel anx-ious to demonstrate its tolerance" (Torode 2009).

The case of the Hebrew Israelites raises interesting questions about identity claims. As Fernheimer asks, "When two groups claim legiti-macy through ancestral descent, how *does* one decide whose claims are authentic?" (Fernheimer 2014). She demonstrates how they disrupted, if not overturned, the dominant narrative of Judaism as white and Eu-ropean by "shifting emphasis from religious practices to ancestral links" and then argued that these links gave them a privileged status:

> By associating with an earlier group of individuals with a set of practices they viewed as closer to biblical prescriptions, in their eyes they trumped Rabbinic Jews' legitimacy. They also challenged the authority of Rabbinic Jews as the only legitimate community descending from the biblical He-brews. . . . In the very act of *not* playing by the Jewish rules, Ben Ammi calls attention to the multiple ways Jewishness is constructed (for exam-ple, by race, ancestry, or religion) and the controversial structure of the Law of Return (and the State of Israel by implication). He simultaneously asserts both a new conceptual grounding for black self-determination and autonomy and a broader definition of Jewish identity. His dissocia-tive innovation and appeals to the Law of Return, if accepted, would thus transform the whole conceptualization of the universal Jewish audience. (Fernheimer 2014)

Ben Ammi and his followers articulated a set of symbols, rituals, prac-tices, and rhetorical strategies unfamiliar to Israeli Jews. For while they denied that they were Jews, preferring to make their ancestral claims as original Hebrews, they nonetheless made a political claim as being racially (ancestrally) Jewish to the Israeli government under a law meant for the return of Jews (Fernheimer 2009). And they smoothly blended the Afro-American longing for equality, liberation, and a return to the motherland in Africa—an idea fully embraced by the Garvey movement—with the Jewish notion of exile and eventual return of the lost children of Israel. But this ancestral claim to Judaism under the Law of Return was predicated on a racial definition rather than a religious definition of who is a Jew, a definition that would, if accepted, effectively expand the boundaries of Jewishness (Fernheimer 2014).

For Ben Ammi and his followers, America was not the promised land but a metaphorical Egypt where they were the modern-day Hebrews. And Israel was not in the Middle East but in northeast Africa. Transforming Frantz Fanon's ideas about the decolonization of the Negro mind into a modern-day exodus out of America, he transported his congregants back to biblical days as true ancient Israelites in the flesh, thus constructing what we might call his own *midrash*—an interpretive process through which biblical text is revisited and reexamined in order to make room for and respond to contemporary problems. Such interpretive work is demonstrated by Ben Ammi's statement below, as cited by Reform Rabbi Israel Gerber:

It's like we've been slaves, and now we're in the wilderness as in Moses' time, and soon we're going to cross over into the Holy Land. Liberia was a stopover to rid ourselves of our Negrotism [*sic*], our slave thoughts, so we could start a new life as our ancestors did when Joshua led them across the Jordan River. (Gerber 1977)

The voices of Black Hebrews and Israelites provided here illustrate the centrality of the Old Testament in shaping the narratives of black Americans. While the biblical story of the children of Israel and their exodus from Egypt has long served as a metaphor for the experience of black Americans, early Black Hebrew and Israelite sects drew upon the Old Testament to construct parallel, and counterhegemonic, essentialist narratives on race (blacks are the original Hebrews and rightful heirs to Israel). While some groups continue to engage in such racial projects, the more prominent groups today (those emerging from the Commandment Keepers movement) have embraced a nonracial view and recognize rabbinic Jews as their brethren. In the next chapter, we will hear from black converts to Judaism and explore what drew them to rabbinic Judaism.

5

Your People Shall Be My People

Black Converts to Judaism

The first time I walked in a synagogue, I just, I mean, it's totally different than being in church. And I was kind of shocked, frankly. . . . You know, when you're in church, like people all pray together, and when you're in temple, who knows what people are doing. . . . Anything goes. I mean, kids are running around. People are talking to each other. They stand up in the middle of the service, and they'll walk around. And they hug, and they kiss . . . You know what I mean? It's like a meeting place.
—Black female convert to Judaism, interview excerpt[1]

Bagels and lox is not the Torah. For some people, this is how, you know, this, this is how you make yourself legitimate. And quite frankly, people ask me, well sometimes ask me, well how do you have a Jewish cultural identity? Simple, I always had one.
—Michael Twitty, interview excerpt[2]

American Jewry defines itself in religious terms through its varied institutional frameworks and their respective rules of membership. Yet for many Jews, being Jewish is more than a religious identity, and they describe themselves in multiple ways, including as an ethnic group, a cultural group, and a nation (Biale, Galchinsky, et al. 1998). Therein lies the challenge for anyone who converts to Judaism, but for African Americans, it can be especially daunting.

Rabbi Neal Weinberg, the rabbinic director of Judaism by Choice in Los Angeles, is well acquainted with these challenges. When I first met him in January 1999, he was directing the Miller Introduction to Judaism Program at the American Jewish University (formerly the University of Judaism). While the program attracted a diverse group of people exploring Judaism—he noted the large numbers of Hispanics and Asians—African Americans represented just a handful of enrollees. One factor that might account for the relatively low numbers, he felt, was the cultural importance of the church among black Americans: "So even though a black person may not be religious, they still feel that cultural tie to the church."[3] He also noted the stigma of being a black Jew: "I think still in some, in a lot of blacks' minds, there is a perception that it is like a joke to be black and be Jewish. I mean Sammy Davis Jr. made a joke of it."

Still, among those blacks who were drawn to Judaism, there were distinct motivating factors that distinguished them from other converts. Rabbi Weinberg noted that they tended to view Christianity as a slave religion that was

> put upon them by their masters, that this was not something that they chose for themselves, so they identified with Jewish history because of the exodus. And then a lot of them don't want to become Muslims because Muslims were involved and still [are involved] today in the black slave trade in Africa. And so, they believe in God, they have values that come from the Bible, so to them it makes sense to become Jewish.

He noted the unique challenges that black converts face, including the neighborhoods in which they live:

> Do you live in a Jewish neighborhood, in which case you are going to stick out as being black? But if you live in a black neighborhood, you are going to stick out being a Jew because, you know, everyone is very church oriented.

One important factor that Weinberg did not discuss was the significant costs associated with converting to Judaism. Converts must join a synagogue (whose membership fees can be considerable), as well as take classes and purchase books and religious articles. These costs may be prohibitive for many African Americans, who represent a much smaller segment of the middle and upper classes.

Few studies have explored conversion to Judaism, and fewer still have focused on black converts to Judaism. As social demographer Nava Lerer and historian Egon Mayer observe, scholars have overwhelmingly relied on the "Pauline experience" of conversion, a model based on the Christian narrative of Paul the Apostle, who had a revelatory encounter with the resurrected Christ on the road to Damascus (Lerer and Mayer 1993). The Pauline model posits a passive subject whose conversion is brought on by a miracle or experience over which one has no control (Richardson 1985).

Sammy Davis Jr.'s conversion to Judaism is often interpreted through this Pauline lens. As the story goes, while recuperating in November 1954 from a near-fatal auto accident in which he lost sight in his left eye, Davis was visited by his friend Eddie Cantor, who spoke to him of the similarities between black and Jewish culture, thus sparking his interest in Judaism. By early 1957, rumors had spread that Davis had become a Negro Jew. In the December 26, 1957 issue of *Jet* magazine, he published a two-page article entitled, "Why I Became a Jew," writing, "Why did I become a Jew? The answer is simple. I became a Jew because this religion offers me more than any other." He went on to state, incorrectly, that his Reform rabbi was called a "priest" and that there was no ritual for converting to Judaism. But in fact, it was years later, in 1961, that Davis underwent a formal Reform conversion.

The sociologist James T. Richardson has written extensively about the passive and active paradigms of conversion. In the latter case, the convert actively seeks meaning and has self-determination (Richardson 1985). As new religions formed in the 1960s and 1970s, scholars such as Loftland and Skonovd developed a descriptive model that takes into account the historical and cultural contexts for conversion. This model encompasses the "revivalist" motif, which refers to transformative experiences that occur in emotionally charged groups; the "coercive" motif, which reflects the conditions of brainwashing or mind control; and finally, the "intellectual motif," which is characterized by "ideologies and ways of life that eschew social involvement" with coreligionists (Lofland and Skonovd 1981). Later scholarship applied a rational-choice approach to describe the context in which actors weigh the rewards of converting or not converting (Gartrell and Shannon 1985). Yet none of these paradigms fully explain the processes at work among those converting to Judaism. Becoming Jewish means adopting a set of responsibilities within a community that has chosen to follow Mosaic law and live an ethical life. Jewish identity is produced through social experience, that is, by acting in ways that are socially identifiable as Jewish. Unlike the sudden and transformative Pauline experience, becoming a Jew is accomplished over time.

Lerer and Mayer (1993), as well as many rabbinic scholars, prefer to use the biblical story of Ruth as the exemplar for converts to Judaism. As the story goes, after the deaths of their husbands, Naomi (an Israelite) implores her daughter-in-law Ruth (a Moabite) to return to her people and the land of her birth, but Ruth refuses, pledging instead to follow Naomi back to the land of Judea: "Where you go I shall go, your people will be my people, your God will be my God and where you die there I shall lie down also" (Ruth 1:16–17; see Lerer and Mayer 1993). Later, Ruth marries the Israelite Boaz and becomes the progenitor of King David.

The significance of this story lies in Ruth's willingness to leave her people and, by implication, her religion and cultural identity to become a Jew. She exemplifies the "righteous convert" because she took on a new identity as part of the people of Israel. Among the Orthodox—who believe that the first spiritual conversion occurred thousands of years ago at the foot of Mount Sinai, when Israel was born anew as a people—her story is frequently used to assert that all Jews are righteous converts.

In the rabbinic context, becoming a part of the Jewish people has meant being subjected to a loose set of rules that began evolving during the sixth century, when the Talmud first defined the Hebrew term for "stranger" (*ger*) as "proselyte." In fact, there is no term for "proselyte" in the Hebrew Bible. Prior to the destruction of the First Temple and the beginning of the Babylonian exile in 586 BCE, a *ger* was defined simply as a stranger who lived among the Israelite community and followed most, but not all, of its laws. And among the first Talmudic scholars, no uniform opinion existed on conversion or about the status of converts. Some considered them special Jews, possibly more righteous than born Jews, while others remained skeptical and held them apart (Forster and Tabachnik 1991).

During the early Roman period, when Jewish proselytizing was widespread, rabbis questioned the status of the proselyte even as they publically asserted that he was equal in all ways to the native-born Israelite.

Did, for example, the scriptural phrase "man of Israel" include the proselyte? According to *tannaitic* law (oral law recorded from roughly 10 to 220 CE), the answer was no. A proselyte "has no share in the land of Israel and is unable to say in his prayers 'Our God and God of our fathers'" (Cohen 1999). As Jews themselves became strangers in a strange land, the question shifted to how they would manage the *ger*, or stranger, amongst themselves. Debates ensued over the status of the convert. For some rabbis, they held a certain kind of second-class status as Jews: "In sum, the rabbis regarded the proselyte as a Jew, an adherent of the true faith, but they were not entirely sure that he was an Israelite. To the extent that Jewish self-definition depended upon national affiliation, to that extent the proselyte was anomalous: an Israelite without tribe or land" (Cohen 1999).

Restrictions on the convert are also found in the Mishnah (the legal commentary on the Torah). In Bikkurim, the section concerning the first fruits that must be brought to the Temple and given to the *Kohen* (priest), the convert can bring the fruits but is excluded from reciting certain words:

> These people bring, but do not recite: the convert brings but does not recite, for he is unable to say [in the biblical recitation] "[the land] that God swore to our fathers to give to us." And if his mother was from Israel, he brings and recites. And when he prays by himself, he says [in place of "the God of our fathers"] "the God of the fathers of Israel." And when he is in the synagogue, he says "the God of your fathers." And if his mother was from Israel, he says "the God of our fathers." (Mishnah Bikkurim 1:4)[4]

While these restrictions are no longer upheld, they attest to a deep-rooted bias towards converts (Cohen 2014). They also establish the preeminence of ancestry from early on. Religion scholar Gary Porton cites the restrictions on converts in early rabbinic literature as evidence of "the importance of Israel's ethnicity and the fact that the rabbis viewed Israel as both an ethnic group and a religious community (Porton 1994). Anthropologist Susan Kahn argues that opposing concepts of Jewishness—kinship versus religious commitment—have always been in tension. Matrilineal descent reinforces the idea that one's Jewishness resides in the body, just as conversion undermines this idea, "suggesting that however embedded Jewish identity may be, it is an identity that can be willfully assumed by a non-Jewish body" (Kahn 2010).

The privileging of kinship over religious commitment persists in the United States. According to the 2013 Pew Research Center survey of US Jews, 66 percent of American Jews consider that "being Jewish" is more about culture and ancestry than religion. Interestingly, this view was shared by both secular and practicing Jews: Even among "Jews by religion" (those who identify as Jews "on the basis of religion," as opposed to "Jews of no religion," those who "describe themselves as having no religion and identify as Jewish on the basis of ancestry, ethnicity or culture"), "more than half (55%) say being Jewish is mainly a matter of ancestry and culture, and two-thirds say it is not necessary to believe in God to be Jewish" (Pew Research Center 2013). Moreover, one in five Jews (22 percent) describe themselves as having no religion (i.e., secular Jews). This trend has grown with each generation. Seven percent of Jews born before 1927 describe themselves as having no religion, compared with 19 percent of baby-boomer Jews (born between 1946 and 1964), 26 percent of Generation X Jews (born between 1965 and 1980), and 32 percent of millennial Jews (born after 1980) (Pew Research Center 2013).

Social scientists have long conflated and interchanged American Judaism (religion) and Jewish ethnic identity, using religious observance as an indicator of Jewish assimilation (Wirth 1927; Phillips 2016). It is true that, until recently, most of American Jewry has largely defined itself in religious terms, and although contemporary Jewish identity has shifted from its historical religious core, religion continues to serve as the benchmark. Becoming a Jew, for people who have chosen Judaism, often reflects years of nurturing a religious Jewish identity. Prior to formal conversion, which culminates in immersion in a *mikveh*, converts typically study the Hebrew language and learn about Jewish law, holidays, and rituals. Male converts undergo circumcision as they symbolically become Israel and a direct descendent of Abraham, who—as some scholars have suggested—was the first convert to Judaism:

> More revealingly, however, the convert's name is changed to "ben Avraham" or "bas Avraham," son or daughter of Abraham. The convert is adopted into the family and assigned a new "genealogical" identity, but because Abraham is the first convert in Jewish tradition, converts are his

descendants in that sense as well. There is thus a sense in which the convert becomes the ideal type of the Jew. We not only do these things because we are this thing but we are this thing because we do these things." (Boyarin and Boyarin 1993)

From the second century BCE through the early fourth century CE, Judaism was a proselytizing religion, yet many Jews see themselves as a culturally distinct "people," a group biologically descended from Abraham. Still, at its foundation, Judaism remains a covenantal community of choice. "Jewishness disrupts the very categories of identity," say scholars Daniel and Jonathan Boyarin, "because it is not national, not genealogical, not religious, but all of these in dialectical tension with one another" (Boyarin and Boyarin 1993).

Recent advances in genetic technologies, championed by Jews themselves, have only reinforced biological notions of Jewishness. Susan Kahn describes these technologies as seductive to a community long preoccupied with its origins, boundaries, and self-definition (Kahn 2010). These technologies also bolster the "ascribed" (inherent) versus "achieved" basis of Judaism, ensuring that even the most secular Jews can claim equal status with the Orthodox, at least genetically. And while many Jews today exercise choice in the ways in which and the extent to which they observe Judaism (Cohen and Eisen 2000), their Jewishness "is often perceived as a given and hence as a biological imperative" (Tenenbaum and Davidman 2007).

Historian Susan Glenn has examined the ways in which Jews continue to use "blood logic" to "Jewhoo," or claim one another, even extending membership to those who have rejected their Jewish identities or converted to other religions (Glenn 2002). In *The Jew Within*, sociologist Steven M. Cohen, along with the Judaic studies scholar and chancellor of the Jewish Theological Seminary, Arnold Eisen, found a high degree of tribalism among moderately affiliated Jews, who asserted "that they are Jews because they are Jews, period—that is, because one or both of their parents are Jews" (Cohen and Eisen 2000). Likewise, sociologists Shelly Tenenbaum and Lynn Davidman found that many "unsynagogued" Jews (i.e., Jews not affiliated with any synagogue) placed "a strong emphasis on the inherent, inalienable nature of their Jewishness" (Tenenbaum and Davidman 2007). Subjects were more likely to embrace biological understandings of Jewish identity than more observant Jews, thus assuring that "their Jewishness is absolute and cannot be increased or lessened by any level of practice or belief" (Tenenbaum and Davidman 2007). Despite their minimal ritual practice and lack of religious belief, respondents claimed that their biology was enough to make them feel essentially Jewish for life, and some questioned whether a person could convert and become "really" Jewish (Tenenbaum and Davidman 2007). This, along with the presumed whiteness of Jews, makes conversion to Judaism fundamentally different from conversion to purely faith communities like Christianity and Islam.

Converting to Judaism also means inheriting a new cultural framework that includes taking on the mantle of descent from Abraham and the ancient Israelite people. It is this focus on peoplehood—as exemplified through the story of Ruth—that further distinguishes conversion to Judaism from other religious conversions and makes necessary a different theoretical discourse. As Lerer and Mayer point out, "The story of Ruth portrays a model of religious conversion that has little to do with either the ecstasy of divine revelation or with a gradual, purposive quest for a new religious identity. Rather, Ruth's conversion seems to emerge out of a profound human bond of a family relationship" (Lerer and Mayer 1993). Lerer and Mayer apply this "family-centered" paradigm, which rests on a "desire to keep the family system intact," to the conversions of a non-Jewish spouse. They find, in fact, that 25–30 percent of marriages between Jews and gentiles result in the conversion of the non-Jewish partner: "Moreover, these studies have shown that about 95% of all conversions to Judaism occur within the context of intermarriage" (Lerer and Mayer 1993).

Prior to World War II, Jewish out-marriage rates were low, as was conversion to Judaism by non-Jewish partners (Forster and Tabachnik 1991). Yet since the 1960s, both have risen significantly. Conducted under the auspices of the Council of Jewish Federations from 1970–1972, the National Jewish Population Survey (NJPS) was the first comprehensive and statistically representative sample of adult Jewish households in the United States. The NJPS brought to the forefront of public discussion the concerns of Jewish out-marriage, the fading away of Jewish identity, and other supposed threats to the survival of the Jewish people. By 1979, the Task Force on Reform Jewish Outreach was formed by the Union of American Hebrew Congregations (now called the Union for Reform Judaism). Starting in the early 1980s, Jewish family services agencies, Jewish community centers, and Reform congregations began establishing outreach programs (Mayer 1995). According to the 2013 study *American Jewish Population Estimates: 2012*, conducted by Steinhardt Social Research Institute at the Cohen Center for Modern Jewish Studies at Brandeis University, the number of Jews in America has grown to 6.8 million, despite the rising rates of out-marriage, which now surpass 50 percent (Tighe, Saxe, et al. 2013).[5]

Jewish attitudes caught up with shifting demographic realities as the crossing of boundaries through both out-marriage and conversion increasingly became the norm. Scholars reported that 30 percent of non-Jewish spouses married to a born Jew were formally converting to Judaism, while another 20 percent were identifying as Jews on surveys (Forster and Tabachnik 1991). Despite the predictions of social scientists that Jewish identity would soon disappear, recent surveys show that younger generations of adults who say they have one Jewish parent and one non-Jewish parent are more likely to claim Jewish identity than older generations (Pew Research Center 2013).

Although much of the recent scholarship on conversion to Judaism points to the family-centered paradigm, the black converts in this study were overwhelmingly single and had been independently drawn to Judaism. Many found resonance with Jewish values and ideas. Some believed they had an ancestral link to Jews.

Alice, a forty-one-year-old single mother and former student of Rabbi Weinberg, attributed her comfort around Jews to some unknown Jewish ancestry, a view that, interestingly, reinforces essentialist notions of Jewishness and emphasizes the biological and genetic basis of Jewish identity.[6]

> I feel that there had to be someone in my family, frankly, I think there's someone Jewish in my family. I think that my grandfather may have been Jewish. . . . He was from Portugal, . . . my father's side of the family, . . . and the reason I say that is that I think that there had to be something there for me to feel as comfortable as I feel with being Jewish. I can't say that I feel like Julius Lester, how he describes having found himself. I just feel so comfortable being Jewish.

Alice's interest in Judaism had been sparked years earlier, when she was dating a Jewish man and "noticed the differences in what his thoughts were about religion versus what, how [she] had grown up as a Christian." Her interest outlasted the relationship, so when she finally decided to explore Judaism, she turned to the telephone book:

> I just actually pulled out the phone book and started calling different temples and telling them that I wanted to learn about Judaism. And somewhere along the way, someone suggested that I try Stephen S. Wise Temple. . . . It's a very large Reform congregation. Happens to be next door to the University of Judaism. And so, I called there, and then they directed me to the UJ.

Afroculinarian Michael Twitty, who described himself as "an African American convert to Judaism with Jewish ancestry" (his mother's grandfather was Jewish), was seven or eight years old when he declared he was Jewish:

> My father took me to Williamsburg [in Brooklyn] when I was a little kid . . . and I remember taking my tri-cone hat and fashioning it into a *kippah*, *yarmulke*, and I had this robe. I was a hilarious kid. I was so dramatic, a total actor, and I think I had seen *The Chosen*, and I knew that is what I wanted. I knew that is me.

Twitty had grown up in a "nominally Christian" home in Montgomery County, Maryland, a quiet suburban community that was both "very Jewish and very black." His aunt was a Jehovah's Witness, and his mother was baptized Lutheran, although her parents were Episcopalian. His second cousin was a bodyguard for Louis Farrakhan. At the same time, he had many Jewish friends and attended several bar mitzvahs: "I have *kippahs* from every last one of those." He attended Howard University— the historically black university in Washington, DC—where he studied anthropology and African American studies, and he went on to become a culinary historian. Today, he has fashioned a unique Judaism steeped in African American and Sephardi traditions, which he expresses through what he calls "Afro-Ashkefardi" cooking and "Kosher/Soul." As he writes on his blog, *Afroculinaria*, "Being Kosher/Soul is about melding the histories, tastes, flavors, and Diasporic wisdom of being Black and being Jewish."[7]

Former civil rights activist Julius Lester was also drawn to Judaism at a young age. In one haunting passage of his memoir, he recounts the piercing beauty and pain he experienced as a child when playing, on the piano, "Kol Nidre"—the hauntingly beautiful prayer/song recited on the eve of Yom Kippur:

> I love Bach's music more than that of any composer, but my favorite com-
> position is in a thick book Momma bought me. There is no composer's
> name and I do not know how to pronounce the title because it is in a for-
> eign language. Every day after I finish practicing, I play it over and over.
> It is not lines or chords; neither does it move, but it does not stand still. It
> simply is. It is happy and sad at the same time. I play and beauty becomes
> pain and then beauty again and in a half-step is inverted into pain once
> more until beauty and pain wrap around each other like the braids of
> a girl's hair, and beauty and pain become a piercing that holds me pin-
> ioned and I feel old like "In the beginning," old as if I was never born and
> will never die. The music winds itself around me and wants to take me
> somewhere, but I am afraid and do not go. When I stop playing there is
> a painful yearning in my stomach, a wishing for something I have never
> had and thus do not know what it is, or a wishing for something which I
> had once and have forgotten what it was. The name of the composition is
> "*Kol Nidre*." It is a Hebrew melody. (Lester 1988)

Lester, who died shortly before this book's publication, was the son of a Methodist minister and grew up in Missouri during the height of Negro segregation, in the 1940s and 1950s.[8] Like Twitty, he learned early on that he had Jewish ancestors—his maternal great-grandfather was a German Jew named Adolph Altschul—although it would be years before he embraced Judaism for himself. In speaking to me of his journey into Judaism, he emphasized the personal over the ancestral connection that ultimately motivated him to convert: "I like being able to pray in song. Because being able to pray in song means that there is a way for me to express my feel-ings, and it is through feeling . . . that for me a connection is made to the divine." He also found great comfort in the daily and life-cycle rituals of Judaism, which brought a heightened consciousness to every moment:

Very central to Judaism is finding the way to make the ordinary fully visible. . . . My religious inclination . . . has always been towards wanting a religion which I could live on a daily basis and not just by going to a building on a certain day of the week and praying and what have you. That's what Judaism certainly gives me. My connection to nature, Judaism certainly supports that just in terms of the cycle of the Jewish year. . . . The Jewish calendar makes much more sense to me than having New Year on January 1st, where ain't nothing changing on January 1st, but in the fall, things are changing, and the old year is dying, and so the rhythm of the Jewish year certainly means a lot to me.

For Lester, Judaism enriched more than his spiritual consciousness. It enriched his black consciousness: "Judaism continues to really make my life richer. It has a great impact on my writing, even when I'm writing about blacks. The things that I've learned as a Jew have opened up to see things as a black experience, as something I wouldn't have seen otherwise."

Cleo, a thirty-five-year-old woman and former student of Rabbi Weinberg, had also discovered Judaism in her childhood.[9] She started attending Hebrew school when she was eight. Her Jamaican Catholic mother and African American Episcopalian father had no objections. Her parents were well educated and cosmopolitan. Her father had served in the Special Forces, and her family had lived in San Francisco and Japan before making their home in Denver, Colorado. They had moved into an all-white neighborhood, and many of her new friends were Jewish:

I went to Hebrew school with my girlfriend, Cathy. . . . And they had Shabbat every Friday night. No matter what. And I was at that house every Friday night for Shabbat . . . with the challah and the candles and the prayers. I mean, I knew the *bracha* [blessing] when I was eight years old. She [Cathy] also knew the Our Father and the Hail Mary because she would come to my house and go to church with me.

When Cleo was ten, her parents divorced, and she and her mother moved to a black neighborhood near Fitzsimons Army Base. For the first time, she felt that she didn't fit in:

I didn't know I was different when I was living in the white neighborhood. How's that? I mean, I blended in with my Jewish friends, and I had no problems with my Jewish friends. Everything was fine. They accepted who I was. We played. I slept at their house. Took baths together. I mean, where in white American would they let a little black child get in the tub with their little white child? . . . We slept in the same bed. . . . I didn't have any problems with not fitting in. The minute we moved to this black neighborhood, I didn't fit in. I didn't speak the way they did. I didn't listen to the same music they did. I didn't wear my hair the way they did. I didn't dress the way they did. My mother wasn't on AFDC [Aid to Families with Dependent Children] the way theirs was. . . . I was called an Oreo.

After one year, Cleo transferred to an integrated school, where everyone was bused: "And if you lived across the street, you were sent across town. I mean, this was integration extreme." She felt just as out of place at her new school and described every day as a nightmare. In seventh grade, she was cornered by a couple of black girls in the bathroom, and they cut off one of her pigtails. One asked, "What color's your mama?" Her mother, in fact, was very light, what Cleo described as "a coolie from West Indies. She's not black. She's white ancestry with a little bit of Indian mixed in. She's very red. She looks like a Pakistani." In fact, Cleo was identified as both "Indian and Negro" on her birth certificate, although her mother always told her to check the "other" box: "Do not check 'black.' Do not check 'white.' Do not check anything but 'other' because they don't need to know."

Although Cleo was dating a Jewish man when she began studying with Rabbi Weinberg, she did not convert with marriage in mind. In fact, before her chance encounter with an Israeli woman, she had never thought of converting:

I'm sitting in Jerry's Deli one day, and . . . this lady's on the other side, and she's reading an Israeli newspaper. And I was still a private investigator. My pager went off. And I turned to her, and I said, "Excuse me. Could you tell the waitress I'll be right back?" . . . I left my purse on the chair, . . . and [when] I came back, she goes, "Don't you ever leave your purse anywhere." I said, "Yeah, but I left it next to you. You can't be bad, you're reading a Hebrew newspaper. You're obviously Jewish, and you can't be bad." Just intuitively, I was fine with her. . . . So we got into this heated conversation about, "I don't care where you are. Just because I'm Jewish doesn't mean . . ." I said, "Yes it does. Because you're innately good." . . . She said, "Well, how do you know so much about Jews and their beliefs?" And I said, "Well, because I have friends that are Jewish . . . and I've always wanted to be Jewish." And she said, "Well, why don't you convert?" And it never dawned on me to convert to Judaism, this whole entire time. From the first guy that I dated that said, "Oh, I could never bring you home because you're not Jewish." It never dawned on me, well just go right up the hill right there and you can convert. Because I always drove by the University of Judaism. But I never, I thought it was a rabbinical school or, you know, like Oral Roberts University. . . . And she said, "Well, go to the University of Judaism and take classes." . . . The minute I left Jerry's Deli, I called [boyfriend] and said, "Guess what? I'm converting . . . I'm converting to Judaism. I found out where I can do it." And he goes, "Well, don't just do it for me." And I go, "I'm not doing it for you. I'm doing it for me. What do you mean doing it for you?" I hadn't even thought about marriage.

Her boyfriend ended up attending the classes with her "because he didn't want me to know more than him." Still, she noted, he used the class to regain his own sense of Judaism: "It came at the perfect time for him to reinvent Judaism for himself, to find out where he was in his religion. So, it actually was *beshert*" [a Yiddish word meaning "destiny"].

Unlike many of Cleo's classmates, who were converting "under the direction of the mother-in-law" and afraid to tell their own parents, Cleo rushed to tell her parents, and they embraced her decision:

I called my mom and said, "Guess what? I'm converting." My mom said, "Oh good. You always wanted to be Jewish." I called my father and said, "Guess what? I'm converting." "Oh good. You always wanted to be Jewish." They were happy to hear something positive. And my mom said, "Well, at least it's the same God." I wasn't going into some Shinto kind of [thing].

Ultimately, what drew Cleo to Judaism was the emphasis on the family: "What I like about the Jewish religion is that it starts in the home more so than Christianity, which is not home-based. . . . You're living a Jewish life because your home is Jewish."

Many interview participants spoke of being drawn to the strong ethical values and intellectualism of Judaism. Alice, who had converted to Conservative Judaism three years earlier, explained:

> I think, frankly, a lot more people would turn to Judaism if they actually understood what the base of the tenets of Judaism revolved around. Because it makes sense. And it stands for everything that's good in the world. And I think people would be attracted to it if they knew what Judaism is. And I'm not saying that's a bad thing about Judaism; however, people do not know anything about Judaism. Judaism, I think, because of the discrimination the Jewish people faced throughout, since time began, actually, it's a closed society. It's almost like a secret society, in a way. And unless you're Jewish you have no access to it. . . . Judaism has such a way of verbalizing and describing. And maybe if I had been born Jewish, it wouldn't have been so well described to me. Because I think a lot of people that are born Jewish take it for granted. But having been taught about Judaism and all of the guidelines and everything just described to me and explained to me in detail so that I could get an understanding, obviously it became very clear to me, the purpose of why you do certain things.

Scholars have argued that converts often engage in solitary expressions of Jewish culture, such as collecting Judaica or watching films with a clear Jewish theme (Forster and Tabachnik 1991). Yet Alice was clearly drawn to the communal aspects of worship and fraternity with other Jews; she loved the liveliness and informality of the synagogue, which were in stark contrast to the staid Lutheran and Catholic churches in which she was raised and where "you sit down, and you're quiet, and you don't say anything." She described her first experience attending synagogue services:

> Everyone was . . . praying out loud. And sometimes one might be praying, and . . . somebody else might be catching up on the prayers. They're [all] in a different place. And there was just so much activity going on in the synagogue. So, I was like, "What is this?"

Other converts, such as Julius Lester, were drawn to the "Jewish way of thinking" that comes from actively engaging with the Torah:

> I like that there is a Jewish way of thinking about things. . . . One of the courses I do is a course in Judaic studies called "Biblical Tales and Legends," . . . and basically, we study various things in the book of Genesis. And getting the students to look at a text and take every word seriously, even "the" and "a," that's a rabbinic way of thinking, is that nothing here is without meaning or without importance, and that the meaning is not preordained by some authority, that the meaning comes from what's your relationship to the text. . . . The other thing that I do in the course is to show them how to use the imagination to open up a text. . . . And so, that's one of the things I love about Judaism, that it's not a matter of faith, it's not a matter of belief, it's a matter of an ongoing relationship. And what's so amazing about Torah study is that it's really a mirror about you, and so you can read the same text for ten years, and then one day you will see something you have never seen before. The text ain't changed, the words are the same. So what changed in you that you're now able to see something in this text that you didn't see before? So, I love that dynamic process.

If Torah is, as Lester put it, a mirror to the self, each year revealing a fresh nuance, a new depth of understanding, then it tells a rich and complicated story when interpreted through his lens. He studied English at Fisk University, a historically black college in Nashville, Tennessee, and went on to become a folksinger and civil rights activist (serving as field secretary for the Student Nonviolent Coordinating Committee in 1968), as well as a nationally acclaimed author. His first book, *Look Out, Whitey! Black Power's Gon' Get Your Mama* (1968), was one of the first to explain the new term "black power," connecting it to the historical legacies of Martin R. Delany, Frederick Douglass, Marcus Garvey, and W. E. B. Du Bois. In 1968, he incurred the wrath of the Anti-Defamation League after airing an angry, anti-Semitic poem on his weekly radio show at New York's WBAI-FM. Years later, he converted to Judaism and became an outspoken critic of anti-Semitism among blacks, drawing much criticism from his colleagues in the Afro-American Studies Department at the University of Massachusetts Amherst. From 1991 through 2001, he served as lay religious leader for Beth El Synagogue in

St. Johnsbury, Vermont. He has published over two hundred essays and reviews and forty-three books (Lederman 2009).

Reflecting back on the condemnation he has drawn, alternately from Jews and blacks, he visualized an inner thread tying all of his actions together:

> I really feel like I have followed, the image that I am having is an inner thread, and I have followed that inner thread, and so that those who saw me as an anti-Semite during the BAI incident were wrong. I did not advocate anti-Semitism, and the FCC [Federal Communications Commission] backed me up on that. And those who want to see me now as some kind of latter-day Jewish hero are also wrong. Somebody attacked the black community the way the teachers' union was doing in New York then, somebody attacks the black community that way now, I will respond with the anger I did then. And somebody attacks the Jewish community as folks were doing, I will, as black folks have been doing, I will respond. Both are wrong. Both are the same thing. There is no contradiction. I think I have been very consistent in terms of what my values are.

Like Julius Lester, Michael Twitty spoke of the personal and interactive relationship with the Torah, which evolved with every reading:

> I did not come to Judaism because I wanted the answer. It is not a religion of answers. Judaism is a religion of questions. . . . It is about questions that come from questions, and answers that come from questions, and questioning those answers. And as somebody who was always bookish, I loved that. . . . It made it possible for me to see myself in the text. Judaism is the only religion where people become books, and books become people. . . . It was finally OK to read a book twelve times. Because, guess what, you read the Torah your entire life. Every single year until the day you die. You are always going to die more than likely in the middle of the damn thing. So, you are never going to finish, and all my life, for example, I read *The Color Purple*. My father got angry at me one time and said, "Why do you have to read books over and over again?" And I am going, "Because I want to understand, if I want to write, if I want to read well, I want to understand what they're saying and I want to be able to see it from different perspectives. The first time I read this is not the same way

as this time I am reading it. As a person, I am coming to the text with different things." Well, in Judaism you don't have to apologize for that.

He saw Judaism as totally compatible with his blackness:

> There is a Yoruba proverb that says, "The Chameleon changes its color according to the leaves." I have to be to survive. I am an African American. I am a Jew. Don't have to put one in front of the other. . . . I can embrace those parts of my heritage.

He also saw his blackness as compatible with Judaism and likened the Jewish people to "a big challah braid, . . . and we think that we are just one type of bread, but really, we are all these different braids pulled into one. Like in one solid loaf of people." When asked if he saw his conversion as a purely religious process or whether the notion of joining a people resonated as well, he said that there was a cultural, social element and that he recognizes in himself certain mannerisms that are culturally Jewish:

> I didn't see it until friends of mine see it. . . . My friend, my boss here, he always tells me, "You are so Jewish." And I am thinking to myself, how am I so Jewish? As I'm talking to you right now, I'm moving my hands around, making these gestures, with my hands and the way I talk, the things I say, the jokes I make, the way I constantly criticize things. A cup of tea is not a cup of tea, right? . . . This tea, it's not warm enough, it's not hot. What is this? I don't want this tea. I want another tea. Like, how Jewish can you get? It is hilarious to me as in they kind of join together, and they are both one and the same. I can code switch, like that [snaps]. Then two seconds later, I'm this. If somebody wastes food in front of me, all of a sudden, I'm my father, my grandfather, "Oh you better not waste that." Then two seconds later, "Oh for God's sakes don't say that, God forbid!" I picked up all these things. They have become a part of me. They are in my cast of characters, that makes up who Michael Twitty is as an average person, and it is just the way it is.

As a culinary historian and historical interpreter, Twitty synthesizes his black and Jewish identities through cooking. In his aforementioned food blog, *Afroculinaria*, he describes his work as a "braid of two distinct brands: the Antebellum Chef and Kosher/Soul." The first is a "reconstruction and revival of traditional African American foodways," which honors the past while promoting a healthy diet for African Americans, resulting in what he calls "culinary justice." The other brand, Kosher/ Soul, involves "identity cooking," which he defines as "how we construct complex identities and then express them through how we eat. . . . Being Kosher/Soul is about melding the histories, tastes, flavors, and Diasporic wisdom of being Black and being Jewish." A variation of Kosher/Soul is Afro-Ashkefardi cooking, which he described in a September 9, 2014 blog post on the website My Jewish Learning:

> From black-eyed pea hummus spiked with homemade horseradish harissa to matzoh-meal fried chicken cooked in shmaltz, to peach noodle kugels touched with garam masala, Afro-Ashkefardi is my way of cooking Jewish. While some of my DNA goes back to old Jewish genes, I converted to Judaism in 2002. For 14 years I've been working on creating a working Jewish identity grounded in my love of being African American and the African Diaspora melded with my love and appreciation for the Jewish people, my other Jewish family. Around my table, only kashrut fences me in. On my plates there are no limits! (Twitty 2014)

For Marissa, a black physician from Philadelphia who was now living in a coastal town in California, it was the emphasis on the here and now that drew her to Judaism:

> I still am really intrigued by the orderliness of it, the sort of sense that what you did on earth did make a difference. That was the thing that really bugged me about Catholicism. . . . You could always confess your sins and that would take off a certain amount of it [sin], but you couldn't take off the rest of it. There wasn't any way to redeem yourself. There was a way to avoid sin, but there really wasn't a push about doing good on this earth. Because really, whatever happens, you can get forgiveness for most of it, and for the other part there was nothing you could do about it. It was always there. This was the sort of dogma of original sin. . . . So, everyone was going to purgatory, unless of course you were a martyr or you were a saint, neither of which I particularly wanted to be. So, every-

body was going to purgatory, and I said this just does not make sense to me. So, having a religion which was really grounded in the here and now [was important].[10]

Marissa had been brought up as a Roman Catholic and had attended Catholic school through the eighth grade. Yet she had struggled with the central premise of Catholic theology: "You have to take this Trinity, you have to believe in the Trinity that are all equal parts." By the seventh grade, she was becoming very spiritual and thinking of becoming a nun, but by the eighth grade, "I was like enough already, I really don't believe in this, I don't know what I believe in. But I don't really believe in this."

In the ninth grade, Marissa transferred to Philadelphia High School, which was heavily Jewish. Most of her friends were Jewish, and she started attending an Orthodox Sephardi synagogue with two sisters to whom she had grown close: "That's where I started. I was still responsible for getting my siblings off to church on Sunday. So, I would go Saturday; I would go to synagogue. And synagogue in a Sephardic *shul* lasts all day." She recalled her first experience in synagogue:

I remember going in being very worried about not doing the right thing. But up there, in this particular synagogue, the women were in the balcony. They had the better seats, I think. There wasn't a *mechitzah* [barrier to separate men and women]. And so, women were upstairs. And there, what I realized was that some of the women really got into *davening*, really got into praying. . . . And what I liked too about Sephardic *shuls* is that the kids run up and down. Under thirteen, girls were allowed to sit with their fathers, the boys were allowed to sit with their fathers. . . . It's a scene because it's a five-hour course of a day. . . . For the adults too, people would take off their *tallis* and go off and talk, and guys would be in the back discussing something or other, and they'd come back and pray some more. And the rabbi would sort of [*Marissa pounds three times on the arm of her chair like a judge using a gavel*], "Alright, alright, we're on page . . . Quiet things down." It would sort of rise and fall and rise and fall, and when he felt like there was just a little bit too much rise and not enough fall, then he'd intervene a little bit.

Quest for Community

It is significant that in a modern context where personal choice characterizes religious membership, there are still people willing to renew a commitment to the meanings, symbols, and aspirations that make up traditional rabbinic Judaism. Some synagogues have seen unprecedented numbers of blacks exploring or converting to Judaism. In 2008, the *Atlanta Journal-Constitution* reported that some 20 percent of students who were enrolled in an introduction to Judaism class in Dunwoody, Georgia, in the suburbs of Atlanta, were black. And at Congregation Shearith Israel, a Conservative synagogue in Atlanta, more than a third of those learning about Judaism were black (Pomerance 2008). That same year, roughly 3 percent of the African American population of the small rural town of Cairo, Illinois, underwent a mass conversion to Reform Judaism. As described in the *Washington Post*, the fifty converts included "former drug dealers, infants, factory workers, old ladies, former gang leaders, lawyers, gunshot victims, high school football players, barge workers, crack addicts, nurses and musicians—a reflection of the diverse, decaying place they call home." For eighteen months, the group packed into "two vans and eight cars" and made the weekly trek to Maryland Heights, Missouri—a distance of 170 miles—to the home of Lynn Goldstein, a Reform rabbi from St. Louis, in order to study and prepare for their conversion (Townsend 2008). Since Goldstein is reported to have been the closest rabbi who volunteered to work with them, it is unclear whether Reform Judaism was the group's preferred denomination or their only option (Siegal 2007).

The black converts whom I have encountered have predominantly converted to more ritually observant movements. This current is consistent with the broader religious trend among African Americans. According to the Pew Research Center's US Religious Landscape Survey conducted in 2007, eight in ten African Americans (79 percent) say religion is very important in their lives, compared with 56 percent of all US adults (Pew Research Center 2009). And in a more recent 2012 General Social Survey, nearly half of all blacks report praying several times a day, compared with only 27 percent of whites (Briggs 2015). Meanwhile, according to the 2013 Pew survey, about three in ten American Jews (including 19 percent of Jews by religion and two-thirds of Jews of no religion) do not identify with any particular Jewish denomination. Another third (35 percent) identify with the Reform movement, while the remaining third include Conservative Jews (18 percent), Orthodox Jews (10 percent), and those identifying with the Reconstructionist and Jewish Renewal movements (6 percent). In a 2014 Pew Religious Landscape Survey, an estimated 44 percent of Jewish respondents identified with Reform Judaism, 22 percent with Conservative Judaism, 14 percent with Orthodox Judaism, and only 5 percent identified with other Jewish movements, while another 16 percent reported no specific Jewish denomination.

While the larger population of converts to Judaism are more often connected to Judaism through their Jewish partners, blacks who make their way to Judaism are often drawn to the spiritual and ethical dimensions and thus lean towards more observant practice. Still, many are met with suspicion or disbelief. Rabbi Weinberg told of a group of African Americans from Chicago who had gone through his program and converted to Conservative Judaism. When they later decided to immigrate to Israel, they encountered resistance:

> About ten years ago, two couples came to my program dressed almost like Abraham and Sarah were dressed, like nomads. These beautiful African gowns. . . . They had biblical names, and they were interested in becoming Jewish under Jewish law. . . . [They] did all the work involved and went through a Conservative conversion. . . . Then they wanted to make *aliyah* to Israel, so they all came, and they were a large family, they came from Chicago to Israel. Now, usually when Jews want to come and live in Israel they are welcomed and there is no problem about becoming a citizen of Israel. Well, because they came from Chicago, they were not sure if they were part of the Black [Commandment] Keepers group, which they're trying to limit, so they held them up coming in, and then they found out they had a Conservative conversion, and they were still holding them up, so then the Conservative movement in Israel started making a big fuss. . . . Yeah, we have a certificate showing that they've been converted to Judaism, so they show their papers, and the Conservative movement got very upset at the Israeli authorities for holding them up now, because it's not even a question of black and white here, it's a question of the legitimacy of the Conservative movement in Israel, of our converts.

In 2008, thirteen members of the Mosley family—the mother, her two sons, the sons' wives, and their children—all converted to Conservative Judaism in Overland Park, Kansas. When they sought to enter the State of Israel under the Law of Return, the Interior Ministry rejected their petition, stating that the family's request raised "serious doubts" by representatives of the Population Registry "about their conversion process and its purpose" (Maltz 2015). After several years, the Mosleys successfully immigrated to Israel and became active members of Kehillat Netzach Israel, a Conservative/Masorti synagogue in the southern coastal town of Ashkelon. Yet despite bearing new offspring there, the family was denied citizenship until May 2015. It appears that officials confused them with members of the African Hebrew Israelites of Jerusalem (called the Black Hebrew Israelites or Hebrew Israelites by the mainstream Jewish press).

In 2015, Michael Twitty was traveling through Ben Gurion Airport after being a guest at the Jewish Film Festival held at the Jerusalem Cinematheque, when he was humiliated at the hands of airport security, who interrogated him rudely, challenged his claim of having come to Israel on a prior occasion on Taglit-Birthright Israel, and detained him for hours (Ben-Ari 2015).[11] Whether Twitty was being detained based on his race or because he was suspected of being a Hebrew Israelite remains unclear.

In the United States, as well, black converts to Judaism have been met with suspicion. Cleo found some congregations more embracing than others. Although she had converted to Conservative Judaism, she sometimes attended Shabbat services at her husband's Reform synagogue. She described one such service, when the rabbi invited her to carry the Torah: "And I went up, and I went up to get the Torah out of the ark, and I could see the [reaction]. . . . 'She's not Jewish! What is she doing up?' I swear to God. There were like five of them that turned, 'She's not Jewish!' So, yeah, you get it from some of the older ones." Still, no one has ever asked her why she was in synagogue or whether she converted: "You're just supposed to accept. If someone says they're Jewish, you're not supposed to say, 'Oh, did you convert?' You're just supposed to say, 'Oh, welcome.' Or not even welcome. Just come over for Shabbat."

Alice's experiences had been much more positive. She described the first day she went to services:

As a matter of fact, I'll never forget the woman that greeted me and offered to get a prayer book for me and showed me where we were in the service and helped me follow along. . . . And, of course, people asked me questions about how I found the synagogue. . . . I think they knew I probably wasn't Jewish. I didn't know the words or anything. . . . I felt very welcomed. And I felt very at home, actually. Even though there was a big culture shock, it wasn't an uncomfortable feeling. It was just an unusual feeling, . . . very different from anything I've ever known. I felt very comfortable. And I could see the warmth in the people that were there in terms of the way they would hug and kiss each other. And just greet each other. So, there was a warmness and a sense of family that was very present.

The *yarmulke-* and *tzitzit*-wearing Twitty preferred the diversity of a Sephardi congregation. His synagogue of choice drew members from Morocco, Tunisia, Egypt, Turkey, and Syria:

When you walk in the room, you have all these Sephardic faces that are brown and light brown. . . . These people would tell you [*laughs*], "I am African American too," but they were serious. Because they are from Morocco, and they had seen people like me in Morocco. There was nothing unusual about me. When I talked to Israelis who had come over, . . . they would tell me, "Oh no. I never thought that you were anything but Yemenite or Ethiopian." Reddish-brown complexion, almond-shaped eyes, my hair is kind of that Euro-Native American, Jewish, African mix.

For Twitty, diversity had always been an innate characteristic of Judaism and could be traced all the way back to Mount Sinai, when "God told six hundred thousand Israelites the Torah and each heard it in his own way." Still, he was frustrated with the prescribed views of what it means to be Jewish in America:

As more and more black people discover the world of the Sephardic and Mizrahim and Ethiopian Jews, then we start to question why has Ashkenazi Jewish America not reframed themselves. It is anachronistic. You have these children's books, I mean go in Jewish bookstores to find books for my kids. I can't buy half the books. Because, forget the fact that I don't look like those people, my kids don't look like those people. They are blondes for God's sakes. I mean how many blonde Jews have I ever seen? I haven't seen that many. If I have, it was a *shiksa* [gentile girl or woman] in the wood pile. There is a problem with that. We have had this twenty-year debate over who controls the academy. It is Eurocentric, and so many Jewish neoconservatives are like, "Well, we are part of the Western tradition." No, you are not! You are only part of the Western tradition via the fact that somebody in Europe decided to pick up the crown of Christianity and carry it. . . . And so, it is this kind of anachronistic whiteness that I am seeing now among Jewish neoconservatives. . . . The Greeks and the Romans thought you all were the most ridiculous, backwards people they had ever seen on the face of the earth. I mean that is how bad it was.

He challenged the singleness presumed by a Jewish identity and pointed to the broad and multilayered identities held by Africans:

When I saw *The Chosen*, and when I read *The Chosen*, and when I saw the Hasidic people dancing, dancing, my heart leapt. When I saw them, you know, "Hi yah, yah yah yah," I knew that it was as much me as "Precious Lord Take My Hand." That is still a part of my background. I didn't convert to Judaism to make myself official in the eyes of Judaism or convert to Judaism because I felt it was better. This is not a hierarchy. I am a true African American. I think in African categories. People in Africa have three or four religions; they may hide one or the other from the eyes of whoever, but they have different religions. They have layers of identity.

Marissa, too, preferred the cultural diversity of Sephardi congregations:

You go into a Sephardic *shul*, and you'll have someone sitting next to you with Farsi and Hebrew, someone with Spanish and Hebrew, someone with French and Hebrew, and someone with English and Hebrew, and they're all praying. It's multicultural. . . . They identified as Jews, as immigrant Jews. They didn't identify with the black community. They didn't identify with the white [community]. They had too thick an accent for the white community. And they were too light and readily identifiable as other in the black community, so they really didn't identify themselves as anything other than Jewish.

As a black, lesbian, Orthodox Jewish woman, Marissa found it challenging to find a single community that met all of her needs: one that was racially diverse, religiously observant, and open to members of all gender identities and sexual orientations. Since no one synagogue fit all of these criteria, she had to build more than one spiritual home.

> I have two home synagogues, . . . three actually: one was the original one, Mikveh Israel in Philadelphia; one was Magain David, which is the one in San Francisco, both Sephardic; and the third one is Sha'ar Zahav, which would nominally be called Reformed, although liturgically or ritually it probably was closer to Conservative. But it was a gay and lesbian *shul* in San Francisco. So those are what I consider my three homes, in a sense. My partner at the time, who I had the kids with, was Jewish, and so, although I am definitely the more active, she's an agnostic at best, but she was culturally a Jew, sort of brought up in a mostly conservative [home]. . . . I came from pretty much an Orthodox background, which said, I want someone who really knows the religion, who I can wrestle with. And that person was Yoel Kahn, who was the rabbi for Sha'ar Zahav. . . . He was the *shul* rabbi there for about ten years. I would come up from here once every couple of weeks for a couple of hours and just sit there with him in his office. . . . I did my conversion with him. . . . It was Reformed. . . . It was a grilling *Bet Din*. . . . Liturgically and ritually, it was probably closer to Conservative, but the problem was the Conservatives, while they accepted the idea and principle of having a woman rabbi, they had not accepted a gay rabbi. And I have a feeling had they done that, Yoel probably would have been a Conservative rabbi. Because that was really what his bent was. But Reformed was the only one that accepted an openly gay rabbi. And Reformed was the only one accepting an openly gay congregation. . . . So, you had people who were Orthodox, Orthodox gay men, who really felt like they couldn't go to the Orthodox synagogues in town without leaving part of themselves there. But they could bring their *goy*, you know, or their less observant individual with them to that *shul*, and everyone would feel comfortable.

Julius Lester discussed how he found a home in Judaism that defied traditional categorization. He used the term "Reconservadox" to describe his particular relationship to Judaism:

I call myself Reconservadox [laughing]. I am really like most American Jews. There are things I like in all the movements, but no one movement expresses for me how I feel about being Jewish. So, I like a much more traditional siddur [prayer book] and liturgy and what have you. But I am much more comfortable with the philosophy of Reform [Judaism]. And so, philosophically I would say I am much more Reform/Reconstruction-ist, but I can't stand the Reform prayer book and liturgy. And so, I am really a mix of traditional and liberal, which I think a lot of American Jews are.

While Lester found his spiritual home in Judaism, his social history as a black man in America precluded a seamless melding of identities. He opted for a dual identity, as black *and* Jewish: "I don't see myself as a black Jew or a Jewish black. Both are nouns, neither one is an adjective describing the other."

When asked about their views on Hebrew Israelites, who make claims to Judaism while electing to not undergo a *halakhic* conversion, the black converts I spoke with were surprisingly accepting, although the reverse is not necessarily true. Michael Twitty reported:

I honestly feel that they have as much right to this tradition as anybody else. I did run across one particular gentleman who he didn't identify himself as Hebrew Israelite, but after I mentioned, "Well hey, so I have a *kippah* on?" he says, "Are you Hebrew?" And I said, "No, I am Jewish." Because I am an anthropologist, don't tell me any of the anachronistic terms. I'm not Israelite cause Israelites are gone. A Hebrew is an archaic term. I am Jewish because I am from the line of Judah. That is the way it goes. He got ruffled with me: "Huh, there's no such thing as Jewish. You are either Hebrew, or you are not."

Still, Twitty defended their legitimacy and felt that they played a role in the Jewish community: "These guys are doing real Judaism, here. The issue is, are they *halakhic* enough for the American Orthodox commu-nity? . . . But I really do feel like they are just as much black Jewish as I am, even though most Jews would disagree with me."

Alice recounted how she had once spotted a black man who wore a Star of David. She approached him and asked him if he was Jewish:

He was one of those, what did you call them? . . . Black Hebrews. Well, he went into this whole thing about white Jews aren't Jewish. They're the devil and this whole thing. . . . And I was like, "Oh God, oh God, oh God, what have I started? Oh God, oh God." Because I said I'm Jewish. "No. You think you are." And I'm like, "Oh, . . . get me out of here."

Differences in the self-conception of those who have chosen to undergo a *halakhic* conversion and Black Hebrews and Israelites, who openly reject the term "Jew," have remained a pivotal source of tension. Still, identifying as black is a constant among them all.

Aviva, a black American convert to Orthodox Judaism and one of the original members of the Alliance of Black Jews, strongly identified as both Jewish and black. In fact, she described herself as an Afrocentric Jew. Yet when confronted with the claims of self-identified Black Jews, she responded as an Orthodox Jew. She shared a recent experience in which she was visiting a black woman in New York: "I thought she was a legitimate Jew. And then the more I got into it, the more she's Hebrew. You know, one of these Ethiopian Hebrews. Because they don't accept Jewish law. Jewish law says you light candles at sundown. They light candles whenever they felt like it."

Aviva had dismissed earlier signs, like the picture of Black Moses in the woman's house and other Afrocentric symbols, which she herself could relate to. "But I'm an Orthodox Jew," she pointed out, "so it started a bit of a conflict. . . . If a person doesn't keep strict Shabbat, you're not supposed to eat in their home because you can't trust that they're kosher. So, I was certainly in a predicament because I was staying with this lady." The next day was Shabbat, and the woman took Aviva to an Orthodox synagogue in the Flatbush section of Brooklyn. It was a "regular white synagogue," with a white rabbi, and the men and women were separated as in any other Orthodox synagogue, but to her surprise, half of the congregants were black, and many of them were dressed in traditional African garb:

And I was in shock because there were so many blacks in this synagogue. I've never seen such a thing. . . . On the one hand, I was very happy. We were happy, but there was so many of them we started to wonder what is this? And when we got talking to the people, because we started talking to them immediately, everything was "sister" and "brother" and everything.

While this was familiar talk in her black circles, it wasn't among normative black Jews: "They don't get into a black thing." It turned out that they were Hebrews. When she questioned the rabbi later, he explained: "Well, there is a problem. . . . There's a problem because they think they're Jews. They have a Jewish heart. . . . They keep kosher, they keep the Shabbat, they do all kinds of things that Jewish law will say a Jew does. But they have no proof of coming from anything. They're just sprang up."

Aviva insisted that the rabbi's reluctance had nothing to do with race: "It's not about them being black. It was about them." She pointed out that another black Orthodox woman who had attended services that day felt the same skepticism towards the visitors. The rabbi asked the two of them to speak to the visitors after the service (likely because Aviva and her friend were black and could serve as ambassadors in this situation):

> So here we are, these two African American Orthodox Jews. Me dressed in some kind of African clothes that I always have anyway. The other lady was completely in regular straight clothes and everything with sleeves down to there. And we're trying to tell them, "Look you got a gem here."

Aviva emphasized her ability to authenticate herself using a legal strategy: "I'm an Orthodox Jew. We've got pictures to prove it. We are always falling back on that. 'Where are your papers?' And we've got papers to prove it. You don't have a black Jewish mother or any type of a Jewish mother. But we have Orthodox . . . we have papers. And not any Jew in the world can deny that we are Jews."

The Jewish sages might have described today's African Americans as a God-fearing people. Indeed, while the US is generally considered a highly religious nation, African Americans are more observant on a variety of indicators, including the importance of religion in their lives, their attendance at religious services, and their frequency of prayer, when compared with other racial and ethnic groups (Pew Research Center 2009). And for many African Americans, the people of the book hold a hallowed place within a cosmology where religion is a force for both personal liberation and moral guidance. Given their religiosity and the growing recognition of racial and cultural diversity (and the diminishing religiousness among postmillennial Jews), black converts offer a unique opportunity to reinvigorate and sustain the historical religious core of American Judaism.

Studies have shown that, within the general population, most converts to Judaism have a Jewish spouse (Lerer and Mayer 1993), yet the black converts with whom I spoke had sought out Judaism on their own and expressed deeply personal connections with the religion. Some cited the interactive relationship with the Torah, others the clear ethnical system or the music that stirred their hearts. Many knew of, or suspected, Jewish ancestry. Each made their journey independently. The next chapter will explore the journeys of biracial Jews and the many challenges they encounter in both legitimizing and negotiating their dual identities as blacks and Jews.

6

Two Drops

Constructing a Black Jewish Identity

I was born Jewish but I had to become black.
—Josh, interview excerpt[1]

Through being black, I realized my Judaism.
—Seymour, interview excerpt[2]

Dana could easily be taken for a Sephardi Jew.[3] She is light-brown com-
plexioned, and her fine features are framed by distinct Yemenite-style
curls. Her mother's family had emigrated from Lithuania during the late
nineteenth century, her dad's had migrated to Chicago from the Southwest. She had attended private Jewish day schools in Chicago but had
also been immersed in the black church, attending Sunday services with
her grandmother. She now belonged to a Conservative synagogue and
had a strong self-identity as a Jew. "I love the way that we are responsible
for finishing the world, the work of the world," she told me. "I love the
mutuality of Judaism, that we are part of the creation process. That God
needs us as much as we need God. And a kind of call and response to
mixed traditions that that calls up. That we can call into question God's
decisions."

At the same time, Dana had developed a strong political identity as an
African American and rejected the "biracial" label: "I dislike that whole
movement. . . . I think it's historically inaccurate, or at least historically
myopic, that black folks have taken in folks of multiple races, for years
and years and years, and I think most of the attempts to separate out
have been about trying to play on a kind of privilege and escape a kind
of discrimination, the stigma of being really black, and I just don't believe in a politics of exception." When asked how she identified herself,
she answered, "You know, people used to say you're half black and half

Jewish, and since the time I was a child, I would correct them and say I'm all black and all Jewish. And you know, Robin Washington says I'm two hundred percent."[4] Shais Rison, a.k.a. MaNishtana, the Orthodox Jewish and African American blogger and humorist, makes a similar point in his "not-autobiography," entitled *Thoughts from a Unicorn: 100% Black. 100% Jewish. 0% Safe*: "There IS no-such thing as just Jewish," he writes (MaNishtana 2013).

While demographic, economic, and social forces have made it possible for children of interracial unions to claim a multiracial identity, Dana has opted for a double minority status. Like many of the biracial Jews interviewed for this book, she chose *not* to identify with the "host society," as white and/or Christian, and embraced two stigmatized social statuses as black and Jewish. Indeed, the identities of biracial Jews might be understood as a wrestling with two forms of double consciousness, one created by the veil of blackness, the second through being the Jewish "other."

Rebecca, a former director of a Sunday school at a Reform day school in her hometown of Milwaukee, grew up just around the block from the Lubavitcher families.[5] Both of her parents were Jewish; her mother was born Jewish, and her African American father had converted. Her family celebrated Shabbat every weekend: "My mother would make challah and do *Kabbalat Shabbat* [liturgical tradition of greeting the Shabbat Queen]." Her parents had given her a strong Jewish education—she'd gone to Hebrew day school from kindergarten through the eighth grade and had attended a Jewish high school for two years—and she identified strongly as a Jew: "I came up . . . being really involved and feeling very comfortable in very different Jewish settings. I went to an Orthodox day school, but I went to this totally secular Labor Zionist summer program every year." The Holocaust figured prominently in her identity, as did Israel: "I had a lot of Israeli teachers when I was young and some very close Israeli friends." She felt secure in both Jewish and black communities and echoed Dana's reluctance to relinquish either identity:

I do not experience being a Jew separate from being a black person or from being a woman or anything else. . . . And I certainly don't feel any kind of divided loyalties or that I have had to choose, although it certainly is one of the ways that mixed-heritage people are targeted. That we're

made to feel like we have to choose and make an impossible decision. . . .
I've really done a lot of thinking about this social identity stuff, and I
think I'm pretty clear about where the stuff comes from and how we're
forced into playing roles as targets of the oppression or of agents of the
oppression or intercolluding with oppression, buying into it and so forth.

While she didn't identify as a "kind of diehard, you know, I'm a Black
hyphen Jew, capitalize the *B* or anything like that," she was committed to
helping multiracial Jews connect with one another:

And that's one of the things that's so fantastic about what's happening
on the Internet with black Jews, is suddenly people have community.
Whereas before it was . . . the kind of cartoon representations of crowds
of people where you have one brown face here and one brown face there.
I think that that's been the experience for a lot of black folks who are
Jewish.

A long history of intermarriage between European and Sephardi
Jews, combined with an influx of Jews from northern Africa (Libya, Morocco), Suriname, and other Caribbean locals, undermines the dominant narrative of Jewish whiteness in America. Still, race is often used as
a marker for group membership, and many American Jews continue to
define "looking Jewish" as embodying an Ashkenazi stereotype.

According to most scholars of American society and culture, race
has trumped religion as the most significant and resilient barrier to social mobility and to the establishment of primary social relationships in
American society (Farley and Allen 1987; Mills 1999; Steinberg 2001a;
Feagin 2014). Blacks have, by and large, remained outside the American mainstream, a status that has fostered the maintenance of a distinct
racial identity and shaped the organization of social boundaries (Demo
and Hughes 1990; Haynes 2006; Rockquemore and Brunsma 2007;
Khanna 2010).

While other historical contexts have shaped Jewish identity in America, including the memory of the Holocaust and the formation of the
State of Israel, it was the shift from a mythological Jewishness imbedded
within the Jewish body to a cognitive Jewishness rooted in choice that
marked the most significant change in postwar Jewish identity. As the

historian David A. Hollinger points out, as Jewishness came to be associated with Europe and whiteness, maintaining a Jewish identity became a choice rather than an imposition (Hollinger 1998). In contrast, the persistence of the one-drop rule has long constrained Americans with any African ancestry from exercising comparable choices. In her essay "On Being and Not Being Black and Jewish, " the philosopher Naomi Zack—the daughter of a Jewish mother and an African American father—reflects on the point at which the one-drop rule and the law of matrilineal descent collide:

> A person who has at least one black ancestor and a Jewish mother is considered racially black in the United States. But, on the basis of her Jewish mother, she is considered Jewish, because Jews define a Jew as someone who has a Jewish mother. . . . Most contemporary American Jews and gentiles designate Jews as racially white. So is the person who is black and Jewish with a Jewish mother white? No, she is black, and in terms of official racial designation, her whiteness is obliterated. (Zack 1996)

The ability of biracial (black/white) individuals to choose their identity—as biracial, multiracial, or black—is a recent phenomenon in the United States. It has been the shifting landscape over the past hundreds of years that has made these new identity options possible.

Out of the Margins: From Mulatto to Black to Multiracial

Well into the twentieth century, the offspring of Europeans—some of whom were also Jewish—and Africans were consigned to an intermediate racial category: mulatto. The term "mulatto" shifted from a signifier of color in the seventeenth century to one of biological marginality in the nineteenth century. The mulatto was regarded as an inferior mixed species, like mules. These ideas were codified in the late nineteenth-century theory of "hybrid degeneracy," which held that racial groups make up distinct biological types and that mixed unions produce inferior, unnatural beings (Brown 2001). Social Darwinists adopted this theory as a direct argument against race mixing (Nakashima 1992).

Meanwhile, America was rapidly transforming from a largely agrarian to a largely urban society. In the late nineteenth century, massive immigration and migration more than doubled the populations of cities like Chicago within a single decade. Chicago became a center for the study of urban ecology and migration patterns, and scholars at the University of Chicago rejected the biological arguments of the social Darwinists, although they did adopt their basic binary logic, applying it to the realm of society and culture and supplanting the concept of hybrid degeneracy with that of marginality. The concept of the "marginal man," first coined in 1928 by urban sociologist Robert Ezra Park, described a "cultural hybrid, a man living and sharing intimately in the cultural life and traditions of two distinct peoples; never quite willing to break, even if he were permitted to do so, with his past and his traditions, and not quite accepted, because of racial prejudice, in the new society in which he now sought to find a place. He was a man on the margin of two cultures and two societies, which never completely interpenetrated and fused" (Park 1928).

The concept of the marginal man had been anticipated by earlier scholars, including Park's teacher, the German Jewish sociologist Georg Simmel, who introduced the idea of "the stranger" in his 1908 essay of the same name:

> [The stranger] is a part of the community, like the poor, or various "enemies within," but a part whose position is simultaneously that of an outsider and a counterpart. . . . Being of another country, city, or race is not something wholly individual. A foreign origin is something that many strangers share, whether actually or potentially (Simmel 2016, 176–179).

The Austrian phenomenologist Alfred Schutz later suggested that the marginal man was simply a particular example of the stranger (Schutz and Wagner 1970). The concept of the stranger remains a useful way to characterize the duality inherent in being at once insider and outsider, an often-important dimension of bicultural identities (McVeigh and Sikkink 2005).

Just as Simmel saw the European Jew as the prototypical stranger, Park regarded the modern "emancipated" Jew as the prototype of the marginal man (Park 1928). Park's student Louis Wirth—a German-born Jew—further explored the marginality of the Jew. In his classic 1928 work, *The Ghetto*, Wirth wrote that the Jew "lived on the periphery of two worlds, and not fully in either. . . . His self is divided between the world that he has deserted and the world that will have none of him" (Wirth 1998). Still, the concept of the marginal man soon came to be associated with individuals of mixed race.

Although Park first coined the term, it was his student Everett V. Stonequist who popularized it with his 1937 book, *The Marginal Man.* Park wrote the introduction, stressing the negative psychological and disorganizing aspects of this modern personality that was caught between two antagonistic cultures (Stonequist 1935; Goldberg 2012). During the mid-1940s, the concept was applied to individuals who straddled two occupational statuses and were unable to attain acceptance in either of their assumed roles (Goldberg 2012). But after World War II, the sociologist David Golovensky cautioned that "multiple loyalties need not be conflicting or disorganizing," touting American Jews as an exemplar. Here was a group that had managed to hold more than one loyalty (Golovensky 1952). While Park once saw bicultural difference as a disadvantage, he came to recognize that marginal men could be agents of social change and leaders of national or racial mass movements (Goldberg 2012). Golovensky echoed Simmel, arguing that only the most marginal men responded to their circumstances with a positive value that inspired "creative living" and "cultural cross-fertilization." Biculturalism, hyphenism, and dualism were stepping stones, not stumbling blocks. Harking back to Horace M. Kallen, Golovensky suggested that if American Jews were conflicted as hyphenated Americans, then all Americans were equally marginal and conflicted.

Unlike W. E. B. Du Bois, who recognized the power of history and social forces to define "who is black," the marginal man theorists largely saw a racial psychological dilemma residing within the mulatto psyche (Du Bois 2015). Yet both the marginal man thesis and Du Bois's thesis of double consciousness saw the individual as torn between two bounded cultural groups. The Negro, like the Jew, could be cast into psychological conflict when forced to see through the eyes of the majority white mainstream. While Du Bois recognized global colonial relationships as dominating race politics and consciousness, he also articulated an essentialist view that the Negro had unique gifts to contribute to civilization as a racial group; such thinking paralleled the Chicago school's treatment of racial groups as transhistorical and primordial.

By mid-twentieth century, mainstream social scientists downplayed the socially constructed nature of race and the social basis of racial identity. Mixed-race persons came to represent the quintessential marginal man, a cultural hybrid in psychological crisis (Nakashima 1992). For much of the century, scholars on multiracial identity reproduced arguments that paralleled nineteenth-century notions of hybrid degeneracy. Their focus had shifted from biological inferiority and sterility to psychological maladjustment, and the hierarchical privilege afforded to white biology was now bestowed upon white culture (Nakashima 1992).

The civil rights movement brought enormous change to race relations in America. As Paul Spickard, an authority on the history of intermarriage in the United States, notes, blacks became both more visible and more attractive to nonblacks. By the early 1970s, a small number of blacks were inching their way into the middle class and even into white suburbs (Spickard 1989). A significant rise in interracial marriages occurred during this period as well, especially following the *Loving v. Virginia* Supreme Court decision of 1967, which invalidated state laws criminalizing intermarriage. Black-white marriages reached 77,000 in 1970, and by 1980, the figure had nearly doubled (Spickard 1989; Daniel 2001). In 1980, just 6.7 percent of marriages were interracial, but during the 1990s, their numbers steadily increased. The 1990 US census counted some 1.3 million interracial marriages, of which 252,000 were between whites and blacks.[6] Twenty years later, a whopping 15 percent of all new marriages in the US were classified as interracial (Qian and Lichter 2011; Minchin 2013; Kim and Leavitt 2016). With these changes came new possibilities for the children of black-white marriages to claim a biracial or multiracial identity. In fact, the 1990 census identified nearly two million children living in homes where the primary adults were of different races—more than twice the number reported in 1980 (DaCosta 2007, 7).[7]

In fall 1993, when *Time* magazine announced "The New Face of America" and declared the nation a "multicultural society," intermarriage was on the rise and the "browning of America" in full force.[8] During this time, a number of advocacy groups, along with self-identified mixed-race people and the parents of mixed-race children, began lobbying the Office of Management and Budget, which oversees the US census. Arguing that the biracial experience was unique, they petitioned for a multiracial category on the approaching 2000 census (Daniel 2001). While the lobby failed to achieve its goal, the new census allowed respondents to check more than one race. The change, heralded as "the greatest in the measurement of race in the history of the United States" (Farley 2002), broke a two-hundred-year tradition. By March 2001, the Census Bureau announced with great fanfare that nearly seven million people, or more than 2 percent of the US population, had chosen to identify with more than one race from the six available categories (Schmitt 2001). Still, only a fraction of respondents—0.41 percent—claimed both black and white ancestry, "a gross underestimation," argues sociologist Nikki Khanna, "given that most African Americans have some degree of white and/or Native American ancestry" (Khanna 2011). In fact, one recent genetic study reports that African Americans have, on average, 24 percent European ancestry and 0.8 percent Native American ancestry (Bryc, Durand, et al. 2015). The majority of census respondents with black and white ancestry identified as black only, a reflection of the persistence of the one-drop rule (Khanna 2011).

The notion that racial categories and their boundaries have been shifting over time has prompted scholars to shift as well (Daniel 2001; F. J. Davis 2001). Many now argue that identities are situational, constructed, fluid, multiple, and located in the group (Brubaker and Cooper 2000). Still, most have focused on the shifting landscape of race relations and the supposed positive consequences of individual social identity. Scholars have even prophesized the complete abandonment of racial identity and the dawning of a new transracial America (Wynter 2002). Some deem racial categories meaningless (Clegg 2001), while others describe a humanistic "postethnic" society that transcends racial and ethnic particularisms (Hollinger 1998; Gilroy 2002; Hollinger 2006). Following the 2008 election of Barack Hussein Obama to president of the United States, numerous journalists and pundits proclaimed that we had finally transcended the racial divide in politics (Nagourney 2008; Thernstrom and Thernstrom 2008). Yet the victory of Donald Trump eight years later and the ascendency of Steve Bannon—the former executive chairman of *Breitbart News* known for anti-Semitic, racist, and sexist views—to chief strategist to the president, shattered any such illusions of a race-free America.

Passing as Black

Recent empirical studies of racial identity formation have suggested that biracial individuals view their social identities in multifaceted ways that may go beyond the census's ability to measure (Daniel 2001; Rockquemore and Brunsma 2007). While more people self-identify as multiracial, there is ample evidence that the once-rigid color line may be merely fading or shifting rather than completely disappearing (Lee and Bean 2010). One analysis of the 2000 census found that over 50 percent of parents of interracial children opted for an interracial identity for their children, checking off both "black" and "white" categories (Roth 2005). Yet in a separate study in which biracial adolescents were asked to choose "the best single race" category, subjects chose "black" almost 75 percent of the time (Harris and Sim 2002). A more recent study, conducted by Khanna and Johnson, found that while most black-white biracial subjects self-identified as biracial or multiracial, in certain contexts they opted for the monoracial category of black (Khanna and Johnson 2010).[9] Indeed, 76 percent of subjects selecting the monoracial category self-identified as black. The authors refer to this phenomenon as "passing as black" and cite the desire to fit in with black peers and educational and employment opportunities in "the post-civil rights era of affirmative action" as motivating factors (Khanna and Johnson 2010). Unlike the conventional notion of passing (as white), where individuals defied prevailing social norms, biracial individuals who identify as monoracial blacks present no challenges to the norms, since they are already identified as black; the transgression is more internal: "Thus, to qualify as passing, the identity does not have to be one in which they were barred by societal rules . . . but it does at least have to be one that contradicts how they understand themselves racially (e.g., they understand themselves as biracial, but in some situations, consciously conceal their white ancestry to present themselves as black)" (Khanna and Johnson 2010).

In today's multiracial context, where even blackness has taken on socially positive connotations, "passing" into a black world has become possible and at times even desirable. Indeed, the biracial Jews whom I interviewed selectively identified themselves as black when it was advantageous to do so. Nadine's experiences, below, capture the contextual factors in opting for a monoracial identity.

Nadine—the daughter of a dark-skinned Arab Jew from Beirut, Lebanon, and an African American father from Charleston, West Virginia—had been raised on New York's Upper West Side, which she described as on the "cusp of gentrification," with tennis courts on one side of the street and a project on the other.[10] In order to ensure admittance to the better Catholic schools, she and her brother had been baptized Catholic when they were young. Until she applied for college, she had never identified herself as African American: "Because up until then, I didn't really have to do it. Like SATs give you that option. I'd always leave it open." Yet the competitiveness of college applications made her reconsider. When she asked her brother for advice, he told her, "Are you kidding? You'd better mark that box down." She wrote "Lebanese American-African American" on the application, thus "killing two birds with one stone," as she put it. Now, at nineteen years old, she reflected back on that moment and noted, "I think that was probably one of the first times that . . . I categorized myself."

While mixed-race applicants may think that there is a clear advantage to identifying as black rather than biracial or multiracial, there is rarely such a need, since institutions will often pool them as black anyway. "Being biracial is often enough to qualify for these programs," Khanna and Johnson explain, "which tells us that in some measure, the one-drop rule is still at work; if one checks both black and white boxes, he/she is frequently reclassified as black and is racially positioned to potentially benefit from affirmative action programs. However, unaware of how racial data are reaggregated, they strategically conceal their white/biracial ancestries in order to present themselves as black" (Khanna and Johnson 2010).

Constructing a Black Jewish Identity

In her classic study of fourth- and fifth-generation European immigrants, the sociologist Mary C. Waters found that the process of ethnic identity formation is different for racially ascribed groups. While individuals classified as "white" retain a set of "options" to choose their identity, nonwhite groups are ascribed to a racial category and offered restricted options (Waters 1990). Those persons who are defined racially, she argues, are constrained to identify with the part of their ancestry that has been socially defined as "essential" (Waters 1996).

In fact, early researchers argued that the offspring of interracial (black/white) unions had but two options for constructing a racial identity: "black" or "biracial." Yet scholarship reveals a more varied set of options available to them (Harris and Sim 2002; Rockquemore and Brunsma 2002; Khanna and Johnson 2010). Sociologist Kerry Ann Rockquemore argues that black-white biracials choose one of four different identity options: a singular identity (exclusively black or exclusively white); a border identity (exclusively biracial); a protean identity (sometimes black, sometimes white, sometimes biracial); and a transcendent identity (no racial identity). These identities can shift over the life course and are very fluid. In fact, the way one publically self-identifies may be more a reflection of social expectations than core beliefs about one's identity (Rockquemore and Brunsma 2002). According to Michael Thornton, a professor of Afro-American studies and an expert on multiraciality, "I choose 'black' from a list because I know that is what society calls me. This selection may reveal only that I can correctly choose the socially approved term. It may say nothing about my core identity" (Thornton 1996). Yet biracial people have considerable agency in shaping and asserting their racial identities. Sociologist Theresa Kay Williams argues, "Not only do biracial individuals 'get race done unto them,' but they also do race as well" (Williams 1996).

My data reveal that individuals exercise their choices within specific social contexts, sometimes opting for the "multiracial" descriptor, other times adopting a singular black identity, and still at other times constructing new, hybrid categories. When asked about their personal identities—with regard to race only—more than half (55 percent) of our eleven biracial participants self-identified as "black," the remainder as "multiracial," "biracial," or "interracial." Yet among the latter group, 73 percent reported checking the "black" category on official forms, applications, or surveys.

Hannah, a biracial Jew in her mid-twenties, expressed a range of identities during our interview.[11] While on standardized forms she marked off the "other" box—"and if they don't have 'other,' then I'll just write 'other' . . . or 'interracial, mixed race'"—context mattered. In some settings, she might emphasize one part of her identity over another. At one point, she stated, "I, a black woman, am also a Jew," but added that she would also describe herself as a Jewish African woman or as an African American Jew who's female: "It depends on the context. Who am I talking to." Hannah had been raised on the Upper West Side of Manhattan and attended elite private schools and an Ivy League university. She was exposed to some Jewish religion while growing up, "but it was very home based." The family celebrated Passover and the High Holidays and sometimes lit candles for the Sabbath. "I have a cultural identity, but in my own personal religious and spiritual life, I'm not a Jew," she said. Her mother always tried to instill pride in both her Jewish and African American heritages, but her father worried that she'd grow up without a strong black identity: "So, he would push stuff on me. But by pushing stuff on me, he would make me really want to move away from it." One example was a book he gave her when she was seven years old:

And he opens it up straight to this picture of a black man who's been lynched. And he's on the ground, and yet you can see his guts coming out of him. He's on a bed of fire. And all around him are white people. And they're standing there, and one of the guys is smiling and holding his son. And my dad says to me, "See, this is what white people do."

Growing up with a biracial identity had been difficult, especially when interacting with black kids, who resented that she called herself interracial: "I had to choose, and I was a traitor. And to my race. I was like, 'If I go with you guys, that means I have to forget the fact that my family was slaughtered by the Cossacks in Russia. I think not. I won't cut myself off from my family history.'" In college, she found many of the black student organizations "exclusive" and unwelcoming to whites who wanted to support their causes: "It was like the minority kids were segregating themselves out. And kids who didn't segregate themselves out were shunned by the minority kids." Even now, she found herself struggling with the same issues. As an artist, she tried to create work that synthesized her disparate identities, to create "an underlying unity," but she was often pigeonholed: "If I'm black and female, then that must be my audience. And that was an argument I used to have a lot when I was in school." Her white professors told her she had to choose her audience, to decide to whom she was talking: "And I would say, 'I'm talking to people.'" Even in her friendships, she was pushed to choose. She spoke about one black male friend from graduate school:

> He had never met someone who identified as interracial who didn't secretly want to be one or the other, and so he was always coming in and challenging me. . . . His push was for me to choose which one I wanted to be more. And I said, "I don't want to be one or the other more, I want to be me." Why should I ignore this fabulous wonderful history . . . and culture I have on both sides?

Sociologist Wendy Roth argues that racial schemas at a subconscious level shape the ways that migrants use cultural knowledge to perform the race to which they believe they belong (Roth 2012). Not unlike Latino immigrants, who display cultural knowledge through speech, multiracial and biracial black Jews sometimes adopted Jewish expressions or black English vernacular to publically signify membership in one or the other community. Roth calls these "racial strategies," and to varying degrees the biracial Jews I met applied an insider's cultural knowledge in strategic ways to claim membership in what most people consider to be two mutually exclusive social groups (Roth 2012). One participant explained that many (white) Jews had to be clued in that she was Jewish: "The bagel and lox, and probably the tone of voice I used when I talked about my mother. You can do this kind of Jewish thing when you're talking about your mother, and lunch." The sociologist Erving Goffman calls this "the art of impression management," and it is accomplished primarily through managing social gestures and racial performance (Goffman 1959). Even the code switching that many biracial Jews deployed in various social situations might best be described as a form of bicultural fluency that enabled a kind of "situational passing," the strategic revealing or concealing of a portion of one's identity (Roth 2012). Khanna and Johnson maintain that in addition to concealing a stigmatized identity, individuals may highlight a preferred identity, which they call "accenting" (Khanna and Johnson 2010).

Seymour, who grew up in Morningside Heights—the location of Columbia University and just on the outskirts of Harlem—exhibited speech patterns and a demeanor that reflected his Harlem roots, yet he also casually mixed in Jewish cultural expressions.[12] After attending a local, predominantly black public school for five years, he enrolled in one of the city's top private schools. He felt stifled there, and in his junior year of high school transferred to a progressive alternative school. He described his early teenage years in the late 1960s as an "initiation" into black culture. He became "caught up in the black power salute, . . . you know, 'black is beautiful,' embracing the whole concept. And it was just a wonderful thing. There was a wonderful nationalism and a sense of identity and being proud."

When he graduated from high school, he moved to Israel, although the decision was not entirely his own:

> When I was in the twelfth grade, I was definitely doing some pretty wild things . . . that were extensions of me searching out in the neighborhood, and just reacting, possibly rebelling. My father said, "Look, you're leaving. You're either going into the army"—and this was too close to Vietnam, and I wasn't going there—"or you're going to Israel." . . . So, I chose Israel.

Seymour spoke of the reinforcing ties between his black and Jewish identities: "Being black and Jewish impacts me as a black and Jewish person." Now a husband (his wife converted to Judaism) and a father, he has sought to reinforce these ties with his son: "Every Friday, I practice. I shouldn't say practice—observe. I celebrate the Jewish holidays. I light candles every Friday. I try to go to synagogue once a month. I'm active. My son goes to Sunday school. He's in his fourth year now. . . . [I] expose him to all that I can offer him, the best that I can offer, being black and being Jewish."

Jake, who grew up in a secular yet culturally Jewish household on Long Island, was often hesitant to publically assert his Jewish identity: "In a weird way, it's probably similar to the whole idea of passing. It's just easier being so light skinned, you can get away with being called white. And sometimes I guess you might admit it, but the fact [is] that I'm mostly kind of passing as not Jewish in some sense."[13]

Unlike Seymour, who saw his black and Jewish identities as mutually reinforcing, Josh felt that his Jewishness "modified" his blackness: "Probably for the simple reason that one is more immutable than the other. For better or for worse. I mean, what is passable, what is not." He quickly added that he didn't see himself as "a self-hating Jew," but admitted that he didn't feel "particularly nurtured or nourished or enriched by the Jewish experience that I think I'm successor to now." Another factor was the need to legitimatize himself as a Jew: "I don't want to have to say, 'Well, my mother's Jewish.'"

Josh's parents had divorced when he was young, and he was raised by his Jewish mother and (white) stepfather in the highly segregated Long Island suburbs: "I was going through the first of several identity crises around eight years old, when kids in school would say, 'Are you Jewish or Christian?' I wasn't really sure what I was." He finally asked his mother, "What am I?" Most of his friends at school were Jewish and had already begun Hebrew school. He told his parents he wanted a bar mitzvah, and he began assimilating into the world of his friends. He remained actively involved in Judaism through his mid-teens, attending retreats and youth programs: "I shared a culture, if nothing else. I knew the prayers. I knew as much as the other students there, so I was kind of on equal cultural footing, equal religious footing."

It wasn't until he applied for college that he began asserting a black identity: "My struggle until then on those standardized test forms was not really knowing. . . . I knew I wasn't white. I didn't feel entitled to be black, or kind of legitimate as a black. And 'other' was just too fractional. I didn't want to be part of some other. . . . It was actually a hugely emotional kind of liberating to finally decide I'm black." He described this transformation as a reversal of primary and secondary identities:

> I was born Jewish, but I had to become black. I had to figure out what being different really meant. What is this difference? You know, being raised in, not in a white family but in a white neighborhood with white parents. . . . I was also . . . a black Jew. And then I guess through that kind of a transitioning, the Jewish black. My fundamental identity—my primary versus secondary identity—kind of switched places.

Like other biracial males with whom I spoke, Josh acknowledged that relationships with black women reinforced his budding black identity: "It wasn't until junior year of high school, when I had a car and started dating a black woman, you know, some sort of subtext somewhere, a big part of defining myself was probably through women."

While scholarship has examined the various Afro-American religious communities that practice forms of Judaism (Brotz 1952; Brotz 1970; Berger 1978; Lounds 1981; Baer and Singer 1992; Wynia 1994; Hare 1998; Chireau 2000; Chireau and Deutsch 2000; Singer 2000; Fauset 2002; Landing 2002; Rubel 2009; Dorman 2013; Jackson 2013), only two studies focus on biracial (black/white) Jews. The first is an unpublished dissertation in social psychology (Segal 1998). It explores how biracial adults of African American and Jewish American parentage negotiate their mixed heritages in a society hostile to interracial unions. The study identified multiple factors contributing to the personal identity of biracial Jews, including parental attitudes towards race and identity, neighborhood and school environment, and phenotype ("looking Black"). For example, individuals who were perceived as black more often identified as such, but those perceived as white were more likely to identify as white or biracial. Interestingly, the study found that while one's closeness with the black parent was not necessary for him/her to identify as black, closeness with the Jewish parent was a necessary condition for identification as a Jew.

The second study—*Black, Jewish, and Interracial: It's Not the Color of Your Skin, but the Race of Your Kin, and Other Myths of Identity*, by Katya Gibel Azoulay—draws on the works of Sartre, Arendt, Fanon, and the contemporary political philosopher Seyla Benhabib to argue that the public discourses (discursive arenas) surrounding black-Jewish relations, intermarriage, and crossracial sexual relations, shape identity (Azoulay 1997). Drawing on the theories of Pierre Bourdieu, Azoulay argues that identity categories take their "value" from their "position in a hierarchically organized system of titles" (Azoulay 1997). Using this framework, Jewish and black social categories are relational and conditioned by negation; the Jew is not a gentile, and the black is not white, and these identities take shape when their "potentiality" is denied (Azoulay 1997). Thus black-Jewish identity is reinforced when individuals reconstruct symbolic boundaries of inclusion and exclusion around blackness and Jewishness (Azoulay 1997).

A third related literature has emerged that explores questions of color, culture, race, and identity within American Jewry (Tobin, Tobin, et al. 2005; Kaye/Kantrowitz 2007; Sicher 2013). While situated within a discourse that continues to reify race (Gilman 2013), this literature seeks a way out of the black/white binary that has dominated discussions of American Jewish identity, replacing it with a vocabulary that offers multiple, hybrid, and diasporic descriptors for Jewish identity. The recent study noted earlier, *JewAsian: Race, Religion, and Identity for America's Newest Jews*, explores how the biracial (Asian/Jewish) individuals "are challenged by, and in turn, challenge traditional notions of Jewish authenticity. . . . Yet, rather than bend to these challenges, we find that interviewees' responses to such encounters result in an assertion, often creative and subversive, of their Jewish authenticity and one that emerges as a more expansive, rather than limited, understanding of what it means to be Jewish" (Kim and Leavitt 2016). Such assertions of authenticity were also in evidence among the black/Jewish biracial individuals interviewed for this book.

The coordinated strategies in which many biracial Jews have engaged to assert their dual identities might be seen through the prism of racial projects. Most reject the either/or dichotomy of racial essentialism, asserting either singular, undivided black-Jewish identities or cosmopolitan multiracial identities. Yet their racial self-awareness and distinct experiences as black Jews have led many to mobilize along racial lines through what Winant calls "strategic essentialism," which is distinct from "the essentialism practiced in service of hierarchical social structures" (Omi and Winant 1994; Winant 2004; Omi and Winant 2014). Such strategic essentialism has led to new social-structural racial projects, which have been greatly facilitated by the Internet (which was just beginning to gain momentum at the time of my interviews in the late 1990s). Groups like Ayecha, Black and Jewish, MORESHET: Network for Jews of African Heritage Jews, and Aframjews—the self-proclaimed "premier online community for Jews of African Heritage"—have provided a forum for exchanging information and addressing issues of cultural and color diversity within the Jewish American community.

Us and Them

Social actors don't merely possess personal identities; rather, people signal membership in social groups by drawing symbolic boundaries that distinguish "us" from "them." The categories themselves link the individual narratives to the public narratives of particular social groups.

Claiming to be Jewish in public is more than simply asserting an identity through stories; it requires that significant others recognize the legitimacy of those claims. As Dashefsky points out, being a Jew depends on the congruence of one's definition and the definition of others (Dashefsky, Lazerwitz, et al. 2003).

For Olga, a biracial Jew who grew up in a secular household, the acceptance she felt among Jews reinforced her own sense of identity as a Jew.[14] Her father was a black filmmaker, and when Olga was in her early teens, the family moved from Manhattan's Upper West Side to Southern California, "in the poor part of Beverly Hills." At her new high school, she found herself drawn to the Jewish students: "There was something I felt comfortable around. . . . I don't know if they physically were able to identify that I was black or that I had something in me other than black. I don't know if they saw me as the dark-skinned Jewish person, but once they found out I was Jewish, it was like I was in." She identified as white and Jewish, which she saw then as the markers of success:

> I think I felt a little, slightly stigmatized by my father being black. I really, really loved my mom and wanted to be like my mom, and I wanted to be like my friends at school who had houses and [whose] parents drove Mercedes, and it turned out they were white and they were Jewish, and I wanted that.

One of her friends was Orthodox, and Olga began celebrating the Sabbath with the family: "I would go over to her house, and they'd say the prayers over the Sabbath candles, and I learned about Shabbos. It was great! I loved it, and they were happy to tell me about this stuff." Her friend always told her, "You're Jewish, you can have this, you can go to Hebrew school":

> I think the one thing that I got . . . with other Jewish people was that I felt very welcomed. And I hadn't felt that same welcoming before into a culture, into a people, and being in Beverly Hills, I didn't have the black experience. I didn't have the equivalent black community to say, "[Olga], come here, we love you." . . . I had always noticed how people would become so happy when they found out I was Jewish. They loved it. . . . I knew the Jewish thing would get me certain places whereas if they didn't

know I was Jewish. Yeah, I was nice, I was pretty, but for all they knew I was, you know, *shvartz*, I was black. . . . By the end of high school, . . . the Jewish thing was stronger than it had been, it was the biggest part of my identity.

Yet it troubled her that none of her close friends were black. She transferred to a more racially diverse school in Los Angeles and became active in both the black and Jewish student organizations, as well as a multicultural student group. Most of the black kids in high school, she found, weren't interested in joining the Black Student Union since "they didn't have to go to assert or affirm their black identity. They knew they were black." The black students who did join the BSU tended to be the better students and saw it as a résumé builder for college, and "those weren't necessarily the people who I really wanted to befriend." She made friends with "a particular population that was more black," but she was never completely comfortable:

I was walking in between two different communities, . . . but there were certain things I wasn't able to do, such as change the way I talked. . . . I wasn't comfortable going into black lingo, per se. I felt like it was really fake, and I felt like I didn't have to do that just to hang out with other black kids.

Although Olga described her first social identity as very "interracial" and "diverse," she also noted that in elementary school, she always had white friends. "For some reason, I always gravitated towards white kids. I think that largely had to do with the fact that my mother was my primary caretaker. My parents were married. Um, I didn't like my father, I had a lot of problems with my father, even though I was close to my father's family and my mother's family, and I got a lot of love from both of them."

It wasn't until college—a small elite school on the East Coast with "a large percentage of students of color"—that Olga truly explored her identity. She joined an interracial discussion group and began to deal with issues around race and her relationship with her father: "And that allowed me to date black guys. . . . I just felt a lot more, a lot more balanced, so that the inside and the outside were one in terms of being interracial." Now, when people asked her, "What are you?" she'd answer, "I'm black, and I'm Jewish. . . . And even though I know that those two aren't completely consistent, those two qualifiers, it's fine for me, you know. I'm speaking of Jewish in terms of the cultural sense and black in the cultural sense."

Pnina, born to a Jewish mother of German descent and an Ethiopian Jewish father, was one of two biracial participants with two Jewish parents.[15] She was extremely knowledgeable about Jewish history and immersed in Jewish culture. She had been one of the founding members of the Alliance of Black Jews and remained active in organizations for multiracial Jews, including the San Francisco-based community-building project Be'chol Lashon.

She grew up in a fairly suburban neighborhood in Los Angeles and described her Jewish upbringing as "High German Reform." There was a lot of turmoil at home, and in her early teen years, she was sent to a Catholic boarding school. Interestingly, there were several other Jewish students at the school, as well as a fair number of blacks. Although Pnina was visibly black, she had not been exposed to black American culture in her home (since her father was African) and was often rejected by other black children at school:

> The black kids didn't accept me because I wasn't black. That was in the days of, you know, Stokely [Carmichael] and H. Rap [Brown]. And, you know, you had to only listen to Motown. I can't dance, never could. Look stupid, you know. But when Evelyn Callan told me in seventh grade I couldn't be black because I couldn't dance, it made me upset. You know, she had a big old Afro. . . . And she, I remember she took a razor blade and cut her boyfriend's name into her leg. And I thought to myself, "If that's being black, thank you, no." But it's just being stupid.

Her family had internalized many of the negative stereotypes associated with blacks and used the term *shvartze*, as well as the "N-word": "They would say, 'You don't want to behave like a nigger.'" While her father also used the term, he harbored his own preconceptions about white Jews and would warn her to stay away from them "because they will break my heart. They would eat me up and spit me out, . . . because it's America. Everything is about race. And there was no permission for him to transcend this. . . . He doesn't say he's Jewish. No one knows he's Jewish, but black he couldn't do nothing about."

Her father's experiences as an Ethiopian Jew in America had a profound impact on Pnina, and she believed that (white) Jews were myopic in their understanding of the diaspora:

> Why is it possible . . . for Jews to turn left at Yemen and end up wherever they end up and still be Jews, but they turned right at Yemen and went down the coast they can't be Jews anymore, you know? You look at the practice of the *Bene Israel* in India. Does that resemble anything like Jewishness? That's up to the Jews. You look at the practice of Ethiopians, doesn't resemble anything like rabbinic Judaism. Problem. Can someone explain that to me? Two groups of people not practicing rabbinic Judaism, . . . the same historical catastrophe created both communities. One is considered Jewish, one is not.

On the other hand, she viewed the homegrown Black Jewish movements in the United States with suspicion. Becoming a Jew was not simply a matter of adopting a faith. It meant joining a people:

> There's no problem for me for somebody to wake up one morning and say, "I have a Jewish soul. I have to lead a Jewish life." But then you have to do more than just say it. And you have to learn a little bit more. And you have to be willing to accept what people are telling you. If you want to join a club, you have to follow the rules. . . . You want to be a Mouseketeer and wear the ears, you got to do what the Mouseketeers do. . . . If you want to join a movement, you have to accept the movement. It has to be mutual. Otherwise, you're creating your own movement. So, create. You're welcome to create your own movement, just don't come and tell me that I have to accept it.

Dana, who referred to herself as all black and all Jewish, echoed this sentiment, distinguishing the religious and cultural dimensions of Judaism:

> I think there's a difference between recognizing someone's humanity and their choices as an individual and recognizing the legal and social structures that organize the way that we recognize each other politically, so-

cially, and ethnically. Being Jewish is a serious endeavor. It has a history of oppression that goes with it. You need to be aware of this before you decide to join a people, right? I understand that, and it makes sense. You're not just joining a religion, you're also joining a people when you join Judaism. . . . Judaism is clearly a cultural identity. It clearly has historic ramifications that are, you know, distinct from religious identification.

Jonathan, on the other hand, a patrilineal Jew whose status in religious circles was sometimes questioned, believed that Judaism's emphasis on distinctions led to racial exclusion:

The problem with Judaism is that . . . it's a religion of purity. And it's a problem. I mean, Judaism is a religion of distinctions between the week and the Sabbath, between culture and trade, Jew and non-Jew. And so, when you have ethnic nuances or cultural nuances, it's sometimes hard for people to reconcile. The fact is though, the Jews have been, have always been a diverse people, nationally, culturally, ethnically, racially. . . . And in fact, you can even say that Judaism is the perfect balance between a continuous culture and a diverse population.[16]

Many men reported that their black identity evolved as they entered their adolescent years, just as their political consciousness began crystallizing. This finding is consistent with Mary C. Waters's observation that ethnic self-awareness increases and identity solidifies in the late teen years (Waters 1990). Seymour, who saw his blackness and Jewishness as reinforcing, spoke of his early teenage years as an "initiation into black culture," while Josh experienced the liberation of declaring himself black when he applied for college. Allen, a native New Yorker, experienced a shifting of identities as he approached high school.[17] He had spent much of his youth in a tree-lined, picturesque neighborhood in Washington Heights—the northernmost tip of Manhattan—where many Polish, Hungarian, and German Jews had settled after World War II. His parents—a Boston-born Jewish mother and a West Indian father—divorced when he was still very young. He lived with his father in Jamaica from ages four through eight but then returned to New York and was raised by his mother. He briefly attended public school before heading off to an elite prep school where "ninety something percent of the kids were

Jewish." As he grew older his primary identity shifted from Jewish to black, although he first had to go through "the tragic mulatto" stage: "I'm not accepted here, and I'm not accepted there, you know, but some of it went with just the angst of growing up." It wasn't until high school that he grew comfortable with identifying himself as black: "I came to the realization that as an American, I had to be a black American. . . . That's what people were looking at and seeing and deciding and judging."

While Allen checked the "black" box on surveys and applications, he described his identity as a mixture of black and Jewish. He added, as an afterthought, "You know, I'm also white and Christian, although it's not in that order." His identity as a black Jew emerged from a parallel history of oppression:

> I very strongly identify with the sense of Jews as a persecuted people, you know, and also, you know, the black diaspora and what happened with them. I mean both things are things that I feel strongly about.

Jonathan, was in his mid-twenties and completing a graduate degree in African American studies. He strongly identified as both a Jew and an African American and noted the psychological connections between the two cultures: "Our anxieties, our concerns, our pleasures, our joys, or even our neuroses, which are very Jewish, are sort of sponsored by being black. . . . Being black forced me to realize that I was not a part of this culture [American] in a fundamental way, . . . that I was marginal." He echoed Seymour in acknowledging the reinforcing relationship between his racial and religious identities: "Through being black, I realized my Judaism."

Both Jonathan and his brother, Andrew, grew up in the Philadelphia suburb of Mount Airy—a "refuge for aging hippies and folkies and civil rights workers."[18] Their black mother held a master's degree in art and had studied in Israel for a year because, according to Jonathan, she was "attracted to the culture and the religion. . . . I know that her closest friends have been consistently Jewish. Her best friend now is Jewish. And she takes great pride that her sons are Jewish, although I'm not sure really what that means to her." Their father was an atheist, a "Jewish-influenced secular humanist," who had been raised in an upper-middle-class household. The grandfather had come from Galicia, an area between Hungary and Poland, the grandmother "from an old, established German Jewish Philadelphia family, which included artists and printers."

Despite his secular upbringing, Jonathan became interested in Judaism at age eleven. He remembers arguing with his father about the existence of God: "'No Dad, there actually is a God. There's a God, and his name is *Emunah*.' And I don't know where I got that from but *Emunah* actually means "faith" in Hebrew." By the time of his bar mitzvah, he had become quite knowledgeable about Judaism and started wearing a *yarmulke*.

Over the years, Jonathan developed "a very strong tribal attachment to Judaism, . . . a strong sense of loyalty to Judaism" but was also very conscious that, as a patrilineal Jew, his status could be questioned. In addition to undergoing two bar mitzvahs and a formal conversion to Judaism, Jonathan became involved in the local Chabad. He described his "moves" to gain legitimacy as a Jew: "I went right to the top. I went to the Orthodox, Orthodox, Orthodox, to seek my legitimation, . . . you know, ultra-ultra-ultra-ultra-Orthodox, right? Who the hell is going to tell me I'm not Jewish? Some American Jew is going to tell me I'm not Jewish? [Name of Chabad rabbi] thinks I'm Jewish. And I know, I feel like it's worked, at least in terms of my own security which is what it's all about."

Like Josh, Jonathan had struggled to find acceptance among blacks during his adolescent years:

I was kind of disconnected from the black world in a way that was really jarring to me. And I also had the stirrings of adolescence. And I think it was Dr. Alvin Poussaint that said, "When an interracial child becomes an adolescent, the blackness is forced to the surface." Because you're interested in girls or boys, depending. And, you know, you're interested in something. You're interested in expressing yourself. And therefore, society demands that you declare yourself. I've actually found, to my great delight, that as I get older that I'm finding more and more acceptance in the black community, on my terms. Like when I was in my late teens and early twenties, I felt that in order to be accepted by black people I would have had to change myself, the way I talked, the way I walked, the way I dressed. Which is ridiculous, and I've never been willing to play that kind of authenticity game.

Just as he had pursued legitimacy as a Jew through relationships with ultra-Orthodox rabbis, Jonathan found legitimacy as a black man through his black (and non-Jewish) girlfriend: "And where's my source of black identity? You know, it's through [name of girlfriend] who is an African princess. Who's going to tell me that I'm not black? She thinks I'm black. Some African American is going to tell me I'm not black?"

* * *

Soon after interviewing Jonathan, I met his brother, Andrew, two years Jonathan's senior. Andrew had recently returned from Germany, where he had spent many years studying and working. He explained how his self-identity, as a black person and a Jew, was a product of place and that blackness carried very different meanings in America and Europe:

> Your identity is different if you are living in a country where being black is a political statement, and where there is a tremendous amount of racism, historical racism that seeps into everyday encounters at every level. That is different in Europe, especially for someone of my background. . . . I remember trying to convince my girlfriend, my first girlfriend, that I was black, and eventually she said, "OK, you can be black here."

"For a German, I am a Jew, period," he added. Andrew described his identity as culturally Jewish and was uncomfortable with categorizing himself into a racial group: "I have to cringe when I get into these situations, especially in America, of course it happens everywhere, where I am forced to say I am X." Still, like many of our biracial participants who resisted racial labels, he had checked off the "black" box on his college and graduate school applications.

Andrew's black identity evolved during his twenties although, as a Jew, he still didn't feel "that welcome in a number of African American circles. I don't feel like a full member." Now in his early thirties, he had come to see himself as "a multicultural person who has . . . critical politics, that believes in social change and thinks racism is a fundamental problem in our society." Unlike his brother, he was not at all religious, although he felt a strong cultural connection to other Jews:

I think that one of the unique things about Judaism is you don't have to believe, it is being part of your community and a part of a historical tradition. . . . You certainly don't have to believe in anything to be a Jew. According to religious Jews, you do have to believe in a lot of things to be a good Jew. But that is different with Christianity where you really have to believe.

Scholars have relied on survey research to emphasize how biracial individuals choose their identities, yet our interviews reveal that identity is not simply a matter of choosing; it requires a reciprocal relationship with the reference group of choice. One may choose but might not be chosen in return, which in turn impacts one's bonds and loyalty to the group. In the next chapter, we examine how a sense of belonging—that is, the extent to which one feels that their claims to both a black and Jewish identity are accepted within their respective reference groups—impacts their responses to charges of Jewish racism and black anti-Semitism.

7

When Worlds Collide

The flash points of black-Jewish relations are ulcers for me.
—Michael Twitty, interview excerpt

I would not elevate my problems with Farrakhan's anti-Jewishness above the other problems I have with him. And it annoys me to no end that white Jews insist that we do.
—Dana, interview excerpt

There is an open hole in the earth boiling with gas and sulfur, and it's in his [Farrakhan's] living room. And the evil in the core of the earth is just bubbling up. I don't like this man.
—Pnina, interview excerpt

He doesn't raise in me the anger and rage that he [does] in . . . the majority of Jews. He actually raises in me . . . just more shame and disappointment. I guess I'm pissed off at him. You know, it's like, "Lou, you make it harder for me."
—Josh, interview excerpt

The biracial Jewish philosopher Naomi Zack observed in her classic essay, "On Being and Not Being Black and Jewish," that the "implicit or explicit 'group mind' message in the face of outside threat is this: If we belong to the same group, my enemies must be your enemies. If you are disloyal to us, you will still be identified as a black or a Jew, but you cannot really *be* a black or a Jew, because from the standpoint of our group hearts and souls, you will not exist" (Zack 1996). But what if one already feels invisible within either or both of the groups? What is the impact of one's perceived status within a group on their allegiance to the group?

As we have seen, identity construction does not operate in isolation; it needs to be affirmed and validated by others, in particular by those who are normative members of the identity group. How does insider/outsider status experienced by biracial Jews, black converts, and Hebrews/Israelites shape the perceptions and responses to black-Jewish conflict? How do they negotiate black anti-Semitism and Jewish racism? Where do their loyalties fall, and what are the key determinants?

In the late 1990s, black-Jewish relations were imploding. In November 1998, the Anti-Defamation League (ADL) released a report on anti-Semitism and prejudice in America, which highlighted the finding that "African-Americans continue to be significantly more likely than white Americans to hold anti-Jewish beliefs," and that "blacks (34%) are nearly four times as likely as whites (9%) to fall into the most anti-Semitic category." Yet the report downplayed the more significant findings: "the overall level of anti-Semitism" among black Americans had decreased from 1992, and black anti-Semitism levels had dropped to 18 percent among the college educated.[1] By lumping together all social classes, the report contributed to the public misconception that black anti-Semitism was on the rise, when in fact it had steadily declined since the 1960s. Other observers continued to propagate the myth that anti-Semitism was widespread and deeply rooted within black attitudes (Shapiro 2005).

Anti-Semitism, at least in the traditional Western canon, is rooted in a particular set of Christian beliefs regarding "Jews as Christ killers," as represented in the Passion and Resurrection stories (Cohen 2007). Yet data gathered in three American cities reveal that not only do black churchgoers consider Jews less prejudiced than other white Americans, but they do not share in the vilification of Jews as Christ killers (Locke 1994). In fact, as we have seen, many blacks favor the Old Testament and identify with the story of the Jews, their plight in Egypt, and their exodus into freedom—an affinity reinforced by their shared experience in the civil rights struggle (Locke 1994; Levine 2007). Yet if the antipathy that at least some blacks feel towards Jews is not classic anti-Semitism, what is it?

From Blumstein's to Hymietown

Some have claimed that black attitudes towards Jews emerge from a particular set of economic relationships: as tenants of Jewish landlords, domestics in Jewish households, employees in Jewish businesses, and customers in Jewish stores (Locke 1994). The dynamic has brought strident condemnation from segments of the black community since at least the 1930s, when Harlemites picketed outside the Jewish-owned Blumstein's Department Store to protest discriminatory hiring practices. While the "Don't Shop Where You Can't Work" boycott was part of a larger initiative that targeted white-owned businesses, Blumstein's—along with other Jewish-owned stores, such as Kress's and Koch's—was located on 125th Street, the major shopping thoroughfare of Harlem. Like many New York department stores, it barred Negroes from employment and even from trying on clothes. The boycott was organized by the flamboyant religious leader Sufi Abdul Hamid, who wanted a "square deal." Jewish newspapers, such as the *Day* and the *Bulletin*, ran stories about black anti-Semitism and called Hamid a "black Hitler" (Hughes 1995). The protest drew support from over two hundred local organizations and community leaders, although organizations considered more mainstream, such as the NAACP, the National Urban League, and even the Socialist and Communists Parties, were reluctant to participate for fear of alienating powerful whites. For this reason, those who did protest were criticized as dissenters from the margins (Greenberg 1991).

The conflict between Israelis and Palestinians has been another lightening rod in black-Jewish relations. Following Israel's victory in the Six Day War, the Student Nonviolent Coordinating Committee ran an article in its newsletter stating that "Zionists conquered the Arab homes and land through terror" and that the House of Rothschild, the eighteenth-century banking enterprise, was part of a conspiracy to create the State of Israel (Zeitz 2007). That same summer, the *Liberator*, a black monthly that claimed a modest circulation of fifteen thousand in a community of more than two hundred thousand, rose to national attention when writer James Baldwin and actor Ossie Davis resigned from the staff, blasting its editor, Daniel Watts, for the "immoral" scapegoating of Jews. The caption of one *Time* magazine article from March 17, 1967, "Black Anti-Semitism," distorted the real story; ironically, the Jewish Telegraphic Agency's *Daily News Bulletin* had more accurately captured it two weeks earlier in its article, "Prominent Negroes Condemn Negro Anti-Semitism; Quit the 'Liberator'" (Jewish Telegraphic Agency 1967; Karp and Shapiro 1999). Political scientist and black intellectual historian Adolph L. Reed Jr. compares the derogatory phrase "black anti-Semitism" to "'Africanized' killer bees" and "crack babies," and he rejects any suggestion that black people have a "particularly virulent" strain of anti-Semitism (Reed 1999).

Still, Jewish scapegoating, by at least some blacks, was on the rise. That same year, the June issue of the Black Panther Party of Northern California's publication, *Black Power*, carried the poem "Jew-Land," which concluded with the following lines (Wolfe 1970):

> In Jew-Land, Don't be a Tom on Israel's side
> Really, Cause that's where Christ was crucified.

Israel was again at the center a decade later, when Andrew Young, the first African American US Ambassador to the United Nations, resigned after making controversial statements about Israel and, in violation of official government policy, met with Zehdi Labib Terzi, the Palestine Liberation Organization (PLO) observer to the UN.

This same period saw the rise in Jewish neoconservatism. In the wake of the identity-based politics and Black Power movement of the 1960s, many Jews became less committed to assimilation and sought to rediscover their own roots (Waters 1990; E. L. Goldstein 2008). It was during this time that the Jewish Renewal Movement was established. Deeply influenced by the Lubavitch Chassidism, it emphasized an "old-time" spirituality and delivered a new sense of ethnic pride to disaffected Jews. Yet this was also the time that mainstream Jewish organizations—including the American Jewish Committee, the American Jewish Congress, and the ADL—embraced market-driven economic policies and rejected the affirmative action strategies favored by blacks (E. L. Goldstein 2008). This shift exacerbated tensions that had grown as Jews moved into the middle class while many blacks remained trapped in poverty by racial barriers.

The neoconservative movement was led by a core of New York Jewish intellectuals who had come of age in the 1930s and 1940s, many of whom had been born to immigrant parents and raised in hardscrabble working-class neighborhoods. Many had attended the City College of New York (during a time when quotas kept most Jews from Ivy League schools) and developed "a fondness for sweeping declarations" and a "suspicion of leftist dogma" (Hartman 2015). These neoconservative intellectuals may, in fact, have been responsible for sowing the "seeds for the disintegration of the black-Jewish alliance" (Diner 1995). Its most prominent leaders included Irving Kristol (founder of the journal *Public Interest*, which questioned the wisdom of liberal government reforms, such as quotas and welfare, that were aimed at eradicating racism and poverty and argued that they would only create more dependency) and the more junior Norman Podhoretz (who served as editor in chief of the conservative Jewish magazine, *Commentary*, from 1960 through 1995). They saw their rise to the middle class as proof of American meritocracy. Abandoning the Jewish liberal values of previous generations, they pointed to their own ability to surmount the obstacles of discrimination and asked why blacks could not do the same (Steinberg 2001b).

Community control has been yet another catalyst of black-Jewish tension. The 1968 New York City teachers' strike, which pitted the heavily Jewish teachers' union against black (and Puerto Rican) parents over control of the public schools, has often been invoked as the key moment of the coalition meltdown.[2] What began as a local dispute over community control in the predominantly black Ocean Hill-Brownsville section of Brooklyn quickly escalated into a thirty-six-day halt to the entire city's school system.

During the summer of 1967, the Board of Education had begun experimenting with "decentralization," an effort to cede more control of inner-city schools to the community by empowering local school boards. The board established three decentralized school districts, Ocean Hill-Brownsville being one of them. Mayor John Lindsay, as well as New Left intellectuals and local communities, were enthusiastic about the experiment, but the largely white and heavily Jewish union viewed the newly empowered schools as a threat to due process, job security, and its collective bargaining power (Podair 2004)—and not without good reason. That next spring, the new board at Ocean Hill-Brownsville abruptly fired thirteen teachers (most of whom were Jewish) and six administrators, which prompted a realignment of relationships across the city, pitting the New Left against organized labor and uniting Catholics and Jews against blacks. Two decades later, sociologist Jonathan Rieder would chronicle how the children and grandchildren of Jewish and Italian immigrants in the closed community of Canarsie would resolve their long-held civic rivalry by collectively resisting the busing of outside children into their community and of their own children into less successful schools outside it (Rieder 1985).

Tensions between blacks and Jews were further exacerbated in December 1968, when Julius Lester—then a radio talk show host on WBAI—read on the air a poem written by a fourteen-year-old student at Ocean Hill-Brownsville. It began, "Hey, Jewboy, with that *yarmulke* on your head, You pale-faced Jew boy—I wish you were dead." Lester's justification for reading the poem was that he wanted people to know how the school controversy was impacting the students, but the incident embroiled him in accusations of anti-Semitism. In a sweeping turnaround, Lester later converted to Orthodox Judaism and, in 1988, he won the National Jewish Book Award for his memoir *Lovesong: Becoming a Jew.* At the time of the book's publication, he was a professor in the Afro-American Studies Department at the University of Massachusetts Amherst. Shortly thereafter, the faculty unanimously demanded that he be removed from the department on the grounds that he had become an "anti-Negro-Negro."[3] One faculty member likened Lester's retention in the Afro-American Studies Department to "Yasser Arafat teaching in the Jewish Studies Department."[4] Ironically, that is just where Lester was transferred.

Discussing the incident a decade later, Lester attributed the conflict with his department to a number of issues that had been brewing long before the book's publication:

> I think a couple of things are at the heart of the conflict. I think one was that . . . they sensed that I betrayed them by telling secrets in public. You know, talking about the shunning that had gone on at the department in '79, when I did the piece in the *Village Voice* about black anti-Semitism.[5] And people didn't speak to me for a year in the department. And then, our differences around [Jesse] Jackson's candidacy [for president], and that was another period of shunning. . . . It really is very effective in terms of making somebody feel very, very isolated. Where before people had been, you know, friends and what have you. And . . . I talk about that in *Lovesong* and express my anger about that. So, I think they felt betrayed. I know that others who have written about the incident attribute anti-Semitism as playing a part. I am not certain about that. On the other hand, I do know that if I had converted to Islam, they would have applauded me, or Catholicism, Buddhism. It wouldn't have bothered them, anything else. And . . . there may be a trace of some kind of passive anti-

Semitism there. I don't want to paint them as any kind of rabid anti-Semites because they are not by any stretch of the imagination. I think there was a sense of betrayal in terms of whom they thought I was, in terms of things that I had written, in terms of black history and black culture and what have you. I think that for a lot of people it's less difficult now, but certainly back then it was very difficult for people to put black and Jewish together, . . . and there were people who said you can't be both. And so therefore if you are Jewish, then you are not black anymore. That is just ridiculous. But that's what happens when we have political definitions of what it means to be black.

Decades later, some academics continued to view Lester's conversion as suspect. The political theorist Alyson Cole gave a searing critique of his memoir in her 2003 essay "Trading Places: From Black Power Activist to 'Anti-Negro Negro,'" characterizing his conversion as "a search for a pure victim position" and his embrace of Judaism and Jewishness as "a type of racial crossing that I call 'Jewface'"—a play on "blackface and other forms of 'racechanges'" (Cole 2003). She argued that, like Jewish vaude-villians who performed in black face and thus magnified the distance between themselves and blacks, Lester appropriates Jewish culture and religion to separate himself from blacks:

> Lester's "ethnic transvestism"—his appropriation of Jewish history, Jewish food, music and other forms of *Yiddishkeit*—inverts this cultural device. His performance is fundamentally an act of individuation, not simply an assimilationist gesture or an attempt to pass. If Jewish performers wore the black mask to merge into the white mainstream, Lester dons the *yarmulke* to distinguish himself from Blacks and ultimately to guarantee his double marginality. He achieves this position by combining two "identities"—African American and Jewish—that have become dramatically opposed in American society. (Cole 2003)

However, when viewed through this lens, many Israelites of the 1930s, who were steeped in Garveyism but who also studied Talmud and Yiddish, would be suspect as well. For Cole, Lester's rebirth as a Jew was nothing more than an inauthentic performance of Jewishness and "a racial conversion more than a religious one." She claimed that by appropriating Judaism he appropriates the victimhood of the Holocaust. Her logic is an affront to anyone—black or white—who has ever contemplated converting to Judaism. In her mind, the desire for victimhood would always supersede any spiritual purpose.

A few years before Lester's memoir was released, blacks and Jews collided on the national stage. In January 1984, presidential candidate Jesse Jackson undermined his own political aspirations during an off-the-cuff conversation with a black reporter from the *Washington Post*. Presuming that he was speaking off the record, Jackson referred to Jews as "Hymies" and to New York City as "Hymietown." The story broke that February, just days before the New Hampshire primary. Jackson first denied making the remarks but soon recanted and apologized, hoping to put the unfortunate blunder behind him. That next month, however, Minister Louis Farrakhan of the Nation of Islam renewed attention to the incident during a radio broadcast, making veiled threats of retaliation towards Milton Coleman, the *Washington Post* reporter who had broken the "Hymietown" story.[6] As if that wasn't enough to anger Jews, he compared himself to Adolf Hitler while criticizing Jews for making the same comparison. By early April, New York City Mayor Ed Koch, along with other prominent Jews, called for Jackson to distance himself from Farrakhan and his anti-Semitic invectives (Schanberg 1984).

Meanwhile, Farrakhan continued to bask in the national spotlight. In June, upon his return to America from Libya, he was quoted again, this time calling Judaism a "gutter religion," an idea attributed to him since at least 1983: "Now, that nation of Israel, never has had any peace in forty years and she will never have any peace because there can never be any peace structured on injustice, thievery, lying and deceit and using the name of God to shield your gutter religion under His holy and righteous name." Farrakhan claimed he only called Judaism a "dirty" religion, although a tape of the sermon in question, which was later released to the *Chicago Sun-Times*, proved otherwise (Shipp 1984). By October 1985, when Farrakhan took the stage at Madison Square Garden for his POWER (People Organized and Working for Economic Rebirth) campaign, he had become a political lightening rod. The "Hymietown" incident, along with Jackson's refusal to disavow Farrakhan, continued to dampen Jewish support when he ran again in the 1988 Democratic presidential primary; he received a mere 8 percent of the Jewish vote (Greenberg 2010).

Insider/Outsider Status

Amid the turmoil of the 1970s and 1980s, many young biracial Jews were struggling to carve out their identities and reconcile their allegiances within two very different, and often opposing, peer groups. Seymour, the biracial Jew who grew up in the mixed neighborhood of Morningside Heights in Manhattan, had been involved in the Zionist socialist youth movement of Hashomer Hatzair (The Youth Guard), as well as Harlem's graffiti subculture. Now a practicing Conservative Jew, he explained how he had negotiated anti-Semitism from blacks and racism from Jews when he was younger:

> I would sort of defend my black brothers from any sort of attack that might be based purely on the color of their skin, or the way they chose to wear Afros, or the way that they chose to dress a certain way. . . . And to Jews in the face of blacks who would be anti-Semitic, you know, my perspective was that, "Do you like me? I'm Jewish, so what do you really know? How deep is this feeling and what's up with that?" . . . It would shock them to some degree; some brothers who would think that they were in a safe room, so they could talk about Jews.

Seymour's comments reflect the strength of his ties to both communities. He felt confident standing up to fellow Jews and blacks alike in the face of discrimination. In contrast, Josh, a very light-skinned black born to a white Jewish mother and an African American father, reported weak ties to both the black and Jewish communities, but each for different reasons. While he was fully accepted within the Jewish community, the acceptance he sought—and which seemed to elude him—was from other blacks. His tenuous status sometimes led him to overcompensate, even to "pass" as a non-Jew in the presence of other blacks: "I'm not as proud of my Judaism. . . . A lot of times, especially if I'm among, you know, . . . black groups, I just don't say anything about it. I figure that it's something I'm happier to have go unnoticed. In a weird way, it's probably similar to the whole idea of passing. . . . It's just easier." He recalled his feelings of inadequacy during college, when Leonard Jeffries—a black studies professor from the City College of New York who was well known for his anti-Semitism—had been invited to the campus to speak:

They certainly had a whole bunch of nationalists in that group. You know, there were a couple of Nation of Islam members that didn't really welcome me. . . . And my whole kind of thinking then was trying to figure out who I am. I didn't really want to associate with the Jewish community very much. You know, couldn't really join their protesting in front of Jeffries, even though I kind of sympathized with their protests. I just didn't want to be a part of it. I guess in [because of] my own personal insecurities in both communities. Not . . . vocal enough in either one of them kind of, . . . and not feeling entitled to claim membership firmly enough in either of them.

In the end, it was not the strength of participants' identity claims but their status within the group—that is, the extent to which their claims as black or Jewish were accepted by normative blacks or Jews—that impacted their sensitivity to group bias (Haynes 2013).

Dana, the biracial Jew from Chicago, resented the attention she often drew in Jewish circles: "You know, getting questions like, 'Are you Jewish? Why are you here? How did you become Jewish? . . . Every time you encounter Jewish people—white Jewish people—they feel entitled to ask about your Jewish identity if you're darker." She described moments when she experienced herself as the "other," that is, the view of one's self through the eyes of the dominant group, a phenomenon W. E. B. Du Bois called "double consciousness":

> It's the racism one experiences from so-called white Jews that create the internal conflicts of identity. . . . I get enraged as a Jew. And my black self goes, "Oh, yeah, of course. I've seen this before." And it's the only moment I bifurcate. But it's more like the split . . . when . . . you're watching white folks react to you, and . . . you react to their reaction. I don't know if you ever do this, but [it is like] that kind of Du Boisian second-sight thing.

The bifurcation that Dana experienced led to her ambivalence about the (then-recent) public focus on Jews and Jewish suffering. *Schindler's List*—Steven Spielberg's epic film about Holocaust survival—had been released in December 1993. In spring 1994, the film had dominated the 66th Academy Awards, taking home seven Oscars, including Best Picture, Best Director, Best Cinematography, and Best Original Score.

For Dana, it seemed emblematic of Jewish power that an event that did *not* occur on American soil was being memorialized in Washington, while blacks were still unable to wrest recognition for their own "holocaust"—the transatlantic slave trade. She attributed Jews' success in gaining recognition for the Holocaust to their whiteness:

> I'll use the language of feeling here, an intense amount of envy and anger at the fact that the Jewish Holocaust can be counted. And pride, Jewish pride, that Jews will not let people forget this. But intense anger and envy about the privileged position that they have in terms of loss, . . . and the way that cultural memory has been instituted successfully by Jews is both one of our greatest achievements and one of our most serious moments of myopic blindness. . . . While I also understand that it's the Jewish difference that made it happen, but it's Jewish whiteness that allows Jews to, at least the kind of guilt and identification that happens with broader white communities. About the fact that these kids who perished were white, you know, these women who died were white. There's a kind of politics of sympathy that happens in terms of that identification that does not happen for other people's loss. . . . So, it angers me every time I hear it. Every time I hear people being moved by Holocaust experiences. Every time I hear people going back and reading off a hundred names, there is a moment where my heart just goes, "Shhhhhh."

In contrast to the indignation Dana expressed over incidents of racism among Jews, she placed black anti-Semitism within a larger contextual framework:

> And this is what I don't understand about the way that black anti-Jewishness is analyzed. It's analyzed as if it is separate and apart from broader anti-Jewish sentiment. And black folks don't have the power to translate that, and we don't have a history of translating that. It seems to me there are exceptional moments where, you know, you have conflagrations of anti-Jewish feeling, which, in New York, is largely immigrant based, not traditional African American community based anyway, so there's that. But to me, it's how it can become a catalyst for wider anti-Jewish sentiment. . . . Looking at the dynamic interrelationship between the Nation [of Islam]'s anti-Jewishness and how it affirms, confirms, and

legitimizes larger anti-Semitic sentiment in the United States. That's the danger. The danger isn't coming from the black community.

Those whose black authenticity was questioned by other blacks expressed greater indignation or anxiety about black anti-Semitism. Likewise, those whose Jewish credentials were challenged by white Jews were more preoccupied with Jewish-based racism, which they often framed through their personal struggles for legitimacy. Rather than cite instances of conventional white racism, in which blacks are victimized or oppressed, they spoke of not feeling fully recognized or embraced as fellow Jews. At the same time, those who did not seek acceptance or validation from either group were less critical, regardless of their insider/outsider status.

Jonathan and his brother, Andrew, were prime examples of this dynamic. Despite attending a Unitarian nursery school, having a Christmas tree during the winter holidays, and growing up with an atheist father, Jonathan had developed a strong spiritual connection to his Jewish roots by the time he had reached adolescence:

> I guess I always had a Jewish consciousness, which was strange. . . . I'm religious, but I don't believe in formal religion as much as I'm attached to Judaism. . . . It organizes my week, my schedule, which is not inconsistent with Judaism as a legal code. . . . But I did always have this kind of feeling of faith and of connection. And then when I was twelve, I realized that I wanted to express that in real knowledge about Judaism. So, I learned it.

He described his early experiences with his black peers as "jarring":

> I had grown up in a fairly rough school, but I didn't realize it. I didn't realize how much every day there was a threat of basically getting my ass kicked. And I always talked my way out of it. I never got beat up. But when I went to the all-Jewish day school, I kind of like had post-traumatic, like I became very, very fearful of, of going outside. And I became very, very fearful of black people.

As a patrilineal-descent Jew, Jonathan had also experienced rejection from rabbinical authorities. The events leading up to his bar mitzvah had been particularly painful:

The rabbi said, "In order to have a bar mitzvah, you have to convert."
I was like, "Convert to what?" I mean, because you couldn't have told
me that I was not Jewish. . . . And even now, I met with some Orthodox
rabbis that wanted me to reconvert to make sure my conversion's good,
. . . because the rabbis that converted [me], one of them was not observant of the Sabbath, which technically nullifies the conversion. But, you
know, my feeling is the rabbis can really kiss my ass.

Challenges to his authenticity only strengthened his sense of self. He
seemed defiantly, triumphantly Jewish:

You don't have to count me for your *minyan*.[7] You can bury me with
goyim, as if the rabbis can separate dust, you know. You can exclude me
however you want. I know what I am. Actually, one of the real comfort-
ing things I've ever heard anyone say was this, the rabbi in New York, in
Utica, or in Brooklyn: "The pope can decide who's Catholic or not, but he
can't decide who's Christian."

Jonathan's failure to become fully recognized as a Jew may have led him
to emphasize the spiritual over the legalistic interpretation of the boundaries of the Jewish community:

I believe in *halakha*. I do believe. It's like citizenship. You know, you have
to have rules. But I'm not a legalist. I believe in the spirit, which is one of
the reasons I'm attracted to Hasidism. It's because I believe in the letter of
the law is important, but without the spiritual interpretation it's nothing.
It's empty. And I refuse to submit to that kind of legal, I mean for me it
was always legal, it was always legalism. My conversion was always legal,
legalistic. Like, I'm already Jewish.

Andrew, on the other hand, was an agnostic Jew and sought no formal recognition of his Jewish credentials. At the same time, he was a
staunch defender of Jewish legalism and believed that it placed Judaism
outside the boundaries of racism:

One of the interesting things of the Orthodox Jewish community is that
they actually have clear rules which determine who is Jewish and who is

not, which takes race out of it. . . . I mean, to be honest, it is not a community that I could be part of, but on the other hand, they are as close to race blind as you can find in the Jewish community. . . . They do have a lot of irrational beliefs, but if you are looking for a community where nobody is going to say I am not black, or nobody is going to question your Jewishness, it is about the only community I can think of.

While he described himself as multicultural, his critique of Jewish racism and black anti-Semitism reflected his stronger links to the Jewish community, especially in Israel:

There are a lot of Jewish communities where people will embrace you because people don't like the racism. In America, they see a parallel between anti-Semitism and racism, and to be very supportive, if I am honest about my Jewish experience, I don't feel that welcome in a number of African American circles. I don't feel like a full member. . . . There is a lot of real anti-Semitism, . . . you know, the Jews are this, there are certain things like we aren't in the same boat. While in Israel, I mean there are different traditions, yet Israel is a place where being brown, I mean, people are brown. The de facto color is brown.

The distinctions between "white" and "brown" Jews were also noted by some of the black converts with whom I spoke. Yet rather than contrasting American- and Israeli-born Jews, they drew the line between the Ashkenazim and Sephardim. Marissa, for example, felt like an outsider among Ashkenazi Jews, especially when attending synagogue: "I was the *shvartze* there, you know. I mean, I was definitely other." In contrast, she found Sephardi Jews much more welcoming. She attributed the black-Ashkenazi divide to economics, recalling painful memories from her childhood:

It was purely economic. It was people who owned apartment buildings, and . . . cut them in half to have double the number of people who were supposed to be in them. I mean that sort of thing, you know. "That old Jew over there who owns this," because that was, it was the economics of it, because it was really the only interaction they had, we had. And, you know, my grandmother's stories about walking into the store and not being served . . . and hearing the word *shvartze* before she knew what it meant and recognizing that it was something that had to do with her, because they'd look over at her and say it. And then, you know, standing there to buy her wholesale things.

Grappling with the political implications of being both black and Jewish has been difficult for Marissa:

As a black and a Jew, you straddle so many different relationships that I think, you know, it does get very complex. How you pray and who you pray with is sometimes, sometimes is a political statement. For me, it's not a political statement. I mean, why I pray and who I pray with is really more a spiritual necessity. But I don't ignore the fact that it may have political implications that might pull me into the politics, since Jews are a political people. I mean, and so are blacks. And so, you've got a double whammy when you're trying to figure how you fit into these cultures of being, you know, of being something of a spirituality, while not ignoring the fact that your presence or your absence or your payment or your lack of payment will somehow affect, also, how other blacks are viewed, even though you're coming there as an individual. It's very complicated.

Michael Twitty, also a convert to Judaism, is grounded in both the African American and Sephardi Jewish communities. Like Marissa, he has felt marginalized among Ashkenazi Jews and only attended Sephardi synagogues. In his assessment of black-Jewish relations, he voices strong criticism of Jewish anti-racism, while challenging his fellow Jews to deal with it:

The flash points of black-Jewish relations are ulcers for me. Because it is very difficult. One thing that I want to contribute to the Jewish community . . . is there is a double standard between the ways blacks and Jews are treated when they come cuss each other out. . . . When Jewish people called us names, which they did, in the South and in the North. When they defended slavery, because it was in the Torah. When they said in Brownsville, in New York, "We want to keep out jobs, and you guys shut up." When they said in Crown Heights, "We are going to go get the *shvartzes* out of our neighborhood." Why aren't we dealing with that?

Why aren't we confronting that? Why is it when black people have issues with Jews, we get a speech about Jewish philanthropy? . . . "We are nice to you people, but now you are ungrateful." Well black people have the same stories, you know. Hasidic Jews threatening, saying, "Come on, you know you are going to sell us your house, so get out of here." What is that? When it's Hasidic Jews beating up random black young men given to be thugs of some sort, let's get over it. Let's begin to talk about this. Let's talk about the fact that, you know, Israel had a very bad record with South Africa. Bad meaning that they were at certain points in time working with, cooperating with them, working with them as two states. . . . What was weird for me is that Jewish people have not adequately, in my opinion, criticized their own racism against blacks. I think black people have very well been criticized, . . . but I do not think that Jews have adequately been criticized against [for] racism against blacks.

Scapegoats and Interlopers

Hostilities among New York's racial and ethnic groups reached a fever pitch in the last decade of the century. New immigrants challenged neighborhood boundaries and tempers, and Korean merchants became seen as the new interlopers in black neighborhoods. In 1990, two Korean greengroceries in Brooklyn—Family Red Apple and Church Fruits— were boycotted by blacks for more than a year. According to news accounts, the boycotts were sparked by an argument between Family Red Apple's owner and a Haitian immigrant customer over how much she'd paid for her plantains and peppers (Vanderkam 2011). The black activist Sonny Carson helped to organize the "Don't shop with people who don't look like us" campaign. It's not surprising that surveys conducted in 1992 showed that black residents were developing attitudes towards Koreans that paralleled those long held towards Jews. For many residents of poor black neighborhoods such as Harlem and Bedford-Stuyvesant, both Koreans and Jews were interested only in making money and protecting their own group (Min 2008, 83).[8]

In 1991, the Historical Research Department of the Nation of Islam released its own account of Jews' purported dominance of the transatlantic slave trade in *The Secret Relationship between Blacks and Jews, Vol-*

ume One. Jewish involvement in civil rights was reduced to a desire for control that stemmed from the commanding role of Jewish merchants in black communities and oddly linked to Jewish nationalism. Jews were now singled out for playing an instrumental and overrepresentative role in America's greatest moral failing: slavery. Harvard professor Henry Louis Gates Jr. called the book "the bible of the new anti-Semitism," which, he explained, "arises not in spite of the black-Jewish alliance but because of it. For precisely such trans-racial cooperation—epitomized by the historic partnership between blacks and Jews—is what poses the greatest threat to the isolationist movement" (Gates 1992).

Although *The Secret Relationship between Blacks and Jews* referenced second- and third-rate scholars with Jewish surnames to drive home its point, the argument was adopted by several mainstream scholars. Tony Martin—a full professor at Wellesley and author of numerous books—drew outcries from Jewish students for teaching from it in his course on African American history. Martin later published his account of the campus controversy in a provocatively titled essay, *The Jewish Onslaught: Despatches from the Wellesley Battlefront* (1993): "The book [*The Secret Relationship*] documents the considerable Jewish involvement in the trans-atlantic African slave trade, the dissemination of which knowledge they, as Jews, considered an 'anti-Semitic' and most 'hateful' act" (3). New York University professor of history David Levering Lewis, author of *When Harlem Was in Vogue* (1979), had already suggested that the Jewish relationship to black social progress was simply a manifestation of manipulative Jewish self-interest, echoing the cultural and social critic Harold Cruse's analysis of Jewish "political and ideological power over Negroes" in *The Crisis of the Negro Intellectual* (1967). Meanwhile, many Jews assigned blame for the fractured alliance to advocates of black power, some of whom openly trashed the history of cooperation between blacks and Jews and saw Jewish paternalism, complacency with segregation, and opposition to affirmative action and quotas (popular strategies to remedy racial inequality) as evidence of Jewish racism. As the emeritus historian Edward S. Shapiro commented, Cruse's book was an "eye-opener for Jews": "Blacks have resented Jews not because they did not do enough for them, but because they did too much" (Shapiro 2005).

The death knell for black-Jewish relations in New York was sounded in late August 1991 in Crown Heights, Brooklyn, home to many longtime

Hasidic residents and new Caribbean immigrants. A Hasidic motorcade under police escort veered off the road, killing seven-year-old Gavin Cato and severely injuring his young cousin. Both were children of Guyanese immigrants. After the accident, an angry crowd gathered and reportedly attacked the driver of the crashed vehicle. While witnesses differed over exactly what happened next, it seems that groups of West Indians—enraged by both the failure of the city police to arrest the driver and the delayed response of medical workers—began a protest that soon escalated into a riot and attacks on local Hasidic Jews. Mayor David Dinkins, New York City's first black mayor, went to Crown Heights and called for calm but was booed repeatedly by local black residents. City police were outnumbered and did little to quell protests. What began as a peaceful march on Eastern Parkway quickly morphed into rock throwing and three days of chaos and rage that ended in the tragic stabbing death of Yankel Rosenbaum, a twenty-nine-year-old Australian *yeshiva* student. Although news accounts characterized the riots as an anti-Jewish *pogrom*, not all Jews were attacked nor were all blacks the attackers; rather, Caribbean-born residents targeted local members of the Hasidic sect who were part of the police motorcade. Still, it was the perception of Jewish favoritism—the police leading the Hasidic motorcade through the area—that was at the heart of the local outcry and Jewish condemnation. Meanwhile, millions of Jews and blacks watched the melee unfold on the five o'clock news. After the riots, Jews expressed outrage when reports—all false—surfaced that Mayor Dinkins and Police Commissioner Lee P. Brown (both black men) had initially withheld police protection from the Hasidim so that blacks could "vent their rage" (Fried 1995). The city's largest African American paper, the *Amsterdam News*, ran the headline "Many Blacks, No Jews Arrested." Princeton professor Cornel West called the riots a "random act"—spontaneous and not indicative of more deeply held sentiments against Jews. In the aftermath, many blacks and Jews from the neighborhood blamed the riots on outside agitators such as Al Sharpton. Little attention was paid to the simple fact that the conflict was largely between West Indian-born blacks and Hasidic Jews.[9]

Meanwhile, Leonard Jeffries was rising to national prominence for his controversial claim that Jews had financed the slave trade. In August 1991, he delivered an address at the Empire State Black Arts and Cultural Festival that tested the limits of tolerance for anti-Semitism. There, in

New York State's capital of Albany and before the US assistant secretary of education, Diane Ravitch, he linked all of his extremist and fantastical beliefs about rich Jews, the slave trade, Hollywood, and a Jewish conspiracy. His comments ignited another barrage of media commentary and forced the City University of New York Board of Trustees to initiate a process of review. In March 1992, the board voted to remove Jeffries as chair of the black studies department. Jeffries challenged the decision in the US District Court in lower Manhattan and was reinstated as chair the next year; the jury also awarded him $400,000 in damages (Glazer 1995). Then, in April 1995, the appeals court reversed the decision following an appeal by the New York State attorney general, G. Oliver Koppell. By then, Jeffries's term as chair had already expired, and the board simply did not reappoint him for another term.

In November 1993, Nation of Islam spokesman Khalid Abdul Muhammad drew national attention after speaking at Kean College in New Jersey. His comments earned him a congressional reprimand. House Resolution 343, enacted the following year, stated, "Whereas Mr. Muhammad specifically justifies the slaughter of Jews during the Holocaust as fully deserved; disparages the Pope in the most revolting personal terms; and calls for the assassination of every white infant, child, man, and woman in South Africa," the House of Representatives resolved to condemn his speech "as outrageous hatemongering of the most vicious and vile kind," along with "all manifestations and expressions of racism, anti-Catholicism, anti-Semitism, and ethnic or religious intolerance" (H. R. Res. 343, 1994). While his brazenness eventually led to his dismissal from the Nation, it landed him a spot on NBC's *Donahue* talk show and a leadership position in the New Black Panther Party (H. R. Res. 343, 1994; Gearty 1995; Eligon and Robles 2016).

It was during this time that Pnina became involved in relationship building between the black and Jewish communities. Pnina was unique in our sample in that both her parents were Jewish (her mother was of German descent, and her father was Ethiopian). Her diverse life experiences ranged from attending a Catholic boarding school, to living in Iran on the eve of the Revolution, to hunting Nazis at the Simon Wiesenthal Center. Anti-Semitism figured large in her world construct and had even formed the basis for some of her childhood games: "We used to play hiding from the Bolsheviks. That was the kind of game I would want to play. Let's hide from the Bolsheviks. 'What is a Bolshevik?' most kids would say."

As a child, her strong Jewish identity and weaker black identity (as well as her lack of institutional ties to the black church) had alienated her from other blacks. The rejection she experienced continued into adulthood, although the particulars changed. Here Pnina describes her experiences in community building between blacks and Jews:

> I got sort of involved in that kind of reconciliation stuff, . . . black-Jewish stuff. . . . People when I would go into a black community would say, "But you're not an authentic black, you're Jewish. You can't be black if you're not a member of the church." When I would go to speak at churches and little old black ladies would say to me, "You're a very nice girl, but we're praying for your soul. . . . You've lost your black soul."

In 1993, she participated in the symposium "Where Worlds Collide: The Souls of African-American Jews" at the California African American Museum (CAAM) in Los Angeles. The event was planned to complement the Los Angeles showing of *Bridges and Boundaries: African-Americans and American Jews*, a traveling exhibition organized by the Jewish Museum of New York, which explored the complex relationships between blacks and Jews in the twentieth century.[10] This was the culminating session in the series, and it quickly spiraled into what Pnina characterized as an anti-Semitic venting fest. The event drew detractors with assorted agendas. Many were seeking a public platform to air their grievances, however remotely connected to the topic at hand. One woman raised the need for a biracial bill of rights. Another asked how Jews were connected to slavery in the Sudan. Some wanted to know whether there was a color caste system in Israel or if there was any substance to the rumor that Jewish doctors were infecting black babies with the AIDS virus. Most of the panelists—which included an Ethiopian Jew, a Russian black Jew, a black convert from South Central Los Angeles, and a prominent black and Jewish journalist, were visibly rattled—save for Rabbi Capers Funnye, who artfully fielded their questions and made reference to his ongoing dialogue with Minister Farrakhan.[11] "About a hundred people showed up," Pnina said. "Many of them were these Africanists who had been sort of harassing us. . . . And they wanted to talk about Jews in Hollywood. And they wanted to talk about Jews and AIDS. And Jews and crack. And Jews and slavery. Does any of this sound familiar to you?"

Rick Moss, who at the time was CAAM's program manager of history, later discussed the event:

> There were a number of members of an organization that, I forgot the exact name of it. . . . A local group of young brothers in the '60s radical mode, from my point of view, just discovered this revolutionary attitude and felt that now they needed to let everyone else know about it, as if no one on stage or in the audience was aware of this or knew about the kinds of things that they were espousing, the whole new idea, and they had the whole story. And so, their whole point was not to enter the dialogue in any constructive way, it was simply to disrupt it. . . . They didn't want it to continue, so their whole reason for being there was simply to stop whatever discussion was going on. So, they would at various times stand up and instead of asking a question, would begin a long diatribe, about this or that and a statement as opposed to a question. And before they even finished, then another one [would stand up]. They were not sitting together necessarily, so you have a series of popinjays.[12]

Undeterred, Pnina helped found the Alliance of Black Jews two years later. The group received attention from Jewish and black media, including *Emerge* magazine, a now-defunct monthly that had a primarily African American readership. While *Emerge* published a favorable piece on the group, Pnina was critical of some of the contrived tactics it used in its production: "They'd sent a photographer, who took some wonderful candid pictures of individual members, but the editor decided the photos were not Jewish enough. And I wanted to say to them, 'You're doing the same thing that you don't like people to do to black folks. What's a black picture? What's a Jewish picture?'" They wanted members posing with ritual objects, Pnina explained. Feeling exploited, she wondered whether the magazine saw black Jews as an opportunity to recast the relationship: "It's kind of like blacks saying, 'See, we don't have a problem with Jews. We even have black Jews.'"

* * *

The year that the Alliance of Black Jews was founded—1995—was also the year of Louis Farrakhan's Million Man March on Washington, DC, and of the ADL's report, *The Nation of Islam: The Relentless Record of Hate (March 1994–March 1995)*. It was the year that Rabbi Michael Lerner and Professor Cornel West toured the country to promote their new book, *Jews and Blacks: Let the Healing Begin*, and that *Common Quest: The Magazine of Black Jewish Relations* was founded.[13] And it was the year that ended, literally, in flames.

In December 1995, Reverend Al Sharpton of the National Action Network and Morris Powell of the 125th Street Vendors Association had teamed up to protest the planned rent increase and subsequent eviction of the Record Shack, a long-standing black-owned business in Harlem owned by the South African-born Sikhulu Shange. Although the actual owner of the building (and party raising the rent) was the United House of Prayer for All People—a black Pentecostal church founded by "Sweet Daddy" Grace in the 1920s and one of the biggest landlords on 125th Street— Shange was subletting the property from Fred Harari, a Syrian-born Jewish entrepreneur who also operated Freddy's Fashion Mart, a small discount clothing store, next door. Still, local anger over the eviction of the Record Shack was targeted at Harari, and Sharpton was accused of anti-Semitism when he denounced "white interlopers" in black communities (although he later expressed regret for his choice of words). In the midst of this tension, Roland James Smith Jr.—a former criminal with a thirty-year history of mental instability—broke through the line of protesters with a loaded .38-caliber pistol and set Freddy's Fashion Mart on fire, killing seven people. The *New York Times* reported that another four were shot but escaped from the store before it was consumed by flames (Kifner 1995). While the fire was heralded as a manifestation of black anti-Semitism, little attention was paid to the underlying political and class tensions between local factions or the fact that Smith was a lone, crazed individual and did not represent broad community sentiment (Kasinitz and Haynes 1996). Meanwhile, the fire claimed the lives of low-wage workers of color—including Kareem Brunner, a black security guard, and a number of Latino and Guyanese immigrants—the real collateral damage of this public feud.

These high-profile incidents of black anti-Semitism, while deeply disturbing, appear to have been isolated. Most daily interactions between blacks and Jews in New York were routine and civil, much like those discussed by sociologist Jennifer Lee, who was struck by the "sheer ordinariness" of most merchant-customer encounters in Harlem and West Philadelphia (Lee 2006). In fact, survey data collected in the early 1990s by the ADL and the American Jewish Committee showed that "the percentages of the 'most anti-Semitic' among both blacks and whites represent declines from levels" recorded in the 1960s (Rubin 1995).

While it was true that some surveys showed a rise in anti-Jewish feelings among some younger black respondents when compared to whites, these numbers may have reflected recent Caribbean immigration. ADL surveys over the years have failed to distinguish between foreign-born and native-born blacks, and evidence shows elevated anti-Semitism among new immigrant populations. In 2002, the ADL conducted a new survey and found a near doubling in the number of African Americans who fell within the "not anti-Semitic" category (from 14 percent in 1992 to 23 percent in 2002); meanwhile, "forty-four percent of foreign-born Hispanics" fell into the most anti-Semitic category. Indeed, Gary Rubin later concluded that the 1992 ADL survey actually found that "African Americans, like everyone else, became less prone to anti-Semitism as their incomes and education rise" (Rubin 1995).

Whether these ADL surveys measured black resentment towards whites in general or towards Jews in particular is not clear, especially when the reports highlighted sensational points about blacks at the expense of other more profound trends in the data. Nor did the analysis disentangle anti- and philo-Semitic sentiments. For example, participants were typically asked to state the degree to which they agreed with the statement, "Jews stick together more than other Americans." While responses were aggregated to create an anti-Semitism scale, strong agreement with the statement could indicate an admiration for Jews rather than resentment towards Jews. Indeed, since at least the late nineteenth century, black American intellectuals have repeatedly idealized characteristics imputed to Jews, such as superior intelligence, group loyalty, economic acumen, and cultural cohesion.[14]

One Israelite interviewed for this project, an elder with the Church of God and Saints of Christ, put it this way:

Ah, what I love about the white Jews, and the black man if he wants to get somewheres, the white Jew works inside the circle. He don't let no one come inside the circle that is not a Jew. He will go out and get what he wants and come right back into that circle, but you cannot penetrate that circle.

Such philo-Semitism can easily morph into anti-Semitism, as when Farrakhan proclaims that, "No black man or woman becomes a multimillionaire without friendship in the Jewish community."[15]

The Man or the Message?

Perhaps no event created more internal conflict for black Jews than the Holy Day of Atonement, Reconciliation, and Responsibility, a.k.a. the Million Man March. Held in the nation's capital in October 1995, the march brought together hundreds of thousands of black American men, in strength and in unity. It was unprecedented and likely never to be repeated. Yet this moment of glory came at a personal cost to many Jews and at a political cost to many black public figures who relied upon both black and Jewish support. Others, who remained committed to the fledgling relationship between blacks and Jews, grappled with the reality that such a positive and potentially healing event had been organized by an anti-Semitic provocateur.

Ironically, the march's theme of atonement was honed by Farrakhan during a conversation he had with Rabbi Capers Funnye, who later shared the details with me:

He'll never say it, but his statement about "there has been much bloodshed between the PLO and the Israelis," and yet Rabin and Arafat were able to reach across the blood and over the tyranny and to shake hands and to try to seek a path to reconciliation. "Can we not make a bridge over rhetoric?" is what I told him to say. Before the march, he invited me to be a participant in the march, he talked about wanting to atone, and I gave him the Hebrew definition of *kippur* . . . and talked to him about atonement and so forth, and he said he wanted to have the crescent and the star. He wanted to have the Christian cross; he wanted to have the *Magen David* [Shield of David], the Star of David. He said, "Rabbi Funnye, I want you to be there. I really want you to be a part and be a speaker." I said, "I think that your idea, the concept of it is wonderful." I said, "Yes, there needs to be atonement," I said, "but you know, Minister, there's already a day of atonement that we have. It's gonna precede the march. And the date that you have set for the march, if you had spoken with me before you set the date, you know, if you had taken my input, I would have told you I couldn't do it that day."

The march was held during Sukkot, a Jewish festival held in the fall, which is the reason Funnye had been unable to attend. Otherwise, he assured me, he would have participated. In fact, several men from his congregation attended and taped the event for him. After the march, Funnye met with Farrakhan:

And I told him what I saw through the lens of the television. I saw a mist actually descend upon that valley of the thousands upon thousands upon thousands of black men that were there. And it was a mist; it was a heavenly mist. Washington did not know what to expect; they shut down the city. Congress closed. And I have to tell you, leaving Farrakhan's speech and his diatribe for two and a half hours aside, there was a spiritual happening there that was so powerful that I think it sent shock waves. And the men that went didn't go because they were Muslims. There're only fifty thousand members of the Nation of Islam nationally, or worldwide. They went because of the conviction that [they] heard the calling.

Others felt more conflicted. Many black leaders—including United Negro College Fund president William Gray III, controversial New York clergyman Reverend Al Sharpton, New York state senator David Paterson, former New York City mayor David Dinkins, Harlem Democratic congressman Charles Rangel, civil rights leader Bayard Rustin, former NAACP president Benjamin Hooks, and, of course, Jesse Jackson—felt compelled to distance themselves from the intolerant rants of Farrakhan, but some waited nearly two months to do so.[16] Hesitant to publicly disown him, they may have feared a racial backlash from their political constituencies and supporters. Despite his vitriol, Farrakhan was viewed among many black Americans as an uncomfortably necessary longtime agitator in the struggle against white bigotry.

Public pressure on black leaders to disavow Farrakhan's comments actually emboldened black activists and alienated black moderates, who resented being held accountable merely because of their race. Did white folks think that blacks bore responsibility for the actions of other blacks? After all, New York's many different African American communities—Harlem, Crown Heights, Bed-Stuy, Flatbush, and Ocean Hill-Brownsville—were distinct communities made up of multiple organizations and groups and not simply one monolithic racial community, just as the various Jewish communities of the Lower East Side, Riverdale, Flatbush, Borough Park, Crown Heights, and Fort Washington did not together constitute a single Jewish community. The pressure was felt by black and biracial Jews as well (Haynes 2013).

Allen, a New York-born Jew with an Ashkenazi mother and West Indian father, was a journalist for a leading news outlet. Like many black Americans of the period, he resented the Farrakhan litmus test that blacks had to pass: "It's only black people that are responsible for every other black person. I mean, but in our situation, you know, that's the only place where people want to know what an entertainer is doing to repudiate a politician. . . . He's speaking for himself or his group, but no one goes to Jerry Seinfeld and says, 'Well you, you're going to repudiate whoever.' It's just not an issue."[17]

When our conversation turned to the Million Man March, however, he drew an ethical line, stating that he couldn't give support to someone so "wrongheaded." He also expressed disappointment that Farrakhan had failed to later capitalize on the political momentum he had built: "And the interesting thing was really how little has . . . really come out of it. I mean, anyone else who put together, whatever it was, six hundred thousand? Anyone else who had done that, there would have been more to come out of it in terms of real goals within that community."

Josh, too, could not support the march, although he felt cheated from what seemed like a once-in-a-lifetime event:

> I did think of the Million Man March. . . . And again, because I would have wanted to [go] if it wasn't Farrakhan. . . . It's kind of a once-in-a-generation kind of thing. But I couldn't really associate myself with him. I wouldn't have had any self-respect. And again, that's part of the disappointment, you know. You deprived me of my chance to actually be part of something that I'm entitled to partly because you're embarrassing.

Julius Lester saw little difference between Farrakhan and Republican congressman Newt Gingrich, both of whom worked against the interests of black people:

> Why can't people see that Farrakhan is a political conservative? He breathes fire, but he talks family values, whatever the fuck that is. Just look at him with the bow tie and the suit; the man is a conservative. But black people can't see that, because they are taken with the entertainment value, the appeal to their emotions, to their basest emotions. It is an abomination.

Lester rejected the argument, touted by many blacks at the time, that one could separate the man from the message:

> I certainly was very disappointed that Minister Farrakhan is a man who has openly espoused anti-Semitism, and yet all those men went to Washington and probably dismissed it, didn't take it seriously, . . . because I know damn well that if some Jew was going around the country, and part of his message was antiblack, and Jews said, "Well, we don't believe that part of it," or "Don't take that part so seriously," black folks would go to war. And so that kind of moral duplicity really offends me. Because as a black person, I wouldn't accept it if a white person did it. So why do blacks accept it when a black person does it?

Interestingly, my data demonstrates that black Jews who had experienced bias from white Jews (i.e., had their status as Jews questioned) were less critical of Farrakhan. Dana, the biracial Jew from Chicago, had spent her early childhood in the middle-class enclave of Hyde Park. When she was in the sixth grade, her family moved to the South Side and lived just around the block from the Nation of Islam headquarters: "We were always sort of on the lower economic range of all the people we interacted with until we moved to that neighborhood, where we fit in economically very well, but my mother was the only white person in the whole neighborhood." She was conscious of the role that class played in defining her identity and sense of belonging within her Jewish community: "There were class issues that led to not belonging that I think trumped my emotional analysis of the racial issues that were going on in my congregation.

Like many African Americans, she credited Farrakhan with building black communities: "I think there are lots of things that Farrakhan and the Nation are doing that are, you know, that are wonderful for our community in relationship to an increasing prison population which needs positive intervention, you know." Her criticism of the Nation focused on its conservative, bootstraps politics: "The kind of lack of analysis about material reality and social justice issues annoys me to no end." She was equally annoyed by Jews' preoccupation with Farrakhan and their insistence that blacks renounce him:

> I have problems with his gender politics. I have problems with his sexuality politics. . . . I have problems with his heterosexism. I have problems with his African politics. . . . And I have problems with his anti-Jewishness. . . . But I would not elevate my problems with Farrakhan's anti-Jewishness above the other problems I have with him. And it annoys me to no end that white Jews insist that we do, . . . particularly because it affects the African American community, and I don't think his anti-Jewishness affects the Jewish community much. Which is not to say that we shouldn't be upset by anti-Jewishness wherever it appears, . . . but . . . I think Jews have much more serious problems.

Pnina, on the other hand, who had experienced rejection from blacks for much of her life, was vehement in her condemnation of Farrakhan:

> I think he is a master manipulator. I think he's a charlatan. I think he is a murderer. . . . When we, when we were in Chicago and we were having this little conference, [a black Jewish female friend] said, "Oh, let's go look at Farrakhan's house." So, we drove around. And I have to tell you, I have been to Sachsenhausen [concentration camp]. I have been to Dachau. I have been to Bergen-Belsen. I have been to horrible places. I have been to, you know, prisoner of war camps during the Iraq-Iran War. . . . I have dealt with evil, right? And I felt as I was driving around his house at night the way I felt when I was driving around Evin Prison in Tehran [notorious prison in Iran known for torture and brutal interrogations]. That there is an open hole in the earth boiling with gas and sulfur, and it's in

his living room. And the evil in the core of the earth is just bubbling up. I don't like this man.

In contrast, Rabbi Bill Tate, an Israelite who had fought hard—and largely in vain—to be recognized as a legitimate Jew, did not view Farrakhan as an anti-Semite, explaining that "he came from a doctrine where all white people were against black. . . . Even the anti-Semitism amongst blacks amongst us is based on our experience with those wrong Jews." He distinguished Farrakhan's vitriol from his actions—"he's not shooting anybody"—and upheld his message of self-defense: "He's advocating killing you if you bother him. Well, what's the difference between that and an eye for an eye and a tooth for a tooth? Which is Judaic in principle."

Participants who felt secure in both the black and Jewish communities or who did not seek affirmation as a Jew were more dispassionate in their responses and provided a nuanced critique of the debate. Rebecca, for example, a biracial Jew who felt equally comfortable in both communities, downplayed Farrakhan's aggression, viewing him more as a media hound than an anti-Semite:

Look, if I was in the media and trying to get attention, I would attack the Jews faster than anybody. I mean if you're trying to get attention, you know what to do. And, you know, Farrakhan was nowhere in the Jewish press until the Jesse Jackson thing, and he stepped in front of Jesse and said, "If you're going to attack Jesse, you're going to have to deal with me," and then kind of attacked the Jews to, I think, to divert attention and get attention for himself.

In the same vein, Rabbi Ben Levy, who was born into the Black Hebrew faith and had limited dealings with white Jews, questioned whether Farrakhan was really anti-Semitic:

It could be, again, when you start in a community from the ground up, to give them some pride, that may be one method used. You know, to give them pride. Self-worth, you know, had to be one of his methods that's being used a lot. And again, before you can develop and start to deal in other areas, you know, you have to first, you know, crawl. You know, and start to say, "Well, I am somebody." And I think that's what he has instilled in the black community. But as he starts to move them into the religious realm, Islam, when he starts doing Islam, now you're in something totally different. You lose the, the race card when you start dealing there. So, he's in that area where, you know, he's strong with black pride being America and so forth.

Meanwhile, Rabbi Funnye, who serves on the Chicago Board of Rabbis, described himself as "somewhat in the door." He had met with Farrakhan several times and had on occasion acted as an intermediary with the Jewish community. He was more critical of Farrakhan than other Hebrews I spoke with, describing him at one point as having a messiah complex. In his view, Farrakhan invoked anti-Semitism as a tool, "an evil tool to . . . project oneself. . . . But what plays? Teaching the upliftment of all of humanity doesn't play. It's not good ink. It's not good media. People who struggle with each other, that's good media. What's his name, Khalid Muhammad, he makes twenty thousand dollars to lecture on college campuses, to call white folks and the pope a cracker. I can barely get seven fifty or a thousand." At the same time, Funnye maintained that anti-Semitism was useful to the Jewish community—an observation that has also been made by noted Jewish spokesmen like Alan Dershowitz:[18]

> I mean he [Farrakhan] had ADL purchase a full page-and-a-half ad in the *New York Times* to run the diatribe of some of his speeches a couple of years ago. How much would it have cost him to get that run? Then he gets on *Newsweek*, or one of those magazines, where they've got him looking all, you know, monstrous, and he hates Jews. Hell, he can't go a hundred feet in any direction of his house without hitting the house of a Jew. And he can go in any one of several neighborhoods in this city that are predominantly black, that are upper crust, where he can live. So, I know it's rhetoric. [*Laughs*] And I said to the guy at ADL and the guy at AJ [American Jewish] Committee, I said, "if Louis Farrakhan said he was packing bags and moving shop to Ghana tomorrow, you'd say, 'please wait till after this campaign,' 'cause he's helping you raise money.'"

Funnye recognized the universal allure of anti-Semitism, as well as its appeal among blacks:

They [Farrakhan's audience] get charged when there's a defined enemy. . . . It is easier when you can give them a name that you don't necessarily have to put a particular face with. Because Jew can also mean white face in his [Farrakhan's] rhetoric. Because the projection that he's giving is that Jews are white, you see. So, it can actually be code talk.

Like Rabbi Tate, Funnye dismissed Farrakhan as ultimately harmless:

Let me tell you why I don't see him as a threat. He has no power. He doesn't have a police force. He doesn't have an army. For Muslims to desecrate synagogues or Jewish cemeteries or present some type of physical threat to an individual Jewish person or to a Jewish group, there's a no-win scenario, because the law is on the side of the Jew in that instance, who's being attacked. Jews are treating Farrakhan, in some respect, like they are treating political powers in other situations throughout history.

Yet for Josh, a biracial Jew, Farrakhan made everything more difficult.

He doesn't raise in me the anger and rage that he [does] in . . . the majority of Jews. He actually raises in me . . . just more shame and disappointment. I guess I'm pissed off at him. You know, it's like, "Lou you make it harder for me."

When the California African American Museum in Los Angeles held its symposium, "Where Worlds Collide: The Souls of African-American Jews," the panel of black Jews from across the nation never dreamed they would find themselves colliding with blacks from Los Angeles' ghettos. But the forces that pitted poor blacks against middle- and upper-class Jews could not be contained. The largely middle-class panelists were repeatedly placed in the position of defending their racial authenticity and picking sides. Indeed, black Jews in America are regularly asked, by both blacks and Jews, to pick sides. And often they are found wanting. According to journalist Bernard Wolfson, Rabbi Capers Funnye empathizes more with Farrakhan than with "his white Jewish detractors" (Wolfson 2000). Yet in my interviews, I found Funnye and other black Jews to be walking a racial tightrope between allegiance to their white coreligionists and their black brethren.

You may choose but might not be chosen. Challenges to one's racial and religious authenticity influence both personal identity and investment in the reference group. This dynamic, in turn, affects group loyalty, as self-preservation ultimately becomes entwined with group preservation. The extent to which one personally perceives a threat to one's group is based, in part, on the extent to which the group perceives you as a member. The racial and anti-Semitic slights experienced by black Jews, black converts to Judaism, and Black Hebrews/Israelites demonstrate the ascendancy of group insider status, rather than of personal identity claims, in determining the impact of and resistance to racism and anti-Semitism.

The conclusion revisits the concept of racial projects as a paradigm for understanding both European-descent Jews and black Jews in the United States and expands on the concept to argue that not all racial projects yield, or are motivated by the pursuit of, socially allocated goods and resources. In the case of Black Hebrews and Israelites, the desired outcome of the project is a reframing of blacks' contributions to civilization and their central role in the engine of history. The conclusion also examines recent trends within the Reform and Hebrew Israelite movements and considers the ongoing shift in the boundaries of American Jewish identity and its implications for the future of American Jewry.

Conclusion

In August 2015, the Union for Reform Judaism presented a bold new face for the movement: a young biracial Jew rooted firmly in both the Jewish and African American communities. April Baskin was appointed "Vice President of Audacious Hospitality," a title that carries the responsibility of aggressively welcoming Jews who remain disengaged from communal Judaism—a striking 50 percent of the Jewish population. These include Jews of color like Baskin (whose mother is an Ashkenazi Jew and father an African American), as well as Jews by choice, gentiles exploring Judaism, LGBTQ Jews, Jews with disabilities, interfaith couples, multiracial families, Jewish millennials, and Jews who are unaffiliated and uninspired by traditional communal offerings.

In an interview with Baskin in August 2016, she described this demographic as "no longer a wave but the ocean of Jewish life." Her appointment attests to these changes and represents a bold shift from the narrow focus on interfaith couples that once defined Jewish outreach. Today's Reform movement is beginning to boldly reimagine a Jewish community outside the boundaries of Ashkenazi culture, whiteness, and heterosexual norms.

Baskin has also served as acting executive director of the Jewish Multiracial Network, whose mission is to "advance Jewish diversity through empowerment and community building with Jews of Color and Jewish multiracial families." At just thirty-two years old, she joins the ranks of leaders like Yavilah McCoy, a black Orthodox Jew who in 2000 founded the Ayecha Resource Organization, in an increasingly diversifying Jewish world. In May 2016, McCoy and Baskin joined some 140 black, Asian, Latino, multiracial, and non-Ashkenazi Jews at the first "Jews of Color National Convening," a three-day event held at New York's Congregation Beit Simchat Torah. For the first time, representatives of both Mizrahi Jews (with roots in the Arab world) and Sephardi Jews (with Spanish roots) came together with black Jews and other racial minorities under the banner of "Jews of color" to explore racism within and outside the Jewish community. This shift represents a significant organizational development and reflects generational changes in social identity among Jewish immigrants of color who, historically, have rejected identification as minorities.

The convening went well beyond the perfunctory sharing and celebration of culture, arts, and cuisine that typically characterize multicultural events and embraced a bold political agenda, as evidenced by the titles of many of its workshops, including "Introduction to Historical and Systematic Racism in Jewish Communal Life," "Community Organizing: Building a Powerful Racial Justice Movement as JOCs," and "Power, Oppression, and Privilege." The topics reflect not only the shared Jewish values of *tikkun olam* (repairing the world) and social action but also the unique space occupied by Jews of color within the struggle for racial justice.

The Black Lives Matter movement has further provided Jews of color with a strategic opportunity to engage, as both Jews and people of color, in the fight for racial justice. According to Baskin, who has been active in the movement, "Black Lives Matter is a Jewish issue because there are Black Jews. The freedom and safety of black people is tied to our Jewish values for justice and safety for everyone. Our country collectively has not been vocal enough." In July 2016, Jews of color were at the forefront of the Black Lives Matter protests in New York, with many chanting "Black lives matter, black Jews matter" (Simon 2016). Jews for Racial and Economic and Justice, a progressive organization based in New York, described the July protests as "a multiracial gathering led by Black Jewish movement leaders as well rabbis and rabbinic students, and others." The protests culminated with an act of civil disobedience outside the New York City Police Department's 6th Precinct in the West Village, in which "Black Jews, rabbis, and rabbinic students read from Lamentations, blew the shofar and recited the Mourner's Kaddish" (JFREJ 2016).

While the Reform movement has actively pursued a more racially pluralistic vision for Judaism, the 2016 appointment of Rabbi Capers Funnye as chief rabbi of the International Israelite Board of Rabbis marks a significant turning point for the Hebrew Israelite movement and Ethiopian Hebrew congregations. After sixteen years of organizational malaise, the Israelite board selected as its new leader a man who has chosen to seek formal recognition among Conservative Jews, having undergone a *halakhic* conversion in 1985 under both Conservative and Orthodox rabbis. The appointment of Funnye amounts to at least tacit recognition of rabbinic law by the International Israelite Board of Rabbis. At the same time, Funnye remains committed to the right of Ethiopian Hebrews to keep their culture and interpret rabbinic law as they see fit. He views his appointment as an acknowledgment of a broader Jewish collectivity, one he described to me as including European Jews, Ethiopian Jews (in Israel as well as those who remain in Ethiopia), South American Jews, and "West African Jews of the Diaspora."[1]

I flew to Chicago in October 2015 to witness the installation ceremony, a semiprivate event and the precursor to Funnye's formal acceptance in June. The ceremony was held at Funnye's home congregation, Beth Shalom B'nai Zaken Ethiopian Hebrew Congregation. Three large conga drums occupied one side of the stage; on the other, a full gospel choir sang, "All praise be to God, Hallelujah!" Women were dressed colorfully but modestly, with long loose garments that fully covered their bodies. Their hair was covered with simple white wraps or multicolored African scarves; some donned elaborate hats that resembled those worn by church ladies. Some men wore dashikis; others, suits; and still others, flowing robes under prayer shawls. There were a variety of head coverings on display, from Sephardi-style *kippot* to African-style *kufis* to white knit skullcaps to Ashkenazi-style *yarmulkes*. The house was nearly full when I arrived. I acknowledged congregants with the traditional Hebrew greeting for the Sabbath, "Shabbat shalom," and was greeted in return with the words, "Shabbat shalom, brother." I took my seat among the men and was helped by fellow worshipers to find my place in the program. Many around me chanted the traditional Hebrew prayers by heart.

Shortly after the Shabbat services, the installation ceremony for Rabbi Funnye began. As Funnye entered the sanctuary, the congregation sang a Hebrew hymn based on Psalms 133:1, *Hineh mah tov umah na'im, Shevet achim gam yachad* ("How good and pleasant it is, For brothers to sit together"). He was escorted by five Israelite rabbis, all dressed in white robes and white knit skullcaps: Yahat Yehudah, Eliyahu Yehudah, Yeshurun Levi, Baruch A. Yehudah, and Sholomo Levy. Rabbi Funnye's son, Aaron Funnye, also joined the procession.

Funnye's Judaism, which blends rabbinic, African American, and African-centered traditions, reflects his desire to remain free, "to travel in all circles and bring it back to our community." At the same time, his Conservative credentials are likely to bring increased recognition and support for the Ethiopian Hebrews and their academy. In fact, the *Washington Post* headlined its coverage of the event "With New Chief Rabbi, Black Hebrew-Israelites Make Bid to Enter the Jewish Mainstream" (October 30, 2015). In a conversation with Funnye a few weeks after the installation ceremony, he spoke of the attention he was receiving from mainstream Jewish organizations. He had already been approached by some thirty congregations (including a modern Orthodox congregation in Riverdale) and fifteen Jewish leaders, including a Lubavitcher rabbi who asked how they could work together. His vision, as he put it to me, is to "bridge the continental divide together."

The emergence of black Jews in mainstream Jewish organizations and communities reflects how boundaries of American Jewish identity continue to change. In the process of organizing themselves, they are forging alliances and drawing boundaries across and within cultural and *halakhic* lines. The Internet has become a powerful tool for Jews of color to connect and build community and to strengthen their own identities, as witnessed by such websites as Jews in ALL Hues, the Jewish Multiracial Network, Jewnited Nations, and, most recently, Mosaic Matches, an online dating site for Jews of color. And with the recent formation of the Fédération des Juifs Noirs in France, such organizing has taken on an international dimension (Levitt 2007).[2]

With the growing numbers and visibility of Afro-American Jews, the Jewish preoccupation with Jewish celebrities has taken on a new form—one which we might call "Black-Jewhooing," or the naming and claiming of black Jews by other black Jews. Black-Jewhooers call out such celebrities as Daveed Diggs, a star of the Tony Award-winning Broadway musical *Hamilton*; Yitz Jordan (a.k.a. Y-Love), a hip-hop artist (and black convert to Orthodox Judaism), whose music incorporates Yiddish, Hebrew, and Aramaic; and Shyne, a Belize-born rapper who converted to Orthodox Judaism and changed his name from Jamaal Barrow to Moses Levi. Celebrities are important, but Black-Jewhooing also encompasses displaying knowledge about historically significant black Jews, such as Uncle Billy, Ephraim Isaac, and the Reform rabbi Alysa Stanton, often touted as "the first African American female rabbi." Meanwhile, interest in black Jews has grown among the broader Jewish public. Websites, such as "Jew or Not Jew," which specialize in keeping track of Jews, increasingly cite black Jews, and Jewish newspapers and magazines report on the growing presence of black Jews. Throughout February 2016, *Tablet*, an online Jewish magazine, published a series on "Black Jews You Should Know," written by MaNishtana in celebration of "Black History Month 5776." Black-Jewhooing has become a mainstream Jewish practice.

Meanwhile, tens of thousands of Africans who practice Judaism—from Ghana (House of Israel), Uganda (Abayudaya), Zimbabwe (Lemba and Jews of Rusape), South Africa (Lemba), Kenya (Kasuku Jewish Community), Nigeria (Igbo), Rwanda and Burundi (Tutsi-Hebrews of Havila), Cameroon (Beth Yeshouroun), Madagascar (Descendants of David), Timbuktu (Zakhor)—have also become more visible (Bruder 2008; Miles 2013; Parfitt 2013; Brettschneider 2015; Weil 2016). The Igbo in particular have been the subject of recent scholarship. Some thirty thousand of Nigeria's thirty million Igbo identify as Jews and believe that they descend from the ancient Israelites. William F. S. Miles has chronicled the way in which the Igbo Jews (or "Jubos" as he describes them) use Messianic Judaism to bridge the missionary Christianity of colonialism with the Judaism of their ancestors (Miles 2013). Echoing groups like Congregation Temple Beth'El in Philadelphia, the Jubos are both very Jewish and very Nigerian and have been called the first "Internet Jews," since they use the Internet to "retrospectively impute cultural affinities between Jewish and Igbo traditions traceable to a Hebraic ancestry" (Miles 2013). Historian and social anthropologist Daniel Lis (2014) details how Afro-Jewish identities, such as those held by the Igbo, emerged part and parcel with colonialism and transatlantic slavery. The Igbo were viewed by colonists as lighter than (and therefore racially superior to) their neighbors, much like the Tutsi in Burundi (Lis 2014).

Noted ethnologist Ellen Bruder, who traces the elaboration and development of Jewish identities in Africa after the turn of the twentieth century, concludes that African Jewish identities have had a long history. She suggests that "spatial and metaphorical relationships historically connected Africans with Judaism" (Bruder 2008) and that "several sources indirectly testify to the antiquity of a Jewish presence, in particular in western Africa, or a Semitic presence in southeastern Africa" (Bruder 2008). Bruder, who is president of the International Society for the Study of African Jewry (ISSAJ), details a variety of African cultural groups that believe they are returning to Judaism. Like her mentor, Tudor Parfitt, she explores the intertwining of biblical myth and local lore that resulted in reimagining Africans as Jews. The rise of what she calls Judaizing communities is not only a response to colonialism and political antagonisms but also a "sociological transformation akin to ethnogenesis" [the formation and development of an ethnic group] as a psychological, cultural, and political response to shifting local conditions (Bruder 2008).

Here in the United States, both Judaism and Islam have served as political vehicles to challenge the dominant racist representations of black people. As religious studies scholar Edward E. Curtis IV observed in *Black Muslim Religion in the Nation of Islam, 1960–1975*, the new narratives link religion to specific understandings of the historical destiny of black people as a whole (Curtis 2005). This link was clearly voiced by one of my participants, an Israelite elder at the Church of God and Saints of Christ, who described both Islam and Judaism as "black people" religions, explaining, "They go back to the histories of their people. To Israel, far, far back, they go back, if they continue to go back they are going back into black, . . . and that was the original."

Black Jews embody the dimensions of ethnicity, race, and religion and yield new narratives and social identity constructions. Countermemories of a Jewish past can be reconstructed to promote present-day political agendas that rival dominant hegemonic narratives and competing interpretations of history and memory (Zerubavel 1995). Yet the narratives of both normative "white" Jews and Black Hebrews/Israelites might be framed as a political struggle to recover their roots, be it through a national project, as in the case of Israel, or through a racial project, as in the case of Hebrew Israelites. Differences between Black Hebrew and rabbinic narratives, much like those between Palestinians and Jews, stem from their radically different reconstructions of the past (Zerubavel 1995).

While all Black Jews share a broad stroke of historical understanding— that is, "that somewhere in the context of their literature and their thinking and their psyche, they feel that Judaism is an African-born religion and faith and that the matriarchs and the patriarchs were people of color," as Rabbi Funnye put it—there are significant differences in the ways in which they practice Judaism and recognize *halakhic* rules for Jewish membership. We might view each group as situated along a *halakhic* continuum, with religiously observant congregations, such as the Commandment Keepers in Harlem and the Beth Shalom B'nai Zaken Ethiopian Hebrew Congregation in Chicago, on one end and black supremacist groups, such as the Nation of Yahweh and the Israelite School of Universal Practical Knowledge, on the other. Meanwhile, Israelite congregations such as the Church of God and Saints of Christ, which adhere to the tenets of biblical Judaism, fall somewhere in the middle. So too do the Black Hebrews (the Black Jews of Dimona), who reject the hegemony of rabbinic Judaism.

On a countercontinuum, we could plot the degree to which an individual's or group's racial ascription impacts their sense of communal identification with other Jews. Here, the Ethiopian Hebrews, who embrace a universal understanding of Judaism, occupy the low end of the continuum, while black nationalist Israelite groups, who characterize white Jews as imposters, occupy the high end. Those in the middle would once again include the Israelites, who, as one Israelite participant put it, tend to "read race into scripture," as well as the Hebrew Israelites, who "deny that they are Jews . . . yet . . . make political claims to Israeli citizenship under the Law of Return, actions that invoke Jewish identity by default" (Fernheimer 2014).

In a nation that applies a religious definition of citizenship, such counterprojects subvert accepted norms and narratives on blackness and Jewishness and bring into relief the blurred continuum between race and ethnicity. While both terms—race and ethnicity—may evoke inferior social standing, only the former is imbued with a sense of national and political exclusion. We know, for example, that Jews, Italians, and Irish were once considered racial outsiders from a social standpoint, yet they reaped all of the political benefits of being classified as white. The concept of racial projects serves as a viable framework for explaining the ideological work carried out by Black Hebrews and Israelites; it had been modeled with much success by eastern European Jewish immigrants, who cast off the stigma of the Oriental to become Westerners, a prerequisite for whiteness (E. L. Goldstein 2008).[3] It could in fact be argued that Black Hebrews have sought to occupy the space abandoned by European Jews, which provided a direct link to an ancient civilization and elevated blackness to biblical chosenness.

What is new, however, is that for many indigenous Black Hebrew and Israelite groups in the United States, the gains they have sought have been largely nonmaterial. Other than the Dimona Hebrews, most Israelite groups have not sought entry to Israel, nor have they hoped that their claims would bring them any material advantage at home. What they have sought is a new collective narrative, one that challenges the essentialist notions of modern Jews, who presume that Jews are white.

While the Ethiopian Hebrews have deracialized their claims to Jewish identity, the roots of all of these groups are based in a counterhegemonic narrative. Using the exodus story to draw an ancestral line between themselves and the ancient Israelites of the Hebrew Bible,[4] they cite the Old Testament to bolster claims that the ancient Hebrews were not white. Some turn to Leviticus 13, which deals with the plague of leprosy and identifies a bright white spot or the whitening of hair as signs of the plague.

Rabbi Rudolph Windsor, an Israelite and author of *From Babylon to Timbuktu: A History of Ancient Black Races Including the Black Hebrews*, argues that white Jews were likely the descendants of blacks who had been turned white by leprosy (Windsor 1988). The book, first self-published in 1969 and currently in its nineteenth printing, exemplifies the new paradigm of Afrocentricity—an African-based ideological framework that uses rhetoric to re-center thought while critiquing Eurocentric scholarship—that was burgeoning in the 1960s and embraced within the newly forming black studies departments of the period.

Windsor's book is widely circulated among Hebrew Israelites and was often cited by those I encountered in my research. Other books that link blacks to ancient Israel include Father Joseph Williams's *Hebrewisms of West Africa: From Nile to Niger with the Jews* (2013); *The Lost Tribes, A Myth: Suggestions towards Rewriting Hebrew History* (1930)—an obscure work written by Allen Howard Godbey, that can easily fetch one thousand dollars on Amazon; and *We the Black Jews: Witness to the "White Jewish Race" Myth* (1996) by Josef A. A. ben-Jochannan, a self-identified Black Jew. For ben-Jochannan, Moses was "an African (or Egyptian)," and everything he knew about the spiritual realm and "Jehovah" was learned from the Nile valley African theosophy he calls the "Craft of

Amun-Ra" (Ben-Jochannan 1993; Walker 2001). While at first cursing European Jews for hijacking Judaism, he ends with a racial coup, arguing for the black origins of the world religions.

As African, Caribbean, and black American Jews create new collective narratives, we gain a glimpse of how all Jews ultimately create an imagined community. Indeed, the very idea of a "Jewish community," in the sense of a culturally cohesive community of Jews, is a modern invention (Anderson 2006). The classical Talmudic rabbis apparently had little use for the term "Jew" since "in the Mishnah, the term *yehudi*, "Jew"—or its feminine singular, *yehudit*, or masculine plural, *yehudim*—appears in only three passages" (Baker 2005). In fact, the term *yehudim*, which means "Judeans," was an ethnogeographic term that was first used by gentiles and Greek writers to refer to an imagined, covenanted nation in Judea; meanwhile, the Jewish people referred to themselves as "Israel" (Baker 2005). As Israelites in Western nations embraced the language of gentiles and Greeks, they began to call themselves Jews. In the late nineteenth century, the concept of a religious covenant, which the term "Israel" represents, was superseded by the idea of a Jewish community, which integrated new ideas about Judaism from diasporic communities in Europe and the Americas. The new Reform and Conservative movements redefined Judaism and helped to construct a new concept of Jewishness that was independent of, and could even be stripped of, any religious meaning. Jews became cultural and ethnic, and Judaism was reframed as a community of choice.

Sociologist Arnold Dashefsky describes two diverging paths to Jewish identity: the traditional, communal "straight way" journey, embedded in Jewish law (i.e., either Jewish parentage or formal conversion) versus a more Western-influenced "roundabout path," which emphasizes individual rights and choice over communal responsibility (Dashefsky, Lazerwitz, et al. 2003). The latter path emerged after the emancipation of Jews from ghettos towards the end of the eighteenth century, when the formation of Jewish denominations (such as Reform Judaism) spawned new expressions of Jewish religious practice: "New social contacts developed and intermarriage increased in Western countries, resulting in the notion of Jewish identity being divided between a strict *halakhic* religious definition as well as a non-*halakhic*, ethnic definition, which emerged in Israel and the Diaspora" (Dashefsky, Lazerwitz, et al. 2003).

Contemporary Jewish identity has shifted away from its historical religious core, but it is religion that continues to serve as the main gatekeeper to communal belonging. "Becoming a Jew" can only be accomplished through conversion, yet Jewish identity more often reflects ideas about culture and ancestry than religious belief or observance. According to the 2013 Pew survey of US Jews, only 19 percent of American Jews reported that observing Jewish law was an essential part of being Jewish, while 56 percent cited working for equity and social justice as essential, and 73 percent cited remembering the Holocaust (Pew Research Center 2013). Conversion to Judaism may in fact be a viable way of rejuvenating religious Judaism and insuring its future. And as Gary Tobin wrote in his provocative proposal to mainstream Judaism, "Our challenge is to envision a community within the context of America where ethnic and religious walls are permeable. . . . Judaism must become attractive both to those who are born Jews, or they will choose to leave, and to those who were not born Jews, so they will choose to join" (Tobin 1999).

Still, biological definitions of Jewishness persist and are reinforced by modern technologies. DNA has offered more reliable proof of ancestry than oral familial history and is often treated as the final arbiter of "truth" about one's identity (Nelson 2016). Today, forty-three direct-to-consumer DNA-testing services promise to "predict your genetic ethnicity" and reveal "a breakdown of your ethnicity" (Moray, Pink, et al. 2017).[5] Called "recreational genetics" or "vanity tests" by researchers, these recent applications of genetics have reinforced essentialist notions of Judaism. Ironically, our feverish attention to the 0.1 percent of the human genome that is not shared has spawned "Technologies of Belonging," which might be better framed as a "backdoor to eugenics" (Phelan, Link, et al. 2013; Wade 2014).

The very terms that individuals use to express their Jewish identities—"Ashkenazi Jew," "Sephardi Jew," "biracial Jew," "Black Jew," "Hebrew Israelite," or "Jew of color"—are significant for determining relevant group boundaries. In the case of "Black Jews," Janice Fernheimer writes, their "very acts of identifying themselves as Jewish matter not only to themselves but also to the larger collective of Jewish and Black peoples with whom they associate and connect through this claim" (Fernheimer 2014).

[I]dentity claims involve at least a two-step process: In the first step, an individual or group makes a specific claim to an identity and in the second step that claim is recognized, accepted, or rejected by the group with whom the individual or group identifies. (Fernheimer 2014)

In the case of Judaism, the concept of pedigree and documentation imposes a further burden of proof on the individual making the claim. Rabbi J. David Bleich posited that this burden is as old as Judaism itself:

> *Yalkut Shim'oni* [an *aggadic midrash*] reports that at the time of the giving of the Torah on Mt. Sinai the gentile nations became exceedingly jealous. They, too, wished to be the recipients of the revealed word of God and to share in the prophetic experience at Sinai. The Midrash depicts God as brusquely rejecting their claim with the retort, "Bring me the record of your pedigree as My children are bringing." This, declare the Sages, is the meaning of the verse "and they declared their pedigrees after their families . . ." (Num. 1:18). In order to be counted among the members of the community of Israel and to be granted recognition as a Jew it was necessary for each of the wanderers in the wilderness to present documentary proof or to adduce witnesses prepared to testify with regard to the genealogical purity of the petitioner's lineage. (Bleich 1977)

From a *halakhic* perspective, Bleich wrote, the only relevant question with respect to the status of today's black Jews is "whether or not they have established a valid claim to Jewish identity by virtue of either birth or conversion" (Bleich 1975). Bleich is a professor of Talmud at the Rabbi Isaac Elchanan Theological Seminary of Yeshiva University, as well as a professor of Jewish law and ethics at the Benjamin N. Cardozo School of Law. He has written extensively on the application of Jewish law to contemporary issues and is the author of the seven-volume series, *Contemporary Halakhic Problems*. In one essay, entitled "Black Jews: A Halakhic Perspective," he constructs three distinct categories for the purposes of responding to "the various groups of black Jews seeking recognition and legitimization":

> There are some groups whose members maintain that they are the original Jews and that white Jews of European descent are "Edomites," usurp-

ers whose claims to Judaism are spurious. Since these black Jews view themselves as the only true Jews, they see no need, and have no desire, to convert to Judaism. From our perspective, and our view of Jewish history and identity, there is very little that need be said in response to such a claim. . . . There are other black Jews who, regardless of their personal feelings and convictions, recognize that in order to gain acceptance as members of the community of Israel it is necessary for them to undergo the process of conversion. . . . This group poses no *halakhic* problem whatsoever. . . . The area of most concern is with regard to a third category of Black "Jews," comprised primarily of individuals rather than of organized groups. There are significant members of Black "Jews," who, for whatever reason, feel a very close affinity to Judaism. These individuals refuse to undergo conversion either because of an erroneous belief that they are Jews by virtue of birth or because of a feeling that since they have conducted themselves as observant Jews for an extended period of time conversion is superfluous. Resistance to acceptance of the necessity for conversion is based, at least in part, upon the identity crisis such a process would precipitate. (Bleich 1975)[6]

When the first National Jewish Population Survey was conducted in 1971, most sociologists agreed that the American Jewish community was predominantly white, middle class, and of German or eastern European stock (Lavender 1977). Black Jews, along with Sephardi Jews, were labeled "sub-communities," existing on the periphery of American Jewry (Lavender 1977). Six years later, the scholar Robert T. Coleman, himself a black Jew, wrote a passionate essay entitled "Black and Jewish—and Unaccepted," in which he described the rejection, "broken engagements," and snide remarks experienced by black converts (Coleman 1977). That same year, scholars began invoking the term "minority within a minority," observing that black Jews had been "neglected" in studies of the American Jewish communities, much like Ashkenazi and Sephardi Jews had been neglected in studies of American society itself. Today there are hundreds of thousands more black Jews than the eight thousand Coleman identified in his 1977 essay. Once considered to be on the margins of American Judaism, they have advanced closer to center stage and are gaining the attention and respect of Jewish media, institutions, and philanthropic organizations.

We can see how globalization, immigration, assimilation, patrilineal descent, and the blurring of racial boundaries have fractured the idea of any single, coherent Jewish archetype, if one ever truly existed. Today, it is increasingly clear that we can no longer speak of "the Jew" the way sociologist Louis Wirth did in his classic study, *The Ghetto*, when he asserted that modern-day Jewish identity was the product of life in the ghetto (Wirth 1927). In fact, the emancipation of Jews from both the European and American ghettos paved the way for Jewish assimilation, which was soon reflected in rising out-marriage rates that opened up new opportunities for both Judaic practice and Jewish identity (Dashefsky, Lazerwitz, et al. 2003). Today, more than ever, the terms "Jew," "Judaism," "Jewishness," and "Hebrew" have increasingly contested meanings within a uniquely American context where the conflation of whiteness and Judaism can no longer be taken for granted.

While the assimilationist project of European Jews entailed multiple morphings, moving them along an East/West and black/white binary that brought resources and opportunity and that inextricably linked Jewishness to whiteness, the last fifty years have transformed the landscape of American Judaism. The increased visibility of biracial Jews and black converts to Judaism has destabilized the Eurocentric view of Jews, while reforms adopted by the Ethiopian Hebrews and their International Israelite Board of Rabbis attest to the reduced hold of race-centrism among Hebrew Israelites. While blackness remains a stigmatized status and marker of identity in American society, the steady growth and normalization of black Jews, as well as the tendencies towards rabbinic-style Judaism by some Hebrew Israelites, suggest that the answer to "Who is a Jew in America?" is in the process of being rewritten.

ACKNOWLEDGMENTS

Few subjects in American life are as filled with controversy and contention as the relationship between blacks and Jews. This project began in 1998, after I had written about black-Jewish relations in Harlem when I was an assistant professor at Yale University. My interest in Jews of African descent emerged soon after. At the time, my Jewish wife—Syma Solovitch—and I had left New York City for Connecticut. At her lead, we became members of Congregation Beth El–Keser Israel (BEKI), a vibrant Conservative synagogue in New Haven, and it was there that I first encountered African American Jews. Just seeing other black faces in the congregation made me feel at ease, and I too was soon embraced by this warm religious community. I was also inspired by the unshakeable moral convictions of the community's spiritual leader, Rabbi Jon-Jay Tilsen, and I identified with the strong ethical compass that I found in Judaism. In fact, well before committing to doing this research project, I began participating in the Shabbat Learners' Minyans, where renowned Jewish scholars like Steven Fraade—the Mark Taper Professor of the History of Judaism at Yale University—patiently answered my naive questions. I loved that questioning was not only permitted, it was encouraged!

In 2001, when Syma and I moved to Davis, California, we found a new Jewish home at Congregation Bet Haverim. Like the folks at BEKI, Rabbi Greg Wolfe and his congregation provided a welcoming space to learn, question, and cultivate a love and appreciation for rabbinic Judaism. They invited me to participate in community life, and the rabbi spent countless hours nurturing my curiosity of Judaism while gently nudging me towards making a more personal commitment. Meanwhile, a few old-guard members of the community, like Norma and Larry Rappaport, treated me like family and made me feel that I had a place in the community. My gratitude to these two extraordinary communities cannot be overstated.

This work bridges the disciplines of sociology, Jewish studies, and African American history, and I have relied on the collective contributions of many scholars. First, I would like to thank Howard Winant for sharing critical feedback on racial and social theories and the cultural sociology of race, and for championing my work from the start through the very end. Two other scholars deserve special mention: Michael Scott Alexander provided meticulous edits and a wealth of knowledge about Judaism and American religion, while Bruce A. Phillips shared his extensive expertise on the historical demography of American Jewry. I am also grateful to my friend Benjamin Orlove, who applied his expertise in ethnography and cultural identity to my early drafts, and to my colleagues at the University of California, Davis, Bill McCarthy and Diane Wolf, whose critical reviews and insights elevated this work considerably. Finally, Gary and Diane Tobin, founders of the Institute for Jewish and Community Research in San Francisco, supported my participation in the Be'chol Lashon (In Every Tongue) think tanks and provided me with invaluable access to their networks.

A number of individuals became vital links to Jews of African descent and contributed historical references on the population. I am indebted to Rabbi Debra A. Bowen, the late Rabbi Bill Tate, Michelle Stein-Evers, Morris Fred, Ara Francis, Rabbi Capers Funnye, Walter Isaac, the late Julius Lester, the late Rabbi Hailu Moshe Paris, Efraim Sicher, and Michael Twitty.

I write from the perspective of a sociologist, not a religious practitioner. I wish to thank Yale University for a Junior Faculty Fellowship (in 1998), which allowed me to jump-start the project, and the University of California, Davis, which granted me sabbatical leave to complete the book. I also thank my colleagues and friends in the Department of Sociology at UC Davis, who provided feedback on many early drafts of the book.

I am grateful to my team at New York University Press, especially my editor Jennifer Hammer, who pushed me to hone my arguments and conducted scrupulous line editing. I am also indebted to my research assistants, Joan Meyers and Kim Ebert, who meticulously coded my interviews and offered keen insights, as well as Robert Vercoe, who guided me through navigating my early searches on the Internet.

Many close friends provided moral support and intellectually stimulating conversation throughout the duration of this long project. I thank Rebecca Plante, Raúl Aranovich, Gail Wallace, Wendy Simonds, Kenneth Firestein, Stu and Linda Bresnick, Stephan Cohen, Tony Wexler, and the Siegel family. My wife, Syma, was the first to recognize the value of exploring the world of Jews of African descent in America. Her unyielding support, relentless faith, and first-rate editorial assistance transformed what might have been an overwhelming endeavor into a labor of love.

Lastly, I owe special thanks and gratitude to the many black Jews, Hebrews, and Israelites who willingly shared their stories with me; to the many rabbis who shared their knowledge of Judaism and Jewish history with me; and to the families who invited me into their worlds when I showed curiosity. Without you, I could not have written this book.

NOTES

INTRODUCTION

1 The 1990 NJPS was conducted by a team of scholars led by Director of Research Barry Kosmin and performed under the auspices of the Council of Jewish Federations.

2 With weighting procedures, the sample represented 3.2 million American households and 8.1 million individuals, a number of whom were not themselves Jewish.

3 January 7, 1992 correspondence from the files of Jeff Scheckner, research consultant on the 1990 NJPS.

4 Updated estimates were carried out by the Steinhardt Social Research Institute at Brandeis University. The report, *American Jewish Population Estimates: 2012*, published in September 2013, represents the "accumulated findings of research conducted over the last decade." According to the report, approximately 70,000 of 4,206,000 Jewish adults, or 1.66 percent of Jewish adults, were black (non-Hispanic) (Tighe, Saxe, et al. 2013, 13). While this figure is lower than that reported in the 1990 NJPS study, it reflects data collected on Jewish adults only. We can assume if children in the home were also counted, the numbers would be significantly higher and align more closely to those reported in the NJPS study.

5 In April 1998, Michael Gelbwasser reported that a 1990 estimate put the number of black Jews at two hundred thousand. See Michael Gelbwasser, "Organization for Black Jews Claims 200,000 in US," *The Jewish News of Northern California*, April 10, 1998, www.jweekly.com. Also cited in Owen Moritz, "Black Writers Hail Jewish Moms," *Daily News*, May 10, 1998, www.nydailynews.com.

6 Personal correspondence with Bruce A. Phillips, professor of sociology and Jewish communal service at Hebrew Union College-Jewish Institute of Religion, Los Angeles.

7 American Jewish Population Project, "Population Estimates for Jewish Adults by Age, Education and Race, 2013" (Waltham, MA: Brandeis University, Maurice and Marilyn Cohen Center for Modern Jewish Studies, Steinhardt Social Research Institute), www.ajpp.brandeis.edu, retrieved February 14, 2018.

8 See James Landing's *Black Judaism: Story of an American Movement* (2002) for the first use of this convention. Most scholars have used the term "Black Jews" to refer to both Hebrew Israelites and *halakhic* Jews. However, the historian James Tinney includes "those groups who adopt Jewish practice but maintain a Christological perspective." This statement reflects the tendency of scholars to conflate cul-

tural practices of Black Jews with broader cultural themes within black religious practice. Some practices are Christian in orientation, while others are not. For example, the religious music of various black Jews—the "Kosher Gospel" music of Joshua Nelson or the choral style of the Congregation Temple Beth'El choir—demonstrates that many of the aesthetic characteristics of Christian gospel style are imbedded in their sacred music. These aesthetics are not Christian but a part of slave culture and Afro-American cultural repertoire, yet observers associate these styles with the predominantly Christian practices of black American communities. Tinney does argue that Hebrews are more Orthodox and Israelites more nationalist, but I found that the use of terms varied by individual. See James Tinney, "Black Jews: A House Divided," *Christianity Today*, December 7, 1973, 52–54. See also Yavilah McCoy's *The Colors of Water*, a Jewish gospel musical describing the matriarchal journey of four generations of an African American Jewish family.

9 Since the mid-1950s, Karaites from Cairo have settled in Chicago and the San Francisco Bay Area.

10 For all known history, Jewish sects have differed on fundamental matters of theology. The Pharisees believed in the Oral Law, the coming of a messiah who would return the Hebrew people to Israel, and the notion of freedom of choice. The Sadducees, the probable ancestors of modern-day Karaites, rejected the Oral Law and tended to interpret scripture literally. Even the desert-dwelling Dead Sea sect rejected the sanctity of the Temple in Jerusalem (Telushkin 1991, 131–132). Neusner (1995) argues that Orthodox Jews traditionally believe that Moses was given the Oral Law as well as the Ten Commandments at Mount Sinai. The rabbinic tradition maintains that the "orthography and the vocalization of Scripture—its writing and its discourse—are not in Scripture; rather they are the possession solely of rabbinic tradition" (38). While the rabbinic tradition encouraged the masses to study Torah and live in accordance with its teachings in order to be "Israel," it also constructed a Judaism that made the authority of the sages indispensable (39). Among the Orthodox, rabbinic authority remains the "true" legitimate interpreter of Torah. They alone have license to define the Jewish people.

11 As early as 1977, Rabbi David Dore, a reported leader of the Ethiopian Hebrew Congregation since 1973, became the second black to receive a degree from Yeshiva University. Rabbi Dore is the grandson of Wentworth Matthew, the founder of the Ethiopian Hebrews. Numerous others members of the EH, as well as of Congregation Temple Beth'El, have received degrees from *yeshivot* or master's degrees in divinity.

12 The "one-drop rule" is known by anthropologists as "hypodescent" and by the courts as the "traceable amount rule."

13 Between 1977 and 1988, 15,826 Beta Israel reached Israel (Spector 2005, 12).

14 Other biographies and memoirs of Jews of African descent have also appeared, but these have received less notoriety. See Yelena Khanga, *Soul to Soul: The Story of a Black Russian American Family 1865–1992* (New York: W. W. Norton, 1992); Ahuva Gray, *My Sister, the Jew* (Southfield, MI: Targum Press, 2001); Lily Golden,

My Long Journey Home (Chicago: Third World Press, 2002); and Ernest H. Adams, *From Ghetto to Ghetto: An African American Journey* (Bloomington, IN: iUniverse, 2009).

15 International Israelite Board of Rabbis, "Beth Elohim," Black Jews, www.black-jews.org, retrieved October 2015.

16 The term "Ashkenazi" is used by scholars to refer to Jews whose families came from Europe, although most Ashkenazi Jews have likely never thought of themselves as such.

17 The term "Sephardi" is used by scholars to refer to Jews descended from Iberia, such as Ladino speakers from the Balkans and Turkey, or to "Spanish" Jews.

18 This is the translation given in the King James Version of the Bible, which was often favored by early Hebrew Israelite groups. One Hebrew translation, from the Chabad website, is the following: "Gifts will be brought from Egypt; Cush will cause his hands to run to God."

19 The Hebrew word *ayecha* literally means "Where are you?" but is often interpreted as "Where do you stand?" It is the first question that appears in the Torah and was posed by God to Adam (Genesis 3:9). Joshua Venture Group provides fellowships of $100,000 to support "visionary leaders" and to transform their ideas into "stable organizations" that can "scale, grow, and transform Jewish life." See "What We Do: Dual Investment Program," Joshua Venture Group, http://joshuaventuregroup.org, retrieved December 22, 2017.

20 The museum closed in 2008.

21 Hosted by Sheree Curry Levy, a journalist and former university instructor in Des Moines, Iowa, the Facebook group remains active and, as of December 2017, has more than 1,450 members.

22 The Central Committee of American Rabbis declared that the child of one Jewish parent was "under the presumption of Jewish descent" so long as *mitzvot* (commandments) or publically formal acts of identification were performed. See the *Yearbook of the Central Conference of American Rabbis* 94 (1984): 172–173. According to Genesis 17, Abraham became a Jew at the moment he was circumcised, making circumcision an identifier of Jewish males. However, in Leviticus 12:3, God commanded that Jewish males be circumcised on the eighth day. Abraham married Sara and established patrilineal descent as the basis for Jewish lineage through his son Isaac and Isaac's son Jacob. However, following the destruction of the Second Temple, Hebrews turned inward, and by the time that the Mishnah was codified during the era of Roman occupation in the third century CE, Jewish descent had shifted from the paternal to the maternal line.

23 The Nation of Yahweh's founder, Yahweh ben Yahweh (the former Hulon Mitchell Jr., also known to his congregation as Moses Israel), claimed to be the son of God sent to deliver the black people of America. In 1992, Yahweh and six of his followers were found guilty of federal charges of conspiracy to commit fourteen murders, two attempted murders, and arson in order to maintain their multimillion-dollar organization. Ben Yahweh, who died in 2007, had attacked nonblack Jews

as "imposters" and called Jews of European ancestry "the synagogue of Satan." The group has drawn condemnation from the Anti-Defamation League, as well as from the Southern Poverty Law Center, which includes them on its list of hate organizations.

24 The word "Abayudaya" means "descendants of Judah," according to community leader Aaron Kintu Moses. Also known as the Bayudaya, the group began when Semei Kakaungula led his community in Mbale, Uganda, towards embracing and practicing Judaism in 1919.

25 Unlike traditional Orthodox practice, egalitarianism is a philosophy that gives women access to traditionally male roles in religious services and within the synagogue organization.

26 I also have collected data from secondary historical sources and Internet discussion groups, as well as from two focus groups—one with black converts and one with biracial Jews—conducted in November 2000 by Gary Tobin and Alex Karp at the Institute for Jewish and Community Research in San Francisco. Their snowball sample was heavily biased towards San Francisco Bay Area residents.

27 According to Primack (1998, xiii), Kulanu was inspired by the Israeli organization Amishav (My People Return), which was founded in 1975 by Rabbi Eliyahu Avichail.

28 We use the less pejorative Spanish term *converso* (convert) rather than the Portuguese terms *cristão-novo* (new Christian) or *marrano*, which had been used during the fourteenth and fifteenth centuries to label Jewish converts to Catholicism.

CHAPTER 1. JEWS, BLACKS, AND THE COLOR LINE

1 Sand cited in Rita Rubin, "'Jews a Race' Genetic Theory Comes under Fierce Attack by DNA Expert," *Jewish Daily Forward*, May 7, 2013, www.forward.com.

2 William I. Thomas and Dorothy Swaine Thomas, *The Child in America: Behavior Problems and Programs* (New York: Alfred A. Knopf (1928), 572.

3 Eugenics and demography have used statistics in attempting to show the mechanisms of race and racial difference. Tukufu Zuberi has traced the history of the idea of race and its relation to inferential and descriptive statistical analysis in his book *Thicker Than Blood: How Racial Statistics Lie* (Minneapolis: University of Minnesota Press, 2001). Zuberi outlines the role of eugenics and eugenicists in the evolution of both demographic study and modern social statistics and shows that these ideas held merit through the Second World War.

4 See "Entartete Musik," Decca Classics, www.deccaclassics.com, retrieved February 14, 2018.

5 While Lamarck is generally credited with the idea of the inheritance of acquired characteristics, he merely maintained the importance of the theory.

6 The historian David Roediger uses the German term *herrenvolk* to describe the kind of republicanism that unfolded in the United States during this period.

7 Interview with Rabbi Capers Funnye conducted on March 12, 1999, in his office in Chicago. Rabbi Funnye spoke as the rabbi and was interviewed with the under-

standing that I was recording the words of a public person and that they would therefore not remain confidential.

CHAPTER 2. B(L)ACK TO ISRAEL

1 Interview conducted on July 28, 1999.

2 The word "Falasha" is from the Ethiopian language Ge'ez. Isaac (2003, 65) suggests that the term comes from "Falasi, falasiyan, from the Ge'ez roots 'falis'—to immigrate, to be uprooted, and to be exiled. Falasiyan is an ancient Classical Ethiopic Ge'ez term well-attested as a descriptive term for Jewish exiles related to the words galut, goha." Kaplan (1992, 66) argues that the term "Falasha" is best translated as "landless person, a wanderer" and stems from the land policies that removed their rights of ownership.

3 This analysis was the outgrowth of participant observation and information interviews at venues frequented by self-identified Ethiopian Jews between 1998 and 2004. I attended religious services at numerous synagogues and was a participant-observer at Be'chol Lashon think tanks attended by leaders of the Beta Israel religious community. In addition, crucial data was gleaned from secondary historical sources and previously published studies of Ethiopian immigrants to Israel.

4 According to *The Columbia Encyclopedia*, 6th ed. (2012), s.v. "Sahara," "The desert includes most of Western Sahara, Mauritania, Algeria, Niger, Libya, and Egypt; the southern portions of Morocco and Tunisia; and the northern portions of Senegal, Mali, Chad, and Sudan. The E Sahara is usually divided into three regions—the Libyan Desert, which extends west from the Nile valley through W Egypt and E Libya; the Arabian Desert, or Eastern Desert, which lies between the Nile valley and the Red Sea in Egypt; and the Nubian Desert, which is in NE Sudan."

5 Blumenbach called them the "Jalof" or "Wuluf."

6 The location of Ophir has been long debated by biblical scholars, archaeologists, and theologians. Some conjectured it was in southwest Arabia (in today's Yemen), while others placed it at the African shore of the Red Sea. Still others believed it was in Mozambique or Zimbabwe.

7 In 1871, the German explorer and geologist Karl Mauch came upon the Great Zimbabwe in his travels (Tyson 2000).

8 Sometimes called secret Jews, crypto-Jews, or Iberian *conversos*, the term *marrano* was a derogatory Spanish term that referred primarily to forced Jewish converts to Christianity from the late fourteenth to the seventeenth century.

9 In 1915, the American Jewish Committee donated $5,000 to Faitlovitch's group. See "Gives $5,000 for Falashas," *New York Times*, March 17, 1915.

10 See "Rabbis Are Urged to Renew Proselyting," *New York Times*, October 22, 1925.

11 Kaplan identifies three lines of interpretations of the term *ayhud*. One associates it with the Ethiopian religious term for Jews; the second, with rebels against the Solomonic king; and the third, with groups viewed as heretical by the Christian church. Thus, how one reads the term as it changes across the centuries deter-

mines whether one draws a historical link between the Beta Israel and the ancient Hebrews.

12 See the Ethiopian text *Teezaza Sanbat* (The Commandments of the Sabbath) and *Abba Elijah* translated by Wolf Leslau (1951).

13 See "Operation Magic Carpet," Alaska Airlines, www.alaskaair.com, retrieved February 14, 2018.

14 Human Rights Watch estimates that the famine of 1964–65 killed tens of thousands, while the great famine of 1983–85 killed an estimated four hundred thousand in northern Ethiopia (not counting those who were killed by resettlement). See Africa Watch, *Evil Days: 30 Years of War and Famine in Ethiopia* (New York: Human Rights Watch, 1991).

15 Formal recognition of the Beta Israel as Jews first came from the Sephardi Chief Rabbi of Israel, Ovadia Yosef, in 1973. Rabbi Yosef based his judgment on the ruling of the sixteenth-century chief rabbi of Cairo, David ben Solomon ibn Abi Zimra, and the views of Israel's former Ashkenazi chief rabbi, Abraham Isaac Kook (Weinstein 1985, 214; Parfitt 1987, 129).

16 Interview with Aviva conducted in January 1999.

17 See Ori Lewis, "Blood Donation Collectors Thrown Out of Israeli Parliament," *Reuters*, December 11, 2013, www.reuters.com.

18 The term has also been used to describe the dark-complexioned Yemenite Jews.

19 Hellenistic, rabbinic, and targumic literature in Hebrew and Aramaic tends to translate *kush* as "black Africa" (Goldenberg 2003). Rabbinic and targumic literature also refers to the land of Nubia/Ethiopia as "Barbaria," as well as "Africa."

20 Observed by many Ethiopian Jews since 1986, Hazkarah corresponds to the traditional Beta Israel celebration of Sigd, which marks the giving of the Law to Moses on Mount Sinai.

21 See JTA, "First Black Miss Israel Titi Aynaw Reflects Growing Diversity in Jewish State," *Jewish Daily Forward*, March 28, 2013, www.forward.com.

22 In the report, the term "Ethiopian Israelis" refers to Israelis born in Ethiopia and Israelis with one or more parents born in Ethiopia.

CHAPTER 3. BLACK-JEWISH ENCOUNTERS IN THE NEW WORLD

1 Rabbinic legal texts are known as "responsa," a term that refers to a body of written opinions on matters of biblical law that remained inexplicit. Some opinions have concerned life among Muslims and Christians, while others deal with matters like marriage or ritual observance. Today, responsa address questions such as whether a funeral can be held for suicide victims or whether a rabbi can convert an atheist who wishes to become a Jew. Different Judaic movements sometimes have different responsa. In the Reform movement, the Central Conference of American Rabbis has published *American Reform Responsa: Collected Responsa of the Central Conference of American Rabbis, 1889–1983*, while a group of twenty-five rabbis serve on the Committee on Jewish Law and Standards and has set *halakhic* policy for the Rabbinical Assembly of the Conservative movement.

2 Their rights were conferred by Governor Johan Maurits (Klooster 2009, 34).

3 Biblical, Talmudic, and medieval Jewish law all prescribed rules governing relations between Jews and slaves that were recognized by Moses Maimonides and eventually compiled into the *Shulchan Arukh* by the sixteenth-century scholar Joseph Caro. His work was widely adopted across the Jewish world during the seventeenth century.

4 According to the congregational minutes "The taxes the Jewish community imposed on its members included a levy of five soldos for each slave purchased from the Dutch West India Company" (quoted in Faber 1998, 17).

5 See Jacob R. Marcus and Stanley F. Cheyt, eds., *Historical Essay on the Colony of Surinam, 1788*, trans. Simon Cohen, Publications of the American Jewish Archives 8 (New York: KTAV, 1974).

6 "Tudor Parfitt's Remarkable Quest," *Nova*, February 22, 2000, www.pbs.org.

7 See "In the Shadow of the Tower: The Works of Josef Nassy, 1942–1945" (March 24–May 31, 1992," Cooley Gallery Exhibition Collection, Reed Digital Collections, https://rdc.reed.edu, retrieved February 15, 2018.

8 "Josef Nassy," *Holocaust Encyclopedia*, United States Holocaust Memorial Museum, www.ushmm.org, retrieved February 15, 2018.

9 "Founder: Rabbi L. E. Dailey, z"l," Congregation Temple Beth'El, www.bethel-ph.org, retrieved February 15, 2018.

10 See "Black Synagogue Takes Big Step Forward," *CBS News*, April 8, 2009, www.cbsnews.com.

CHAPTER 4. BACK TO BLACK

1 Interview with Elder William Samuel Williamson conducted on January 12, 1999, in Stratford, Connecticut.

2 The House of Israel had been founded by Rabbi Edward Emmanuel Washington.

3 The Ethiopian Hebrew Congregation was founded in 1915 and is Chicago's first Black Hebrew synagogue.

4 Interview with Rabbi Bill Tate conducted on March 23, 1999, in Brooklyn, New York.

5 During the eighteenth century, the Hasidic movement emerged in response to the oppressive conditions experienced by Jews in eastern Europe. The aim of the Hasidim is to follow the commandments of the Torah while reflecting the divine spark of God in all beings and in all things by bringing joy into their daily practice. After the Holocaust, remnants of the movement reorganized in Israel, Europe, and America. The Satmar Congregation Yetev Lev D'Satmar, whose early rabbis originated in Hungary, dominates the Hasidim within the Williamsburg section of Brooklyn, New York. The group gets its name from the Satu Mare region that lies in the multinational corner of Transylvania, Romanian (see Gersh 1959). Much like Israelite groups, the ultra-Orthodox Hasidim follow the teachings of charismatic *rebbes* (rabbis), who are considered to be *tzaddikim* (righteous men). Chabad-Lubavitch is another ultra-Orthodox fundamentalist Hasidic sect,

sometimes known as "Black Hats" for the black fedoras that they typically wear. Chabad is known for its "Chabad-mobiles" and for hosting Shabbat dinners in an effort to return lost Jews to the fold.

6 From a church report to the US Bureau of the Census, 1906 (quoted in Landing 2002, 53).

7 The International Israelite Board of Rabbis was organized in 1970 as an outgrowth of the Ethiopian Hebrew Rabbinical College founded back in 1925.

8 "Beth Elohim History," Black Jews, www.blackjews.org, retrieved February 15, 2018.

9 Interview with Rabbi Benyamin Levy conducted on March 24, 1999, in Queens, New York.

10 Bayard Rustin led a delegation to Israel in January 1980, after attempts by the Israeli government to detain Hebrew Israelites at the airport invoked charges of racism. The delegation of black representatives found no racism. See David K. Shipler, "Israelis Urged to Act over Black Hebrew Cult," *New York Times*, January 30, 1981, www.nytimes.com.

11 The Israeli contingent operates these restaurants in Beersheba, Tel Aviv, and Dimona.

12 Interview with Barbara conducted on August 5, 1999, in Chicago.

CHAPTER 5. YOUR PEOPLE SHALL BE MY PEOPLE

1 Interview conducted in January 1999.

2 Interview with Michael Twitty conducted in December 2001, by phone.

3 Interview with Rabbi Neal Weinberg conducted in January 1999.

4 Acquired from the Sefaria website at www.sefaria.org.

5 The 1990 NJPS, which uses a more restrictive definition for counting Jews, reported fewer numbers.

6 Interview with Alice conducted in January 1999.

7 Michael W. Twitty, "About," *Afroculinaria* (blog), https://afroculinaria.com, retrieved February 15, 2018.

8 Interview with Julius Lester conducted on January 20, 1999, at his home.

9 Interview with Cleo conducted in January 1999.

10 Interview with Marissa conducted in January 1999.

11 Taglit-Birthright Israel is an organization dedicated to offering free ten-day cultural immersions in Israel to young Jewish adults between the ages of eighteen and twenty-six.

CHAPTER 6. TWO DROPS

1 Interview with Josh conducted in January 1999.

2 Interview with Seymour conducted in March 1999.

3 Interview with Dana conducted in January 1999.

4 Robin Washington, the former editor of Minnesota's *Duluth News Tribune*, is the moderator of Black and Jewish, a closed Facebook group.

5 Interview with Rebecca conducted in December 1999.

6 US Census Bureau, "1990 Census of Population and Housing: Public Use Micro-data Samples," www.census.gov, last revised September 28, 2012.

7 Steven A. Holmes, "Study Finds Rising Number of Black-White Marriages," *New York Times*, July 4, 1996, www.nytimes.com.

8 This cover introduced the nation to a composite image of a human face using morphing technology.

9 While Nikki Khanna alone conducted the study in 2005–2006, its findings are reported in an article coauthored by Khanna and Cathryn Johnson (2010).

10 Interview with Nadine conducted in April 2000.

11 Interview with Hannah conducted in April 2000.

12 Interview with Seymour conducted in May 1999.

13 Interview with Jake conducted in May 1999.

14 Interview with Olga conducted in January 1999.

15 Interview with Pnina conducted in January 1999.

16 Interview with Jonathan conducted in March 1999.

17 Interview with Allen conducted in June 1999.

18 Interview with Andrew conducted in April 1999.

CHAPTER 7. WHEN WORLDS COLLIDE

1 *Highlights from a November 1998 Anti-Defamation League Survey on Anti-Semitism and Prejudice in America* (New York: Anti-Defamation League, 1998).

2 For details about the Ocean Hill-Brownsville strike, see Mayor's Advisory Panel on the Decentralization of the New York City Schools, *Reconnection for Learning: A Community School System for New York City York City Schools* (New York: Prager, 1969); Diane Ravitch, *The Great School Wars: A History of the New York City Public Schools* (Baltimore: Johns Hopkins University Press, 2000); Podair (2004, 113–114); Daniel Perlstein, "Community Control of Schools," in *Encyclopedia of African American Education*, vol. 1, ed. Kofi Lomotey (Thousand Oaks, CA: SAGE, 2010), 180–82.

3 "Action at UMass Prompts Cries over Censorship," *New York Times*, May 29, 1988, cited by Cole (2003, 37).

4 Article in the *Chicago Tribune*, June 19, 1988 (quoted by Cole 2003, 37).

5 The *Village Voice* piece to which Lester refers here is the September 10, 1979 essay, "The Uses of Suffering," in which he criticizes the establishment civil rights leadership for standing behind US Ambassador Andrew Young, who met secretly with the PLO.

6 The full text of Farrakhan's radio broadcast is reprinted in "Farrakhan on Race, Politics, and the News Media," On the Record, *New York Times*, April 17, 1984, www.nytimes.com.

7 A *minyan* is the minimum number (ten) of adult male Jews traditionally required for Orthodox communal worship. An adult male Jew is defined as one who has passed his thirteenth birthday. While Orthodox Jews observe this definition, the

Conservative, Reform, Reconstructionist, and Renewal movements recognize women in the *minyan*.

8 Min found that nearly 45 percent of subjects agreed that "Koreans are overly concerned with making money" and that "Koreans care only about other Koreans."

9 This conflict and the attempts of the community to resolve it are depicted in the eighty-five-minute documentary *Blacks and Jews*. Directed by Alan Snitow and Deborah Kaufman, it was broadcast on PBS's *POV* after first premiering at the Sundance Film Festival in 1997.

10 *Bridges and Boundaries* was organized by the Jewish Museum in New York City, in collaboration with the National Association for the Advancement of Colored People. It traveled throughout the country from 1992 through 1994. According to the *New York Times*, the show included more than 350 works of art, artifacts, photographs, documents, film and television excerpts, and press materials. See Sheila Rule, "Exhibition on Blacks and Jews Is Faulted," *New York Times*, April 20, 1992, www.nytimes.com.

11 Based on archival tapes of the event that were loaned to me by Rick Moss, program manager of history at the California African American Museum in Los Angeles.

12 Interview with Rick Moss conducted in January 1999.

13 Founded in 1995–1996 by the American Jewish Committee and Howard University, *Common Quest* magazine folded in 2000 due to lack of funding.

14 For discussion, see Jonathan Karp, "Ethnic Role Models and Chosen Peoples: Philosemitism in African American Culture," in *Philosemitism in History*, edited by Jonathan Karp and Adam Sutcliffe (Cambridge, Cambridge University Press, 2011), 211–234.

15 Louis Farrakhan, June 26, 2010, in Atlanta, Georgia, quoted in "Farrakhan: In His Own Words," Anti-Defamation League, www.adl.org, updated March 20, 2015.

16 See Larry Yudelson, "Black Leaders Distance Themselves from Address by Aide to Farrakhan," *Daily News Bulletin* (Jewish Telegraphic Agency), January 26, 1994, www.jta.org; and Jon Nordheimer, "Angry Echoes of Campus Speech," *New York Times*, January 26, 1994, www.nytimes.com.

17 Journalist Bernard Wolfson first used the "Farrakhan Litmus Test" in his controversial exposé on the formation of the Alliance of Black Jews, "The Soul of Judaism," which was published in the September 1995 issue of *Emerge* magazine and again in Chireau and Deutsch (2000), under the title "African American Jews: Dispelling Myths, Bridging the Divide" (Wolfson 2000).

18 See Alan M. Dershowitz, *Chutzpah* (New York: Touchstone, 1991).

CONCLUSION

1 Based on conversation with Funnye a few weeks following the October 2015 installation ceremony.

2 The Fédération des Juifs Noirs earned recognition from the Conseil Représentatif des Institutions Juives de France (Representative Council of French Jewish Insti-

tutions), an organization that serves as a liaison for Jewish institutions and links French Jews to the World Jewish Congress.

3 Like the Hebrew Israelites, Ashkenazi Jews used "racial rhetoric" to resist being cast out of the human family as nonwhite.

4 Biale (2006) recounts how the *Mekhilta*, an early rabbinic *midrash*, was used to lend support to the idea that the Israelite nation remained biologically distinct during their four hundred years of Egyptian captivity (xviii). The *Mekhilta*'s claim that the Israelites did not violate biblical sexual prohibitions has been used to argue that the Israelites did not intermarry. But historical evidence suggests that during the period of Egyptian captivity, Jews intermarried and even adopted foreign names, like Moses.

5 See the websites for AncestryDNA, www.ancestry.com, retrieved February 3, 2018; and Helix, www.helix.com, February 3, 2018.

6 Also reprinted in Bleich (1977, 315).

BIBLIOGRAPHY

Alexander, M. S. and B. D. Haynes (2016). "The Color Issue: An Introduction." *American Jewish History* 100(1): ix–x.

Anderson, B. (2006). *Imagined Communities: Reflections on the Origin and Spread of Nationalism*. Brooklyn, NY, Verso.

Arendt, H. (1978). The Jew as Pariah: A Hidden Tradition. *The Jew as Pariah: Jewish Identity and Politics in the Modern Age*. R. H. Feldman. New York, NY, Grove Press: 67–90.

Astren, F. (2004). *Karaite Judaism and Historical Understanding*. Columbia, SC, University of South Carolina Press.

Aviv, C. S. and D. Shneer (2005). *New Jews: The End of the Jewish Diaspora*. New York, NY, New York University Press.

Azoulay, K. G. (1997). *Black, Jewish, and Interracial: It's Not the Color of Your Skin, but the Race of Your Kin, and Other Myths of Identity*. Durham, NC, Duke University Press.

Baer, H. A. and M. Singer (1992). *African American Religion in the Twentieth Century: Varieties of Protest and Accommodation*. Knoxville, TN, University of Tennessee Press.

Baker, C. (2005). "When Jews Were Women." *History of Religions* 45(2): 114–134.

Baldwin, J. (1985). Negroes Are Anti-Semitic Because They're Anti-White. *The Price of the Ticket: Collected Nonfiction, 1948–1985*. New York, NY, St. Martin's Press: 425–433.

Barron, S. (1991). *Degenerate Art: The Fate of the Avant-Garde in Nazi Germany*. Los Angeles, CA, Los Angeles County Museum of Art; and New York, NY, Harry N. Abrams.

Baum, B. (2008). *The Rise and Fall of the Caucasian Race: A Political History of Racial Identity*. New York, NY, New York University Press.

Beck, E. M. and S. E. Tolnay (1990). "The Killing Fields of the Deep South: The Market for Cotton and the Lynching of Blacks, 1882–1930." *American Sociological Review* 55(4): 526–530.

Ben-Ari, N. (2015). "Black and Jewish? Try Explaining That to Israel's Airport Security." *Haaretz*, Jan. 6. www.haaretz.com.

BenEzer, G. (2002). *The Ethiopian Jewish Exodus: Narratives of the Migration Journey to Israel, 1977–1985*. New York, NY, Routledge.

Benite, Z. B.-D. (2009). *The Ten Lost Tribes: A World History*. Oxford, Oxford University Press.

Ben-Jochannan, Y. A. A. (1993). *We the Black Jews: Witness to the "White Jewish Race" Myth.* Baltimore, MD, Black Classic Press.

Benor, S. B. (2016). "Black and Jewish: Language and Multiple Strategies for Self-Preservation." *American Jewish History* 100(1): 51–71.

Ben-Ur, A. (2009). A Matriarchal Matter: Slavery, Conversion, and Upward Mobility in Suriname's Jewish Community. *Atlantic Diasporas: Jews, Conversos, and Crypto-Jews in the Age of Mercantilism, 1500–1800.* R. L. Kagan and P. D. Morgan. Baltimore, MD, Johns Hopkins University Press: 152–169.

Ben-Ur, A. (2014). The Cultural Heritage of Eurafrican Sephardi Jews in Suriname. *The Jews in the Caribbean.* J. S. Gerber. Portland, OR, Littman Library of Jewish Civilization: 169–193.

Ben-Ur, A. with R. Frankel (2012). *Remnant Stones: The Jewish Cemeteries and Synagogues of Suriname: Essays.* Cincinnati, OH, Hebrew Union College Press.

Ben-Yehuda, S. (1975). *Black Hebrew Israelites from America to the Promised Land.* New York, NY, Vantage.

Berger, G. (1978). *Black Jews in America: A Documentary with Commentary.* New York, NY, Commission on Synagogue Relations, Federation of Jewish Philanthropies.

Berger, G. (1987). *Graenum: An Autobiography.* Hoboken, NJ, KTAV.

Berman, P. (1994). *Blacks and Jews: Alliances and Arguments.* New York, NY, Dell.

Beveridge, A. (2001). "Redefining Race." *Gotham Gazette,* Feb. www.gothamgazette.com.

Biale, D. (1998). The Melting Pot and Beyond: Jews and the Politics of American Identity. *Insider/Outsider: American Jews and Multiculturalism.* D. Biale, M. Galchinsky, et al. Berkeley, CA, University of California Press: 17–33.

Biale, D. (2006). *Cultures of the Jews: A New History.* New York, NY, Schocken Books.

Biale, D., M. Galchinsky, et al. (1998). *Insider/Outsider: American Jews and Multiculturalism.* Berkeley, CA, University of California Press.

Blassingame, J. (1979). *The Slave Community: Plantation Life in the Antebellum South.* New York, NY, Oxford University Press.

Bleich, J. D. (1975). "Black Jews: A Halakhic Perspective." *Tradition: A Journal of Orthodox Jewish Thought* 15(1/2): 48–79, 308.

Bleich, J. D. (1977). *Contemporary Halakhic Problems, Volume 1.* Hoboken, NJ, KTAV.

Block, R. I. (1999). *A Rabbi and His Dream: Building the Brotherhood Synagogue.* Hoboken, NJ, KTAV.

Blumenbach, J. F. (1997). Degeneration of the Species. *Race and the Enlightenment: A Reader.* E. C. Eze. Malden, MA, Blackwell: 79–90.

Boasberg, L. W. (1989). "Holocaust Art by a Jew Who Was Black: Joseph Nassy's Vision of Nazi Camps Has Its First US Show Here." *Orlando Sentinel,* Apr. 19. www.orlandosentinel.com.

Boyarin, D. and J. Boyarin (1993). "Diaspora: Generation and the Ground of Jewish Identity." *Critical Inquiry* 19(4): 693–725.

Brettschneider, M. (2015). *The Jewish Phenomenon in Sub-Saharan Africa: The Politics of Contradictory Discourses.* Lewiston, NY, Edwin Mellen.

Bridges, K. M. (2011). *Reproducing Race: An Ethnography of Pregnancy as a Site of Racialization*. Berkeley, CA, University of California Press.

Briggs, D. (2015). "Are Black Americans the Most Religious—and Virtuous—of All?" *The Blog, Huffington Post*, Apr. 29. www.huffingtonpost.com.

Brodkin, K. (1998). *How Jews Became White Folks and What That Says About Race in America*. New Brunswick, NJ, Rutgers University Press.

Brotz, H. (1952). "Negro 'Jews' in the United States." *Phylon* 13(4): 324–337.

Brotz, H. (1970). *The Black Jews of Harlem: Negro Nationalism and the Dilemmas of Negro Leadership*. New York, NY, Schocken Books.

Brown, U. M. (2001). *The Interracial Experience: Growing Up Black/White Racially Mixed in the United States*. Westport, CT, Praeger.

Brubaker, R. and F. Cooper (2000). "Beyond 'Identity.'" *Theory and Society* 29(1): 1–47.

Bruder, E. (2008). *The Black Jews of Africa: History, Religion, Identity*. New York, NY, Oxford University Press.

Bruder, E. (2012). The Proto-History of Igbo Jewish Identity from the Colonial Period to the Biafra War, 1890–1970. *African Zion: Studies in Black Judaism*. E. Bruder and T. Parfitt. Newcastle upon Tyne, UK, Cambridge Scholars: 31–64.

Bruder, E. and T. Parfitt (2012). *African Zion: Studies in Black Judaism*. Newcastle upon Tyne, UK, Cambridge Scholars.

Bryc, K., E. Y. Durand, et al. (2015). "The Genetic Ancestry of African Americans, Latinos, and European Americans across the United States." *American Journal of Human Genetics* 96(1): 37–53.

Burkhardt, R. W., Jr. (2013). "Lamarck, Evolution, and the Inheritance of Acquired Characters." *Genetics* 194(4): 793–805.

Calabi, D. (2001). The "City of the Jews." *The Jews of Early Modern Venice*. B. Ravid and R. C. Davis. Baltimore, MD, John Hopkins University Press: 31–50.

Calimani, R. (1988). *The Ghetto of Venice*. Santarcangelo di Romagna, Italy, Rusconi Libri.

Callahan, A. D. (2006). *The Talking Book: African Americans and the Bible*. New Haven, CT, Yale University Press.

Chafets, Z. (2009). "Obama's Rabbi." *New York Times Magazine*, Apr. 2. www.nytimes.com.

Chireau, Y. (2000). Black Culture and Black Zion: African American Religious Encounters with Judaism, 1790–1930, an Overview. *Black Zion: African American Religious Encounters with Judaism*. Y. Chireau and N. Deutsch. New York, NY, Oxford University Press: 15–32.

Chireau, Y. and N. Deutsch (2000). Introduction. *Black Zion: African American Religious Encounters with Judaism*. Y. C. and N. Deutsch. New York, NY, Oxford University Press: 3–14.

Clegg, R. (2001). "Census Sense." *National Review Online*, March 7. www.nationalreview.com.

Cohen, J. (2007). *Christ Killers: The Jews and the Passion from the Bible to the Big Screen.* New York, NY, Oxford University Press.

Cohen, S. J. D. (1999). The Rabbi in Second-Century Jewish Society. *The Cambridge History of Judaism, Vol. 3: The Early Roman Period.* W. Horbury, W. D. Davies, et al. Cambridge, Cambridge University Press: 922–990.

Cohen, S. J. D. (2014). *From the Maccabees to the Mishnah.* Louisville, KY, Westminster John Knox.

Cohen, S. M. and A. Eisen (2000). *The Jew Within: Self, Family, and Community in America.* Bloomington, IN, Indiana University Press.

Cole, A. (2003). "Trading Places: From Black Power Activist to 'Anti-Negro Negro.'" *American Studies* 44(3): 37–76.

Coleman, R. T. (1977). Black and Jewish—and Unaccepted. *A Coat of Many Colors: Jewish Subcommunities in the United States.* A. D. Lavender. Westport, CT, Greenwood Press: 229–232.

Crouch, S. (1995). *The All-American Skin Game, or, The Decoy of Race: The Long and the Short of It, 1990–1994.* New York, NY, Pantheon Books.

Curtis, E. E., IV (2005). "African-American Islamization Reconsidered: Black History Narratives and Muslim Identity." *Journal of the American Academy of Religion* 73(3): 659–684.

DaCosta, K. M. (2007). *Making Multiracials: State, Family, and Market in the Redrawing of the Color Line.* Stanford, CA, Stanford University Press.

Daniel, G. R. (2001). *More Than Black: Multiracial Identity and New Racial Order.* Philadelphia, PA, Temple University Press.

Dashefsky, A., B. Lazerwitz, et al. (2003). A Journey of the "Straight Way" or the "Roundabout Path": Jewish Identity in the United States and Israel. *Handbook of the Sociology of Religion.* M. Dillon. Cambridge, Cambridge University Press: 240–260.

Davis, F. J. (2001). *Who is Black? One Nation's Definition.* University Park, PA, Pennsylvania State University Press.

Davis, N. Z. (2010). David Nassy's 'Furlough' and the Slave Mattheus. *New Essays in American Jewish History Commemorating the Sixtieth Anniversary of the Founding of the American Jewish Archives.* P. S. Nadell, J. D. Sarna, et al. Cincinnati, OH, American Jewish Archives of Hebrew Union College-Jewish Institute of Religion: 79–94.

Davis, N. Z. (2016). "Regaining Jerusalem: Eschatology and Slavery in Jewish Colonization in Seventeenth-Century Suriname." *Cambridge Journal of Postcolonial Literary Inquiry* 3(1): 11–38.

Davis, R. C. (2001). Introduction. *The Jews of Early Modern Venice.* R. C. Davis and B. Ravid. Baltimore, MD, Johns Hopkins University Press: vii–xix.

DeBow, J. D. B. (1853). *The Seventh Census of the United States: 1850.* Washington, DC, Government Printing Office.

Demo, D. H. and M. Hughes (1990). "Socialization and Racial Identity among Black Americans." *Social Psychology Quarterly* 53(4): 364–374.

Diner, H. R. (1995). *In the Almost Promised Land: American Jews and Blacks, 1915–1935*. Baltimore, MD, Johns Hopkins University Press.

Diner, H. R. (2006). *The Jews of the United States, 1654 to 2000*. Berkeley, CA, University of California Press.

Domínguez, V. R. (1993). *White by Definition: Social Classification in Creole Louisiana*. New Brunswick, NJ, Rutgers University Press.

Dorman, J. S. (2013). *Chosen People: The Rise of American Black Israelite Religions*. New York, NY, Oxford University Press.

Du Bois, W. E. B. (2015). *The Souls of Black Folk*. New Haven, CT, Yale University Press.

Duster, T. (2003a). *Backdoor to Eugenics*. New York, NY, Routledge.

Duster, T. (2003b). Buried Alive: The Concept of Race in Science. *Genetic Nature/Culture: Anthropology and Science beyond the Two-Culture Divide*. A. H. Goodman, D. Heath, et al. Berkeley, CA, University of California Press: 258–277.

El-Haj, N. A. (2012). *The Genealogical Science: The Search for Jewish Origins and the Politics of Epistemology*. Chicago, IL, University of Chicago Press.

Eligon, J. and F. Robles (2016). "Amid Broad Movement against Police Abuse, Some Act on the Fringe." *New York Times*, Jul. 22. www.nytimes.com.

Esenten, A. (2009). "Once Reviled, Black Hebrews Now Fêted." *Jewish Daily Forward*, Mar. 18. www.forward.com.

Faber, E. (1998). *Jews, Slaves, and the Slave Trade: Setting the Record Straight*. New York, NY, New York University Press.

Farley, R. (2002). Racial Identities in 2000: The Response to the Multiple-Race Response Option. *The New Race Question: How the Census Counts Multiracial Individuals*. J. Perlmann and M. C. Waters. New York, NY, Russell Sage Foundation: 33–61.

Farley, R. and W. R. Allen (1987). *The Color Line and the Quality of Life in America*. New York, NY, Oxford University Press.

Fauset, A. H. (2002). *Black Gods of the Metropolis: Negro Religious Cults of the Urban North*. Philadelphia, PA, University of Pennsylvania Press.

Feagin, J. R. (2014). *Racist America: Roots, Current Realities, and Future Reparations*. New York, NY, Routledge.

Fernheimer, J. W. (2009). "Black Jewish Identity Conflict: A Divided Universal Audience and the Impact of Dissociative Disruption." *Rhetoric Society Quarterly* 39(1): 46–72.

Fernheimer, J. W. (2014). *Stepping into Zion: Hatzaad Harishon, Black Jews, and the Remaking of Jewish Identity*. Tuscaloosa, AL, University of Alabama Press.

Forster, B. and J. Tabachnik (1991). *Jews by Choice: A Study of Converts to Reform and Conservative Judaism*. Hoboken, NJ, KTAV.

Fredrickson, G. M. (2002). *Racism: A Short History*. Princeton, NJ, Princeton University Press.

Fried, J. P. (1995). "Cuomo Testifies on Crown Heights Rioting." *New York Times*, Jan. 19. www.nytimes.com.

Friedman, M. (1995). *What Went Wrong? The Creation and Collapse of the Black-Jewish Alliance*. New York, NY, Free Press.

Gamerman, E. (1997). "Art Captures the Holocaust Exhibit: Josef Nassy's Paintings and Drawings Document the Bleak Life in a German Internment Camp during World War II." *Baltimore Sun*, May 19. www.baltimoresun.com.

Gartrell, C. D. and Z. K. Shannon (1985). "Contacts, Cognitions, and Conversions: A Rational Choice Approach." *Review of Religious Research* 27(1): 32–48.

Gates, H. L., Jr. (1992). "Black Demagogues and Pseudo-scholars." *New York Times*, Jul. 20. www.nytimes.com.

Gauthie, J. G. (2002). *Measuring America: The Decennial Censuses from 1790 to 2000*. US Department of Commerce, Economics and Statistics Administration. Washington, DC, US Census Bureau.

Gearty, R. (1995). "Khalid Quits the 'Burbs: Farrakhan Pal Moving to Harlem." *Daily News*, May 31. www.nydailynews.com.

Gerber, I. J. (1977). *The Heritage Seekers: American Black in Search of Jewish Identity*. Middle Village, NY, Jonathan David.

Gersh, H. (1959). "Satmar in Brooklyn: A Zealot Community." *Commentary*, Nov. 1959. www.commentarymagazine.com.

Gilman, S. (1991). *The Jew's Body*. New York, NY, Routledge.

Gilman, S. (2013). Foreword. *Race, Color, Identity: Rethinking Discourses about "Jews" in the Twenty-First Century*. E. Sicher. New York, NY, Berghahn Books: x–xvii.

Gilroy, P. (2002). *Against Race: Imagining Political Culture beyond the Color Line*. Cambridge, MA, Belknap Press of Harvard University Press.

Glazer, N. (1995). "Levin, Jeffries, and the Fate of Academic Autonomy." *William and Mary Law Review* 36(2): 703–732.

Glenn, S. A. (2002). "In the Blood? Consent, Descent, and the Ironies of Jewish Identity." *Jewish Social Studies* 8(2/3): 139–152.

Glenn, S. A. (2010). "Funny, You Don't Look Jewish": Visual Stereotypes and the Making of Modern Jewish Identity. *Boundaries of Jewish Identity*. S. A. Glenn and N. B. Sokoloff. Seattle, WA, University of Washington Press: 64–90.

Goffman, E. (1959). *The Presentation of Self in Everyday Life*. New York, NY, Anchor Books.

Goffman, E. (1986). *Stigma: Notes on the Management of Spoiled Identity*. New York, NY, Touchstone.

Gold, R. S. (2003). "The Black Jews of Harlem: Representation, Identity, and Race, 1920–1939." *American Quarterly* 55(2): 179–225.

Goldberg, C. A. (2012). "Robert Park's Marginal Man: The Career of a Concept in American Sociology." *Laboratorium* 4(2): 199–217.

Goldenberg, D. M. (2003). *The Curse of Ham: Race and Slavery in Early Judaism, Christianity, and Islam*. Princeton, NJ, Princeton University Press.

Goldfarb, H. (1977). Blacks and Conversion to Judaism. *A Coat of Many Colors: Jewish Subcommunities in the United States*. A. D. Lavender. Westport, CT, Greenwood Press: 226ff.

Goldstein, D. B. (2008). *Jacob's Legacy: A Genetic View of Jewish History.* New Haven, CT Yale University Press.

Goldstein, E. L. (2008). *The Price of Whiteness: Jews, Race, and American Identity.* Princeton, NJ, Princeton University Press.

Golovensky, D. I. (1952). "The Marginal Man Concept: An Analysis and Critique." *Social Forces* 30(3): 333–339.

Gossett, T. F. (1997). *Race: The History of an Idea in America.* New York, NY, Oxford University Press.

Gotham, K. F. (2000). "Racialization and the State: The Housing Act of 1934 and the Creation of the Federal Housing Administration." *Sociological Perspectives* 43(2): 291–317.

Gould, S. J. (1996). *The Mismeasure of Man.* New York, NY, W. W. Norton.

Green, C. and B. Wilson (1991). *The Struggle for Black Empowerment in New York City: Beyond the Politics of Pigmentation.* New York, NY, McGraw-Hill.

Greenberg, C. L. (1991). *"Or Does It Explode?": Black Harlem in the Great Depression.* London, Oxford University Press.

Greenberg, C. L. (2010). *Troubling the Waters: Black-Jewish Relations in the American Century.* Princeton, NJ, Princeton University.

HaGadol, P. G. and O. B. Israel (1992). *The Impregnable People: An Exodus of African Americans Back to Africa.* Washington, DC, Communicators Press.

Hare, A. P. (1998). *The Hebrew Israelite Community.* New York, NY, University Press of America.

Harris, D. R. and J. J. Sim (2002). "Who Is Multiracial? Assessing the Complexity of Lived Race." *American Sociological Review* 67(4): 614–627.

Hart, M. B. (2011). Jews and Race: An Introductory Essay. *Jews and Race: Writings on Identity and Difference, 1880–1940.* M. B. Hart. Waltham, MA, Brandeis University: xiii–xxxix.

Hartman, A. (2015). "The Neoconservative Counterrevolution." *Jacobin,* April 23. www.jacobinmag.com.

Hattam, V. (2007). *In the Shadow of Race: Jews, Latinos, and Immigrant Politics in the United States.* Chicago, IL, University of Chicago Press.

Hattam, V. (2001). "Whiteness: Theorizing Race, Eliding Ethnicity." *International Labor and Working-Class History,* no. 60: 61–68.

Haynes, B. D. (2006). *Red Lines, Black Spaces: The Politics of Race and Space in a Black Middle-Class Suburb.* New Haven, CT, Yale University Press.

Haynes, B. D. (2009). "People of God, Children of Ham: Making Black(s) Jews." *Journal of Modern Jewish Studies* 8(2): 237–254.

Haynes, B. D. (2013). A Member of the Club? How Black Jews Negotiate Black Anti-Semitism and Jewish Racism. *Race, Color, Identity: Rethinking Discourses about "Jews" in the Twenty-First Century.* E. Sicher. New York, NY, Berghahn Books: 147–166.

Haynes, B. D. and R. Hutchison (2012). Introduction. *The Ghetto: Contemporary Global Issues and Controversies.* R. Hutchison and B. D. Haynes. Boulder, CO, Westview Press: vii–xliii.

Haynes, E. R. (1923). "Negroes in Domestic Service in the United States: Introduction." *Journal of Negro History* 8(4): 384–442.

Hekman, S. J. (1983). "Weber's Ideal Type: A Contemporary Reassessment." *Polity* 16(1): 119–137.

Herder, J. G. (1997). Organization of the Peoples of Africa. *Race and the Enlightenment: A Reader.* E. C. Eze. Malden, MA, Blackwell: 71–78.

Hirshberg, J. (1990). "Radical Displacement, Post Migration Conditions and Traditional Music." *World of Music* 32(3): 68–89.

Hochschild, J. L. (2005). "Looking Ahead: Racial Trends in the United States." *Daedalus* 134(1): 70–81.

Hollinger, D. A. (1998). Jewish Identity, Assimilation, and Multiculturalism. *Creating American Jews: Historical Conversations about Identity.* K. S. Mittelman. Philadelphia, PA, National Museum of American Jewish History: 52–59.

Hollinger, D. A. (2005). "The One Drop Rule and the One Hate Rule." *Daedalus* 134(1): 18–28.

Hollinger, D. A. (2006). *Postethnic America: Beyond Multiculturalism.* New York, NY, Basic Books.

Holmes, K. E. (2006). "Celebrating Being Black and Jewish: A Synagogue in West Oak Lane Revels in Its History and Its Bonds." *Philadelphia Inquirer*, May 27.

Horowitz, E. (2006). "Families and Their Fortunes: The Jews of Early Modern Europe." *Cultures of the Jews: A New History.* D. Biale. New York, NY, Schocken Books: 573–636.

H. R. Res. 343 (1994). 103rd Congress, Congressional Record. www.congress.gov.

Hughes, L. (1995). From *The Big Sea. Voices from the Harlem Renaissance.* N. I. Huggins. New York, NY, Oxford University Press: 370–381.

Hutchison, R. and B. Haynes (2008). "The Ghetto: Origins, History, Discourse." *City and Community* 7(4): 347–352.

Isaac, E. (2005). "The Question of Jewish Identity and Ethiopian Jewish Origins." *Midstream Magazine: A Monthly Jewish Review*, Oct.

Isaac, E. (2013). "Ethiopian History Is Not Three Thousand Years! (Ephraim Isaac, PhD): An Open Letter to an Inquisitive Young Ethiopian Sister." *Awramba Times*, Dec. 28. www.awrambatimes.com.

Jackson, J. L., Jr. (2005). *Real Black: Adventures in Racial Sincerity.* Chicago, IL, University of Chicago Press.

Jackson, J. L., Jr. (2013). *Thin Description: Ethnography and the African Hebrew Israelites of Jerusalem.* Cambridge, MA, Harvard University Press.

Jacobson, M. F. (1999). *Whiteness of a Different Color: European Immigrants and the Alchemy of Race.* Cambridge, MA, Harvard University Press.

Jewish Telegraphic Agency (1967). "Prominent Negroes Condemn Negro Anti-Semitism; Quit the 'Liberator.'" *Daily News Bulletin*, Feb. 28. www.jta.org.

JFREJ (2016). "Largest Ever Mobilization of Jews For Black Lives Matter!" Jews for Racial and Economic Justice, Aug. 12. www.jfrej.org.

Jordan, W. D. (1974). *The White Man's Burden: Historical Origins of Racism in the United States.* London, Oxford University Press.

Kagen, R. L. and P. D. Morgan (2009). Preface. *Atlantic Diasporas: Jews, Conversos, and Crypto-Jews in the Age of Mercantilism, 1500–1800.* R. L. Kagan and P. D. Morgan. Baltimore, MD, John Hopkins University Press: vii–xvii.

Kahn, S. M. (2010). Are Genes Jewish? Conceptual Ambiguities in the New Genetic Age. *Boundaries of Jewish Identity.* S. A. Glenn and N. B. Sokoloff. Seattle, WA, University of Washington Press: 12–26.

Kaplan, S. (1987). "The Beta Israel (Falasha) Encounter with Protestant Missionaries: 1860–1905." *Jewish Social Studies* 49(1): 27–42.

Kaplan, S. (1992a). *The Beta Israel (Falasha) in Ethiopia: From Earliest Times to the Twentieth Century.* New York, NY, New York University Press.

Kaplan, S. (1992b). "Indigenous Categories and the Study of World Religions in Ethiopia: The Case of the Beta Israel (Falasha)." *Journal of Religion in Africa* 22(3): 208–221.

Kaplan, S. (1999). "Can the Ethiopian Change his Skin? The Beta Israel (Ethiopian Jews) and Racial Discourse." *African Affairs* 98(393): 535–550.

Karadawi, A. (1991). "The Smuggling of the Ethiopian Falasha to Israel through Sudan." *African Affairs* 90(358): 23–49.

Karp, W. and H. R. Shapiro (1999). Exploding the Myth of Black Anti-Semitism. *Strangers and Neighbors: Relations between Blacks and Jews in the United States.* M. Adams and J. Bracey. Amherst, MA, University of Massachusetts Press: 660–668.

Kasinitz, P. and B. D. Haynes (1996). "The Fire at Freddy's." *Common Quest: The Magazine of Black Jewish Relations* 1(2): 24–34.

Katz, Y. (2012). "Distrust in Dimona." *Jerusalem Post*, Dec. 8. www.jpost.com.

Kaufman, A. L. (1998). *Cardozo.* Cambridge, MA, Harvard University Press.

Kaufman, H. (2005). "*King Solomon's Mines?*: African Jewry, British Imperialism, and H. Rider Haggard's Diamonds." *Victorian Literature and Culture* 33(2): 517–539.

Kaye/Kantrowitz, M. (2007). *The Colors of Jews: Racial Politics and Radical Diasporism.* Bloomington, IN, Indiana University Press.

Kershner, I. (2015). "Anti-police Protest in Israel Turns Violent." *New York Times*, May 3. www.nytimes.com.

Kessler, D. and T. Parfitt (1985). *The Falashas: The Jews of Ethiopia.* London, Minority Rights Group.

Kestenbaum, S. (2014.). "Rabbi Hailu Moshe Paris, Revered Leader of America's Black Jews, Dies at 81." *Jewish Daily Forward*, Nov. 6. www.forward.com.

Khanna, N. (2010). "'If You're Half Black, You're Just Black': Reflected Appraisals and the Persistence of the One-Drop Rule." *Sociological Quarterly* 51(1): 96–121.

Khanna, N. (2011). *Biracial in America: Forming and Performing Racial Identity.* Lanham, MD, Lexington Books.

Khanna, N. and C. Johnson (2010). "Passing as Black: Racial Identity Work among Biracial Americans." *Social Psychology Quarterly* 73(4): 380–397.

Khazzoom, A. (2003). "The Great Chain of Orientalism: Jewish Identity, Stigma Management, and Ethnic Exclusion in Israel." *American Sociological Review* 68(4): 481–510.

Kifner, J. (1995). "Death on 125th Street: The Overview; Gunman and 7 Others Die in Blaze at Harlem Store." *New York Times*, Dec. 9.

Kim, H. K. and N. S. Leavitt (2016). *JewAsian: Race, Religion, and Identity for America's Newest Jews*. Lincoln, NE, University of Nebraska Press.

King, J., N. Fischman, et al. (2012). *Twenty Years Later: A Survey of Ethiopian Immigrants Who Have Lived in Israel for Two Decades or More*. Jerusalem, Myers-JDC-Brookdale Institute.

Könighofer, M. (2008). *The New Ship of Zion: Dynamic Diaspora Dimensions of the African Hebrew Israelites of Jerusalem*. Vienna, Lit Verlag.

Kosmin, B. and S. P. Lachman (1993). *One Nation under God: Religion in Contemporary American Society*. New York, NY, Crown.

Kurtis, B. (1999). Strangers in the Holy Land. *Strangers and Neighbors: Relations between Blacks and Jews in the United States*. M. Adams and J. Bracey. Amherst, MA, University of Massachusetts Press: 92–99.

Landes, R. (1967). "Negro Jews in Harlem." *Jewish Journal of Sociology* 9(2): 175–189.

Landing, J. E. (2002). *Black Judaism: Story of an American Movement*. Durham, NC, Carolina Academic Press.

Lavender, A. D. (1977). Introduction. *A Coat of Many Colors: Jewish Subcommunities in the United States*. A. D. Lavender. Westport, CT, Greenwood Press: 3–27.

Lazerwitz, B., J. A. Winter, et al. (1997). *Jewish Choices: American Jewish Denominationalism*. Albany, NY, State University of New York Press.

Leclerc, G.-L. (1997). "A Natural History, General and Particular." *Race and the Enlightenment: A Reader*. E. C. Eze. Malden, MA, Blackwell: 15–28.

Lederhendler, E. (2009). *Jewish Immigrants and American Capitalism, 1880–1920: From Caste to Class*. Cambridge, Cambridge University Press.

Lederman, D. (2009). "Former UMass Professor Julius Lester's Collection of Photos to Be Exhibited in Southampton." *Republican*, Jun. 21. www.masslive.com.

Lee, J. (2006). *Civility in the City: Blacks, Jews, and Koreans in Urban America*. Cambridge, MA, Harvard University Press.

Lee, J. and F. D. Bean (2010). *The Diversity Paradox: Immigration and the Color Line in Twenty-First Century America*. New York, NY, Russell Sage Foundation.

Leifer, J. (2015). "Israel's #BlackLivesMatter Moment?" Blog, *Dissent*, May 10. www.dissentmagazine.org.

Lerer, N. and E. Mayer (1993). In the Footsteps of Ruth: A Sociological Analysis of Converts to Judaism in America. *Papers in Jewish Demography 1989*. U. O. Schmelz and S. DellaPergola. Jerusalem, Avraham Harman Institute of Contemporary Jewry, Hebrew University of Jerusalem: 172–184.

Lerner, M. and C. West (1995). *Jews and Blacks: Let the Healing Begin*. New York, NY, G. P. Putnam's Sons.

Leslau, W. (1951). *Falasha Anthology*. New Haven, CT, Yale University Press.

Lester, J. (1988). *Lovesong: Becoming a Jew*. New York, NY, Little, Brown.

Levi, C. M. B. (1997). *Israelites and Jews: The Significant Difference*. Temple Hills, MD, Levitical Communications.

Levine, L. W. (2007). *Black Culture and Black Consciousness: Afro-American Folk Thought from Slavery to Freedom.* New York, NY, Oxford University Press.

Levitt, P. (2007). Redefining the Boundaries of Belonging: The Transnationalization of Religious Life. *Everyday Religion: Observing Modern Religious Lives.* N. T. Ammerman. New York, NY, Oxford University Press: 103–120.

Lewis, M. and K. Wigen (1997). *The Myth of Continents: A Critique of Metageography.* Berkeley, CA, University of California Press.

Lis, D. (2014). *Jewish Identity among the Igbo of Nigeria: Israel's "Lost Tribe" and the Question of Belonging in the Jewish State.* Trenton, NJ, Africa World Press.

Locke, H. G. (1994). *The Black Anti-Semitism Controversy: Protestant Views and Perspectives.* Selinsgrove, PA, Susquehanna University Press.

Loewen, J. W. (2005). *Sundown Towns: A Hidden Dimension of American Racism.* New York, NY, Simon and Schuster.

Lofland, J. and N. Skonovd (1981). "Conversion Motifs." *Journal for the Scientific Study of Religion* 20(4): 373–385.

Lounds, M. (1981). *Israel's Black Hebrews: Black Americans in Search of Identity.* Washington, DC, University Press of America.

Loveman, M. (2014). *National Colors: Racial Classification and the State in Latin America.* New York, NY, Oxford University Press.

Lyman, S. M. (2001). *Roads to Dystopia: Sociological Essay on the Postmodern Condition.* Fayetteville, AR, University of Arkansas Press.

Lyons, L. (2012). "Black Jews Gain Wider Acceptance." *Jewish Daily Forward,* Jul. 23. www.forward.com.

Malkiel, D. J. (2001). The Ghetto Republic. *The Jews of Early Modern Venice.* R. C. Davis and B. Ravid. Baltimore, MD, Johns Hopkins University: 117–142.

Maltz, J. (2015). "African-American Converts Finally Recognized as Jews in Israel: After Challenging Validity of Non-Orthodox Conversions, Interior Ministry Backs Down in Legal Fight." *Haaretz,* May 28. www.haaretz.com.

MaNishtana (2013). *Thoughts from a Unicorn: 100% Black. 100% Jewish. 0% Safe.* New York, NY, Hyphen.

Markowitz, F. (1996). "Israel as Africa, Africa as Israel: 'Divine Geography' in the Personal Narratives and Community Identity of the Black Hebrew Israelites." *Anthropological Quarterly* 69(4): 193–205.

Martin, T. (1993). *The Jewish Onslaught: Despatches from the Wellesley Battlefront.* Dover, MA, Majority Press.

Mayer, E. (1995). From an External to an Internal Agenda. *The Americanization of the Jews.* R. Seltzer and N. S. Cohen. New York, NY, New York University Press: 417–435.

McVeigh, R. and D. Sikkink (2005). "Organized Racism and the Stranger." *Sociological Forum* 20(4): 497–522.

Meir-Glitzenstein, E. (2011). "Operation Magic Carpet: Constructing the Myth of the Magical Immigration of Yemenite Jews to Israel." *Israel Studies* 16(3): 149–173.

Melnick, R. (1980). "Billy Simons: The Black Jew of Charleston." *American Jewish Archives* 32(1): 3–8.

Miles, W. F. S. (2013). *Jews of Nigeria: An Afro-Judaic Odyssey*. Princeton, NJ, Markus Wiener.

Miller, J. C. (2001). Central Africa during the Era of the Slave Trade, c. 1490s–1850s. *Central Africans and Cultural Transformations in the American Diaspora*. L. M. Heywood. Cambridge, Cambridge University Press: 21–70.

Mills, C. W. (1999). *The Racial Contract*. Ithaca, NY, Cornell University Press.

Min, P. G. (2010). *Ethnic Solidarity for Economic Survival: Korean Greengrocers in New York City*. New York, NY, Russell Sage Foundation.

Minchin, T. J. (2013). "'A Sharp Break from the Recent Past'? Assessing the Rise in Interracial Marriage in the Contemporary United States." *Australasian Journal of American Studies* 32(1): 27–52.

Moray, N., K. E. Pink, et al. (2017). "Paternity Testing under the Cloak of Recreational Genetics." *European Journal of Human Genetics* 25(6): 768–770.

Morgan, P. D. (1998). *Slave Counterpoint: Black Culture in the Eighteenth-Century Chesapeake and Lowcountry*. Chapel Hill, NC, University of North Carolina Press.

Muhammad, K. G. (2011). *The Condemnation of Blackness: Race, Crime, and the Making of Modern Urban America*. Cambridge, MA, Harvard University Press.

Myers-JDC-Brookdale Institute (2012). *The Ethiopian-Israeli Community: Facts and Figures*. Jerusalem, Myers-JDC-Brookdale Institute.

Nagourney, A. (2008). "Obama Elected President as Racial Barrier Falls." *New York Times*, Nov. 4. www.nytimes.com.

Nakashima, C. L. (1992). An Invisible Monster: The Creation and Denial of Mixed-Race People in America. *Racially Mixed People in America*. M. P. P. Root. Newbury Park, CA, SAGE: 162–178.

Nelson, A. (2016). *The Social Life of DNA: Race, Reparations, and Reconciliation after the Genome*. Boston, MA, Beacon Press.

Neusner, J. (1995). *Rabbinic Judaism: Structure and System*. Minneapolis, MN, Augsburg Fortress Press.

New York Times (1911). "Here in Behalf of Abyssinian Jews: Ethnologist Seeks to Establish a Branch of Society to Unite Them to Others of the Race," May 1.

New York Times (1931). "Falasha Scholar Paying Visit to City," Jun. 21.

New York Times (1936). "Future of the Ethiopian Jews," Oct. 11.

Nobles, M. (2000). *Shades of Citizenship: Race and the Census in Modern Politics*. Palo Alto, CA, Stanford University Press.

Omi, M. and H. Winant (1994). *Racial Formation in the United States: From the 1960s to the 1990s*. New York, NY, Routledge.

Omi, M. and H. Winant (2014). *Racial Formation in the United States*. New York, NY, Routledge.

Onolemhemhen, D. N. and K. Gessesse (1998). *The Black Jews of Ethiopia: The Last Exodus*. Lanham, MD, Scarecrow Press.

Osterer, H. (2012). *Legacy: A Genetic History of the Jewish People*. New York, NY, Oxford University Press.

Parfitt, T. (1987). *The Thirteenth Gate: Travels among the Lost Tribes of Israel*. Bethesda, MD, Adler and Adler.

Parfitt, T. (2012). "(De)Constructing Black Jews." *African Zion: Studies in Black Judaism*. E. Bruder and T. Parfitt. Newcastle upon Tyne, UK, Cambridge Scholars: 12–30.

Parfitt, T. (2013). *Black Jews in Africa and the Americas*. Cambridge, MA, Harvard University Press.

Parfitt, T. and N. Fisher (2016). *Becoming Jewish: New Jews and Emerging Jewish Communities in a Globalized World*. Cambridge, MA, Cambridge Scholars.

Parfitt, T. and E. T. Semi (2002). *Judaising Movements: Studies in the Margins of Judaism in Modern Times*. New York, NY, Routledge.

Parfitt, T. and E. T. Semi (2005). *Jews of Ethiopia: The Birth of an Elite*. New York, NY, Routledge.

Park, R. E. (1928). "Human Migration and the Marginal Man." *American Journal of Sociology* 33(6): 881–893.

Perez, A. D. and C. Hirschman (2009). "The Changing Racial and Ethnic Composition of the US Population: Emerging American Identities." *Population and Development Review* 35(1): 1–51.

Pew Research Center (2009). "A Religious Portrait of African-Americans." Polling and Analysis, Pew Forum on Religion and Public Life, Jan. 30. www.pewforum.org.

Pew Research Center (2013). "A Portrait of Jewish Americans: Overview." Polling and Analysis, Pew Forum on Religion and Public Life, Oct. 1. www.pewforum.org.

Phelan, J. C., B. G. Link, et al. (2013). "The Genomic Revolution and Beliefs about Essential Racial Differences: A Backdoor to Eugenics?" *American Sociological Review* 78(2): 167–191.

Phillips, B. A. (2016). "Not Quite White: The Emergence of Jewish 'Ethnoburbs' in Los Angeles, 1920–2010." *American Jewish History* 100(1): 73–104.

Podair, J. E. (2004). *The Strike That Changed New York: Blacks, Whites, and the Ocean Hill-Brownsville Crisis*. New Haven, CT, Yale University Press.

Pomerance, R. (2008). "Judaism Drawing More Black Americans." *Atlanta Journal-Constitution*, Jun. 18.

Porton, G. G. (1994). *The Stranger within Your Gates: Converts and Conversion in Rabbinic Literature*. Chicago, IL, University of Chicago Press.

Primack, K. (1998). Preface. *Jews in Places You Never Thought Of*. K. Primack. Hoboken, NJ, KTAV, xi–xiii.

Qian, Z. and D. T. Lichter (2011). "Changing Patterns of Interracial Marriage in a Multiracial Society." *Journal of Marriage and Family* 73(5): 1065–1084.

Quirin, J. (1992). *The Evolution of the Ethiopian Jews: A History of the Beta Israel*. Philadelphia, PA, University of Pennsylvania Press.

Raboteau, A. J. (2004). *Slave Religion: The "Invisible Institution" in the Antebellum South*. Oxford, Oxford University Press.

Ratner, S. (1984). "Horace M. Kallen and Cultural Pluralism." *Modern Judaism* 4(2): 185–200.

Ravid, B. (2001). The Venetian Government and the Jews. *The Jews of Early Modern Venice*. R. C. Davis and B. Ravid. Baltimore, MD, John Hopkins University Press: 3–30.

Reed, A. L., Jr. (1999). What Color is Anti-Semitism? *Strangers and Neighbors: Relations between Blacks and Jews in the United States* M. Adams and J. Bracey. Amherst, MA, University of Massachusetts Press: 24–26.

Reuter, S. Z. (2006). "The Genuine Jewish Type: Racial Ideology and Anti-immigrationism in Early Medical Writing about Tay-Sachs Disease." *Canadian Journal of Sociology* 31(3): 291–323.

Reznikoff, C. (1950). *The Jews of Charleston: A History of an American Jewish Community*. Philadelphia, PA, Jewish Publication Society of America.

Richardson, J. T. (1985). "The Active vs. Passive Convert: Paradigm Conflict in Conversion/Recruitment Research." *Journal for the Scientific Study of Religion* 24(2): 163–179.

Rieder, J. (1985). *Canarsie: The Jews and Italians of Brooklyn against Liberalism*. Cambridge, MA, Harvard University Press.

Ringel, S., N. Ronell, et al. (2005). "Factors in the Integration Process of Adolescent Immigrants: The Case of Ethiopian Jews in Israel." *International Social Work* 48(1): 63–76.

Ripley, W. Z. (1940). *The Races of Europe: A Sociological Study*. New York, NY, D. Appleton.

Robinson, D. (2004). *Muslim Societies in African History*. New York, NY, Cambridge University Press.

Rockquemore, K. A. and D. L. Brunsma (2002). "Socially Embedded Identities: Theories, Typologies, and Processes of Racial Identity among Black/White Biracials." *Sociological Quarterly* 43(3): 335–356.

Rockquemore, K. A. and D. L. Brunsma (2007). *Beyond Black: Biracial Identity in America*. Lanham, MD, Rowman and Littlefield.

Roediger, D. R. (2007). *The Wages of Whiteness: Race and the Making of the American Working Class*. Brooklyn, NY, Verso.

Rogoff, L. (1997). "Is the Jew White? The Racial Place of the Southern Jew." *American Jewish History* 85(3): 195–230.

Roth, C. (1996). *The Spanish Inquisition*. New York, NY, W. W. Norton.

Roth, W. D. (2005). "The End of the One-Drop Rule? Labeling of Multiracial Children in Black Intermarriages." *Sociological Forum* 20(1): 35–67.

Roth, W. D. (2012). *Race Migrations: Latinos and the Cultural Transformation of Race*. Palo Alto, CA, Stanford University Press.

Rubel, N. L. (2009). "Chased out of Palestine": Prophet Cherry's Church of God and Early Black Judaism in the United States. *The New Black Gods: Arthur Huff Fauset and the Study of African American Religions*. E. E. Curtis IV and D. B. Sigler. Bloomington, IN, Indiana University Press: 49–69.

Rubin, G. E. (1995). How Should We Think about Black Antisemitism. *Antisemitism in America Today: Outspoken Experts Explode the Myths*. J. Chanes. New York, NY, Birch Lane: 150–170.

Said, E. W. (1977). "Orientalism." *Georgia Review* 31(1): 162–206.

Said, E. W. (1978). *Orientalism*. New York, NY, Pantheon Books.

Salamon, H. (1999). *The Hyena People: Ethiopian Jews in Christian Ethiopia*. Berkeley, CA, University of California Press.

Salamon, H. (2003). "Blackness in Transition: Decoding Racial Constructs through Stories of Ethiopian Jews." *Journal of Folklore Research* 40(1): 3–32.

Salamon, H. (2006). "Religious Interplay on an African Stage: Ethiopian Jews in Christian Ethiopia." *Cultures of the Jews: A New History*. D. Biale. New York, NY, Schocken Books: 977–1008.

Sales, B. (2015). "Israel Just Approved Immigration for 9,000 Ethiopian Jews—Here's Who They Are." *Times of Israel*, Nov. 23. www.timesofisrael.com.

Salzman, J. and C. West (1997). *Struggles in the Promised Land: Towards a History of Black-Jewish Relations in the United States*. New York, NY, Oxford University Press.

Sand, S. (2010). *The Invention of the Jewish People*. Brooklyn, NY, Verso.

Sanders, E. R. (1969). "The Hamitic Hypothesis; Its Origin and Functions in Time Perspective." *Journal of African History* 10(4): 521–532.

Santamaria, U. (1987). "Blacks Jews: The Religious Challenge or Politics versus Religion." *European Journal of Sociology* 28(2): 217–240.

Sarna, J. D. (2005). *American Judaism: A History*. New Haven, CT, Yale University Press.

Sartre, J.-P. and J. MacCombie (1964). "Black Orpheus." *Massachusetts Review* 6(1): 13–52.

Schaefer, R. T. (1996). *Racial and Ethnic Groups*. New York, NY, HarperCollins.

Schanberg, S. H. (1984). "New York: Jackson as Polarizer." *New York Times*, Apr. 10. www.nytimes.com.

Schmitt, E. (2001). "For 7 Million People in Census, One Race Category Isn't Enough." *New York Times*, Mar. 13. www.nytimes.com.

Schorsch, J. (2009). *Jews and Blacks in the Early Modern World*. Cambridge, Cambridge University Press.

Schutz, A. and H. R. Wagner (1970). *On Phenomenology and Social Relations*. Chicago, IL, University of Chicago Press.

Seeman, D. (2000). "The Question of Kinship: Bodies and Narratives in the Beta Israel-European Encounter (1860–1920)." *Journal of Religion in Africa* 30(1): 86–120.

Segal, J. C. (1998). *Shades of Community and Conflict: Biracial Adults of African-American and Jewish-American Heritages*. PhD diss., Wright Institute Graduate School of Psychology. Dissertation.com.

Seligman, C. G. (1930). *The Races of Africa*. London, Thornton Butterworth.

Semi, E. T. (2005). "*Hazkarah*: A Symbolic Day for the Reconstituting of the Jewish-Ethiopian Community." *Jewish Political Studies Review* 17(1/2): 191–197.

Sennett, R. (1996). *Flesh and Stone: The Body and the City in Western Civilization*. New York, NY, W. W. Norton.

Shapiro, E. S. (2005). *We Are Many: Reflections of American Jewish History*. Syracuse, NY, Syracuse University Press.

Shapiro, H. L. (1960). *The Jewish People: A Biological History*. New York, NY, UNESCO.

Shelemay, K. K. (1986). *Music, Ritual, and Falasha History*. East Lansing, MI, Michigan State University.

Shipp, E. R. (1984). "Tape Contradicts Disavowal of 'Gutter Religion.'" *New York Times*, Jun. 29. www.nytimes.com.

Shulewitz, M. H. (2000). *The Forgotten Millions: The Modern Jewish Exodus from Arab Lands*. New York, NY, Bloomsbury Academic.

Sicher, E. (2013). *Race, Color, Identity: Rethinking Discourses about "Jews" in the Twenty-First Century*. New York, NY, Berghahn Books.

Siegal, J. (2007). "Rural Converts Journey into Judaism." *Jewish Daily Forward*, Dec. 19. www.forward.com.

Simmel, G. (2016). "The Stranger." *Baffler*, no. 30: 176–179.

Simon, A. (2016). "Jews of Color Hold Black Lives Matter March Downtown." *Brooklyn Daily*, Aug. 1. www.brooklyndaily.com.

Singer, M. (2000). Symbolic Identity Formation in an African American Religious Sect: The Black Hebrew Israelites. *Black Zion: African American Religious Encounters with Judaism*. Y. Chireau and N. Deutsch. New York, NY, Oxford University Press: 55–72.

Sirmans, M. E. (1962). "The Legal Status of the Slave in South Carolina, 1670–1740." *Journal of Southern History* 28(4): 462–473.

Sleeper, J. (1990). *The Closest of Strangers: Liberalism and the Politics of Race in New York*. New York, NY, W. W. Norton.

Smedley, A. and B. D. Smedley (2012). *Race in North America: Origin and Evolution of a World View*. Boulder, CO, Westview Press.

Smith, T. H. (1995). *Conjuring Culture: Biblical Formations of Black America*. New York, NY, Oxford University Press.

Snipp, C. M. (1989). *American Indians: The First of This Land*. New York, NY, Russell Sage Foundation.

Somers, M. R. (1994). "The Narrative Constitution of Identity: A Relational and Network Approach." *Theory and Society* 23(5): 605–649.

Spector, S. (2005). *Operation Solomon: The Daring Rescue of the Ethiopian Jews*. New York, New York, Oxford University Press.

Spickard, P. R. (1989). *Mixed Blood: Intermarriage and Ethnic Identity in Twentieth-Century America*. Madison, WI, University of Wisconsin Press.

Star, S. L. and J. R. Griesemer (1989). "Institutional Ecology, 'Translations' and Boundary Objects: Amateurs and Professionals in Berkeley's Museum of Vertebrate Zoology, 1907–39." *Social Studies of Science* 19(3): 387–420.

Steinberg, S. (2001a). *The Ethnic Myth: Race, Ethnicity, and Class in America*. New York, NY, Beacon Press.

Steinberg, S. (2001b). *Turning Back: The Retreat from Racial Justice in American Thought and Policy*. New York, NY, Beacon Press.

Steinsaltz, A. (1976). *The Essential Talmud*. New York, NY, Basic Books.

Stonequist, E. V. (1935). "The Problem of the Marginal Man." *American Journal of Sociology* 41(1): 1–12.

Summerfield, D. (2003). *From Falashas to Ethiopian Jews: The External Influences for Change, c. 1860–1960*. London, Routledge.

Sutcliffe, A. (2009). Jewish History in an Age of Atlanticism. *Atlantic Diasporas: Jews, Conversos, and Crypto-Jews in the Age of Mercantilism, 1500–1800*. R. L. Kagen and P. D. Morgan. Baltimore, MD, John Hopkins University Press: 18–30.

Telushkin, J. (1991). *Jewish Literacy: The Most Important Things to Know about the Jewish Religion, Its People, and Its History*. New York, NY, William Morrow.

Tenenbaum, S. and L. Davidman (2007). "It's in My Genes: Biological Discourse and Essentialist Views of Identity among Contemporary American Jews." *Sociological Quarterly* 48(3): 435–450.

Thernstrom, A. and S. Thernstrom (2008). "Taking Race out of the Race: White Voters' Support for Obama Suggests a Dramatic Change in the Electorate." *Los Angeles Times*, Mar. 2. www.latimes.com.

Thomas, H. (1997). *The Slave Trade: The Story of the Atlantic Slave Trade, 1440–1870*. New York, NY, Touchstone Books.

Thomas, M. G., T. Parfitt, et al. (2000). "Y Chromosomes Traveling South: The Cohen Modal Haplotype and the Origins of the Lemba—the 'Black Jews of Southern Africa.'" *American Journal of Human Genetics* 66(2): 674–686.

Thomas, W. I. (2017). *The Child in America: Behavior Problems and Programs*. London, Forgotten Books.

Thornton, M. (1996). Hidden Agendas, Identity Theories, and Multiracial People. *The Multiracial Experience: Racial Borders as the New Frontier*. M. P. P. Root. Thousand Oaks, CA, SAGE: 101–120.

Tighe, E., L. Saxe, et al. (2013). *American Jewish Population Estimates: 2012*. Waltham, MA, Brandeis University, Maurice and Marilyn Cohen Center for Modern Jewish Studies, Steinhardt Social Research Institute.

Tilly, C. (2007). "History of and in Sociology." *American Sociologist* 38(4): 326–329.

Tinney, J. (1973). "Black Jews: A House Divided." *Christianity Today*, December 7, 1973: 52–54.

Tobin, D., G. A. Tobin, et al. (2005). *In Every Tongue: The Racial and Ethnic Diversity of the Jewish People*. San Francisco, CA, Institute for Jewish and Community Research.

Tobin, G. A. (1999). *Opening the Gates: How Proactive Conversion Can Revitalize the Jewish Community*. San Francisco, CA, Jossey-Bass.

Torode, J. (2009). "The Black Vegan Cult Finally Loved by Israel." *Jewish Chronicle*, Jun. 23. www.thejc.com.

Townsend, T. (2008). "New Jews, New Hope." *Washington Post*, Feb. 2. www.washingtonpost.com.

Treitler, V. B. (2013). *The Ethnic Project: Transforming Racial Fiction into Ethnic Factions*. Stanford, CA, Stanford University Press.

Twaddle, M. (1993). *Kakungulu and the Creation of Uganda*. Athens, OH, Ohio University Press.

Twitty, M. (2014). "An Afro-Ashkefardi Recipe for Rosh Hashanah." *Jewish&* (blog), My Jewish Learning, Sep. 9. www.myjewishlearning.com.

Tyson, P. (2000). "Mysteries of Great Zimbabwe." *Nova*, Feb. 22. www.pbs.org.

Ullendorff, E. (1967). *Ethiopia and the Bible*. New York, Oxford University Press.

Vanderkam, L. (2011). "Where Did the Korean Greengrocers Go?" *City Journal*, Winter. www.city-journal.org.

Vincent, N. (1994). "Two Papal Letters on the Wearing of the Jewish Badge, 1221 and 1229." *Jewish Historical Studies* 34: 209–224.

Vink, W. (2010). *Creole Jews: Negotiating Community in Colonial Suriname*. Leiden, the Netherlands: KITLV Press.

Wade, P. (2014). "Race, Ethnicity, and Technologies of Belonging." *Science, Technology, and Human Values* 39(4): 587–596.

Wagaw, T. G. (1991). "Caught the Web: The Horn of Africa and the Migration of Ethiopian Jews." *Northeast African Studies* 13(2/3): 109–126.

Wailoo, K. and S. Pemberton (2006). *The Troubled Dream of Genetic Medicine: Ethnicity and Innovation in Tay-Sachs, Cystic Fibrosis, and Sickle Cell Disease*. Baltimore, MD, Johns Hopkins University Press.

Walker, C. E. (2001). *We Can't Go Home Again: An Argument about Afrocentrism*. New York, NY, Oxford University Press.

Waters, M. C. (1990). *Ethnic Options: Choosing Identities in America*. Berkeley, CA, University of California Press.

Waters, M. C. (1996). Optional Ethnicities: For Whites Only? *Origins and Destinies: Immigration, Race, and Ethnicity in America*. S. Pedraza and R. G. Rumbaut. Belmont, CA, Wadsworth Cengage Learning: 444–454.

Weil, S. (1997). "Religion, Blood, and the Equality of Rights: The Case of Ethiopian Jews in Israel." *International Journal on Minority and Group Rights* 4(3/4): 397–412.

Weil, S. (2011). Beta Israel Students Who Studied Abroad, 1905–1935. *Proceedings of the 16th International Conference of Ethiopian Studies, Vol. 1*. S. Ege, H. Aspen, et al. Trondheim, Norwegian University of Science and Technology: 209–217.

Weil. S. (2016). "The Unification of the Ten Lost Tribes with the Two 'Found' Tribes." *Becoming Jewish: New Jews and Emerging Jewish Communities in a Globalized World*. T. Parfitt and N. Fisher. Cambridge, MA, Cambridge Scholars: 25–35.

Weisenfeld, J. (2016). *New World A-Coming: Black Religion and Racial Identity during the Great Migration*. New York, NY, New York University Press.

Wilkerson, I. (2011). *The Warmth of Other Suns: The Epic Story of America's Great Migration*. New York, NY, Vintage Books.

Williams, T. K. (1996). Race as a Process: Reassessing the "What Are You?" Encounters of Biracial Individuals. *The Multiracial Experience: Racial Borders as the New Frontier*. M. P. P. Root. Thousand Oaks, CA, SAGE: 191–220.

Willoughby, P. R. (2007). *The Evolution of Modern Humans in Africa: A Comprehensive Guide*. Lanham, MD, AltaMira Press.

Winant, H. (2004). *The New Politics of Race: Globalism, Difference, Justice*. Minneapolis, MN, University of Minnesota Press.

Windsor, R. R. (1988). *From Babylon to Timbuktu: A History of Ancient Black Races Including the Ancient Hebrews*. Atlanta, GA, Windsor's Golden Series.

Wirth, L. (1927). "The Ghetto." *American Journal of Sociology*. 33(1): 57–71.

Wirth, L. (1998). *The Ghetto*. New Brunswick, NJ, Transaction.

Wolfe, T. (1970). "Radical Chic: That Party at Lenny's." *New York Magazine*, June 8. www.nymag.com.

Wolfson, B. (2000). African American Jews: Dispelling Myths, Bridging the Divide. *Black Zion: African American Religious Encounters with Judaism*. Y. Chireau and N. Deutsch. New York, NY, Oxford University Press: 33–54.

Wood, D. (1992). *The Power of Maps*. New York, NY, Guilford Press.

Wynia, E. M. (1994). *The Church of God and Saints of Christ: The Rise of Black Jews*. London, Routledge.

Wynter, L. E. (2002). *American Skin: Pop Culture, Big Business, and the End of White America*. New York, NY, Crown.

Zack, N. (1993). *Race and Mixed Race*. Philadelphia, PA, Temple University Press.

Zack, N. (1996). On Being and Not-Being Black and Jewish. *The Multiracial Experience: Racial Borders as the New Frontier*. M. P. P. Root. Thousand Oaks, CA, SAGE: 140–152.

Zeitz, J. (2007). *White Ethnic New York: Jews, Catholics, and the Shaping of Postwar Politics*. Chapel Hill, NC, University of North Carolina Press.

Zeller, J. and D. Zeller (1998). Fight for the Honor of the Ethiopian Jewish Community! *Jews in Places You Never Thought Of*. K. Primack. Hoboken, NJ, KTAV, 141–43.

Zenner, W. P. (1989). "Chicago's Sephardim: A Historical Exploration." *American Jewish History* 79(2): 221–241.

Zerubavel, E. (2004). *Time Maps: Collective Memory and the Social Shape of the Past*. Chicago, IL, University of Chicago Press.

Zerubavel, Y. (1995). *Recovered Roots: Collective Memory and the Making of Israeli National Tradition*. Chicago, IL, University of Chicago Press.

Zianga, J. (2013). "Black Jews in Academic and Institutional Discourse." *Race, Color, Identity: Rethinking Discourses about "Jews" in the 21st Century*. E. Sicher. New York, NY, Berghahn Books: 182–195.

Zuberi, Tukufu (2003). *Thicker Than Blood: How Racial Statistics Lie*. Minneapolis, MN, University of Minnesota Press.

Zunz, O. (2000). *The Changing Face of Inequality: Urbanization, Industrial Development, and Immigrants in Detroit, 1880–1920*. Chicago, IL, University of Chicago Press.

INDEX

Abayudaya of Uganda, 19, 23, 220n24
Abeta Hebrew Cultural Center, 104–5
Abraham, 82, 103, 219n22; conversion of, 116–17
"accenting," 153–54
Adam, 50
ADL. *See* Anti-Defamation League
adolescence, 178–79; Jewish identity and, 162–63
Africa, 47, 81, 106, 221n4; division of, 48–49; immigration to, 104–5; Uganda, 19, 23, 220n24
African American Hebrews, 12–13
African American Jews, 18; CAAM and, 186–87, 197; diversity of, 17, 22, 134–35
African Americans: genetics of, 148; Jews compared to, 53, 168; religion of, 131, 139–40, 168
African diaspora, 73–76, 129
Africanists, 186–87
African Judaism, 203–4
Africans, 18–19, 203; from Ham, 50; Israelite Jewish identity of, 56–57; Yemenite Jews, 57–58, 161. *See also* Ethiopian Hebrews; slavery
Afro-American Jews, 202–3
Afro-Ashkefardi cooking, 120–21, 129
Afrocentric Jews, 85, 101, 103–4, 138, 206
Airlift, 6–7, 21, 46, 57–62
Alliance of Black Jews, 14, 138, 160, 187
American black Jews, 206; Jewish identity of, 7–9
American early black Jewish sects, 73–77; Beth B'nai Abraham, 78–79; black

Muslims and, 80; chosenness of, 82; exoticism of, 82–83; "Hebrewisms" and, 80, 84; 1919–1930, 78; Old Testament and, 80–82; Temple Beth'El and, 84–85; UNIA and, 78–80
American Jewish University, 111–12
American Jews, 5, 53, 63, 208; in colonies, 74–76; from Europe, 36–37; genetics and, 117; kinship of, 116–18; number of, 119, 224n5; religion of, 116–18, 131–32; secularism of, 16–17. *See also* African American Jews
Amishav, 220n27
anointed, 95–96
Anti-Defamation League (ADL), 168, 189, 219n23
anti-racist racism, 103–4
anti-Semitism, 2, 33, 172–73, 196; at CAAM, 186–87; Christ killers and, 168; decrease in, 189; Lester and, 126–27; in New York City, 183–85, 188; Venetian ghettos and, 35–36
Arendt, Hannah, 38, 42
art, 73, 152–55
Ashkenazi Jews, 8, 134, 219n16; race of, 25, 227n3; Sephardi Jews compared to, 180–81
Ashkenazi stereotype, 143
assimilation, 40, 42, 52, 61, 116, 170, 173, 211
atonement, 190–91
authenticity, 197–98; of Beta Israel, 55–56, 59, 102; of biracial Jews, 156–57; of Hebrew Israelites, 106, 109–10

ABOUT THE AUTHOR

Bruce D. Haynes is Professor of Sociology at the University of California, Davis and a Senior Fellow in the Urban Ethnography Project at Yale University. His publications include *Down the Up Staircase: Three Generations of a Harlem Family* (co-author S. Solovitch, 2017), *The Ghetto: Contemporary Global Issues and Controversies* (co-author R. Hutchison, 2011), and *Red Lines, Black Spaces: The Politics of Race and Space in a Black Middle-Class Suburb* (2006).